One Million
CHILDREN

**CORWIN
PRESS**

The Corwin Press logo—a raven striding across an open book—represents the happy union of courage and learning. We are a professional-level publisher of books and journals for K–12 educators, and we are committed to creating and providing resources that embody these qualities. Corwin's motto is "Success for All Learners."

One Million CHILDREN

SUCCESS FOR ALL

With Contributions By:
Bette Chambers
Cecelia Daniels
Martha French
Barbara Haxby
Kathleen Simons
Barbara Wasik

Robert E. Slavin • Nancy A. Madden

CORWIN PRESS, INC.
A Sage Publications Company
Thousand Oaks, California

For information:

Corwin Press, Inc.
A Sage Publications Company
2455 Teller Road
Thousand Oaks, California 91320
E-mail: order@corwinpress.com

Sage Publications Ltd.
6 Bonhill Street
London EC2A 4PU
United Kingdom

Sage Publications India Pvt. Ltd.
M-32 Market
Greater Kailash I
New Delhi 110 048 India

Printed in the United States of America

Library of Congress Cataloging-in-Publication Data

One million children: Success for All / edited by Robert E. Slavin and
Nancy A. Madden; with contributions by Bette Chambers ... [et al.].
        p. cm.
Includes bibliographical references and index.
    ISBN 0-8039-6802-7 (cloth : alk. paper) — ISBN 0-8039-6803-5 (pbk. :
alk. paper)
    1. School improvement programs—United States. 2. Socially
handicapped children—Education (Elementary) — United States. 3.
Academic achievement—United States. I. Slavin, Robert E. II. Madden,
Nancy A. III. Chambers, Bette.
    LB2822.82 .O54 2000
    372.1826'94   00-008785

This book is printed on acid-free paper.

01   02   03   04   05   06   07   7   6   5   4   3   2

Corwin Editorial Assistant: Kylee Liegl
Production Editor: Diane S. Foster
Editorial Assistant: Candice Crosetti
Typesetter/Designer: Danielle Dillahunt and Barbara Burkholder
Cover Designer: Oscar Desierto

Contents

Preface

Every child can learn. Every school can ensure the success of every child. Statements to this effect appear in goals statements, commission reports, and school district offices. They are posted in school buildings and appear as mottoes on school stationery. But does our education system behave as if they are true? If we truly believed that every child could learn under the proper circumstances, we would be relentless in the search for those circumstances. We would use well-validated instructional methods and materials known to be capable of ensuring the success of nearly all children if used with intelligence, flexibility, and fidelity. We would involve teachers in constant, collaborative professional development activities to continually improve their abilities to reach every child. We would frequently assess children's performance to be sure that all students are on a path that leads to success, and we would respond immediately if children were not making adequate progress. If children were falling behind despite excellent instruction, we would try different instructional approaches and, if necessary, we would provide them with tutors or other intensive assistance. We would involve parents in support of their children's school success, we would check to see whether vision, hearing, health, nutrition, or other nonacademic problems were holding children back, and then we would find a solution to those problems. If we truly believed that all children could learn, we

CONCORDIA UNIVERSITY LIBRARY
PORTLAND, OR 97211

would rarely if ever assign children to special education or long-term remedial programs that in effect lower expectations for children. If we truly believed that all schools could ensure the success of all children, then the failure of even a single child would be cause for great alarm and for immediate, forceful intervention.

Success for All and Roots & Wings are comprehensive restructuring programs for elementary schools designed to make the idea that all children can learn a practical, daily organizing principle for schools, especially those serving many children placed at risk. Success for All, first implemented in 1987, was created to show how schools could ensure that virtually all children can read and write. Roots & Wings, begun in 1991, extends similar principles to mathematics, social studies, and science. This book describes the programs in detail, presents the extensive research evaluating them, and discusses the implications of this research for policy and practice.

The development, dissemination, and evaluation of Success for All and Roots & Wings are the products of the dedicated efforts of hundreds of educators, developers, trainers, and researchers throughout the United States and other countries. Research and development of Success for All has been funded by the Office of Educational Research and Improvement, U. S. Department of Education (Grants No. OERI-R-117-R90002 and OERI-R-117-D40005), and by the Carnegie Corporation of New York, the Pew Charitable Trusts, the Abell Foundation, and the France and Merrick Foundations. Roots & Wings has been funded by the New American Schools Development Corporation, the Dana Foundation, and the Knight Foundation.

The not-for-profit Success for All Foundation, established in 1998 to take on the development and dissemination of Success for All and Roots & Wings, has been supported by grants and loans from the Sandler Family Foundation, the Stupski Family Foundation, the MacArthur Foundation, the Ford Foundation, and the New Schools Fund. Development, research, and dissemination in Britain is being funded by the Fischer Family Trust.

In addition to the authors of this volume, many other researchers have been involved in development, evaluation, and dissemination of Success for All. These include Margarita Calderón, Barbara Wasik, Robert Cooper, Amanda Datnow, and Nancy Karweit of Johns Hopkins University; Barbara Livermon of Notre Dame College; Robert Stevens of Penn State University; Steve Ross, Lana Smith, and Jason Casey of the University of Memphis; John Nunnery of the Memphis City Schools; Marcie Dianda of the National Education Association; Philip Abrami of Concordia University in Montreal; Yola Center of Macquarie University in Sydney, Australia; David Hopkins and Alma Harris of Nottingham University (England); Rachel Hertz-Lazarowitz and Bruria Schaedel of Haifa University (Israel); and Bette Chambers, Barbara Haxby, Kathy Simons, Cecelia Daniels, Eric Hurley, and Anne Chamberlain of the Success for All Foundation.

The development of Success for All and Roots & Wings has also involved too many talented and dedicated individuals to name here, but the current leaders of the development teams, all of whom work at the Success for All Foundation under the overall direction of Nancy Madden, are as follows: For reading, writing, and language arts, development leaders are Holly Coleman, Laura Burton Rice, and Martha

French. Kathy Simons leads mathematics development, and Cecelia Daniels, Susan Magri, and Coleen Bennett lead both WorldLab and middle school development. Bette Chambers is the director of Early Learning development. Barbara Haxby and Susan Milleman direct family support development.

As of this writing, the Success for All Foundation employs more than 200 trainers, without whom the program could not exist. All training is directed by Barbara Haxby, with unit leaders John Batchelor, Susan Boyer, Jane Harbert, Liz Judice, Mark Rolewski, Argelia Carreon, Patrice Case-McFadin, Diane Chapman, Jane Dunham, Jill Ferguson, Connie Fuller, Judy Gill, Norma Godina-Silva, Anna Grehan, Tracy Heitmeier, Irene Kann, Margaret Masten, Wanda Maldonaldo, Carla Musci, Amanda Nappier, Elma Noyola, Wendy Paule, Vicki Pellicano, Saundra Pool, Judith Ramsey, Dorothy Sauer, Carmen Stearns, and Randi Suppe.

About the Authors

Nancy A. Madden is President of the Success for All Foundation. She received her BA in Psychology from Reed College in 1973 and her PhD in Clinical Psychology from American University in 1980. Dr. Madden is the author or coauthor of articles and books on cooperative learning, mainstreaming, Title I, and students at risk, including *Effective Programs for Students at Risk* and *Every Child, Every School: Success for All.* She worked at Johns Hopkins University from 1980 to 1998, where she was the Co-Director of the Success for All and Roots & Wings project and has directed the development of the reading, writing, language arts, and mathematics elements of Success for All.

Robert E. Slavin is currently Co-Director of the Center for Research on the Education of Students Placed at Risk at Johns Hopkins University and Chairman of the Success for All Foundation. He received his BA in Psychology from Reed College in 1972 and his PhD in Social Relations in 1975 from Johns Hopkins University. He has authored or coauthored more than 200 articles and 18 books, including *Educational Psychology: Theory Into Practice, School and Classroom Organization, Effective Programs for Students at Risk, Cooperative Learning: Theory, Research, and Practice, Preventing Early School Failure, Every Child, Every School: Success For*

All, Show Me the Evidence: Proven and Promising Programs for America's Schools, and *Effective Programs for Latino Students.* He received the American Educational Research Association's Raymond B. Cattell Early Career Award for Programmatic Research in 1986, the Palmer O. Johnson award for the best article in an AERA journal in 1988, the Charles A. Dana award in 1994, the James Bryan Conant award from the Education Commission of the States in 1998, and the Outstanding Leadership in Education Award from the Horace Mann League in 1999.

1

One Million Children

Success for All

Despite the constant public outcry about the crisis in U.S. education, every community has one or more outstanding and often widely recognized public school. Some of these appear to succeed because they serve children of wealthy, well-educated parents or because they are magnet schools that can screen out unmotivated or low-achieving students. However, there are also schools that serve disadvantaged and minority children in inner-city or rural locations and, year after year, produce outstanding achievement outcomes. Such schools play a crucial role in reminding us that the problems of our school system have little to do with the capabilities of children; they provide our best evidence that all children can learn. Yet, the success of these lighthouse schools does not spread very far. Excellence can be demonstrated in many individual schools but not in whole districts or communities. An outstanding elementary school benefits about 500 children, on average. Yet, there are millions of children who are placed at risk by ineffective responses to such factors as economic disadvantage, limited English proficiency, or learning difficulties. How can we make excellence the norm rather than the exception, especially in schools serving many at-risk children? How can effective practices based on research and on the experiences of outstanding schools be effectively implemented every day by hundreds of thousands of teachers?

Success for All is one answer to these questions. Born in one Baltimore school in 1987, Success for All is used (as of fall, 1999) in more than 1,500 schools in 48 states, plus schools in five foreign countries. By fall 2000, it will be in about 1,800 schools, serving one million children. These schools are highly diverse. They are in 40 of the 50 largest urban districts but also in hundreds of rural districts, inner suburban districts, and Indian reservations. Most are Title I schoolwide projects with many children qualifying for free lunches, but many are in much less impoverished circumstances.

Success for All is by far the largest research-based, whole-school reform model ever to exist. It is the first model to demonstrate that techniques shown to be effective in rigorous research can be replicated on a vast scale with fidelity and continued effectiveness. Both the research and the dissemination of Success for All pose inescapable challenges to educational policy. If replicable excellence is possible, then how can we accept the abysmal performance of so many children? This is not to say that every school needs to adopt Success for All, but what it does imply is that every school needs to create or adopt some program that is no less effective than Success for All. It is unconscionable to continue using ineffective practices if effective ones are readily available and are capable of serving any school that is prepared to dedicate itself to quality implementation.

This book presents the components of Success for All, the research done on the program, and the policy implications of this research for the transformation of America's schools.

Success for All:
The Promise and the Plan

To understand the concepts behind Success for All, let's start with Ms. Martin's kindergarten class. Ms. Martin has some of the brightest, happiest, and most optimistic kids you'll ever meet. Students in her class are glad to be in school, proud of their accomplishments, certain that they will succeed at whatever the school has to offer. Every one of them is a natural scientist, a storyteller, a creative thinker, a curious seeker of knowledge. Ms. Martin's class could be anywhere, in suburb or ghetto, small town or barrio; it doesn't matter. Kindergartners everywhere are just as bright, enthusiastic, and confident as her kids are.

Only a few years from now, many of these same children will have lost the spark they all started with. Some will have failed a grade. Some will be in special education. Some will be in long-term remediation, such as Title I or other remedial programs. Some will be bored or anxious or unmotivated. Many will see school as a chore rather than a pleasure and will no longer expect to excel. In a very brief span of time, Ms. Martin's children will have defined themselves as successes or failures in school. All too often, only a few will still have a sense of excitement and positive self-expectations about learning. We cannot predict very well which of Ms. Martin's students will succeed and which will fail, but we can predict, based on the past, that if nothing changes, far too many will fail. This is especially true if Ms. Martin's kindergarten happens to be located in a high-poverty neighborhood, in which there are typically fewer resources in the school to provide top-quality instruction to every child, fewer forms of rescue if children run into academic difficulties, and fewer supports for learning at home. Preventable failures occur in all schools, but in high-poverty schools, failure can be endemic—so widespread that it makes it difficult to treat each child at risk of failure as a person of value in need of emergency assistance to get back on track. Instead, many such schools do their best to provide the greatest benefit to the greatest number of children possible but have an unfortunately well-founded expectation that a certain percentage of students will fall by the wayside during the elementary years.

Any discussion of school reform should begin with Ms. Martin's kindergartners. The first goal of reform should be to ensure that every child, regardless of home background, home language, or learning style, achieves the success that he or she so confidently expected in kindergarten, that all children maintain their motivation, enthusiasm, and optimism because they are objectively succeeding at the school's tasks. Any reform that does less than this is hollow and self-defeating.

What does it mean to succeed in the early grades? The elementary school's definition of success, and therefore the parents' and children's definition as well, is, overwhelmingly, success in reading. Very few children who are reading adequately are retained, assigned to special education, or given long-term remedial services. Other subjects are important, of course, but reading and language arts form the core of what school success means in the early grades.

When a child fails to read well in the early grades, he or she begins a downward progression. In first grade, some children begin to notice that they are not reading adequately. They may fail first grade or be assigned to long-term remediation. As they proceed through the elementary grades, many students begin to see that they are failing at their full-time jobs. When this happens, things begin to unravel. Failing students begin to have poor motivation and poor self-expectations, which lead to continued poor achievement, in a declining spiral that ultimately leads to despair, delinquency, and dropout.

Remediating learning deficits after they are already well established is extremely difficult. Children who have already failed to learn to read, for example, are now anxious about reading and doubt their ability to learn it. Their motivation to read may be low. They may ultimately learn to read, but it will always be a chore, not a pleasure. Clearly, the time to provide additional help to children who are at risk is early, when children are still motivated and confident and when any learning deficits are relatively small and remediable. The most important goal in educational programming for students at risk of school failure is to try to make certain that we do not squander the greatest resource we have: the enthusiasm and positive self-expectations of young children themselves.

In practical terms, what this perspective implies is that schools, and especially Title I, special education, and other services for at-risk children, must be shifted from an emphasis on remediation to an emphasis on prevention and early intervention. Prevention means providing developmentally appropriate preschool and kindergarten programs so that students will enter first grade ready to succeed, and it means providing regular classroom teachers with effective instructional programs, curricula, and professional development to enable them to ensure that most students are successful the first time they are taught. Early intervention means that supplementary instructional services are provided early in students' schooling and that they are intensive enough to bring at-risk students quickly to a level at which they can profit from good-quality classroom instruction.

Success for All is built around the idea that every child can and must succeed in the early grades, no matter what this takes. The idea behind the program is to use everything we know about effective instruction for students at risk to direct all aspects of school and classroom organization toward the goal of preventing academic deficits from appearing in the first place, recognizing and intensively intervening with any deficits that do appear, and providing students with a rich and full curriculum to enable them to build on their firm foundation in basic skills. The commitment of Success for All is to do whatever it takes to see that every child becomes a skilled, strategic, and enthusiastic reader by the end of the elementary grades. As Success for All has developed, it now provides materials in math, science, and social studies that can help children achieve success in these areas as well.

Usual practices in elementary schools do not support the principle of prevention and early intervention. Most schools provide a pretty good kindergarten, a pretty good first grade, and so on. Starting in first grade, a certain number of students begin to fall behind, and over the course of time, these students are assigned to remedial programs (such as Title I) or to special education or are simply retained.

Our society's tacit assumption is that those students who fall by the wayside are defective in some way. Perhaps they have learning disabilities, or low IQs, or poor motivation, or parents who are unsupportive of school learning, or other problems. We assume that because most students do succeed with standard, pretty good instruction in the early grades, there must be something wrong with those who don't.

Success for All is built around a completely different set of assumptions. The most important assumption is that every child can learn. We mean this not as wishful thinking or just a slogan but as a practical, attainable reality. In particular, every child without organic retardation can learn to read. Some children need more help than others and may need different approaches than those needed by others, but one way or another, every child can become a successful reader.

The first requirement for the success of every child is prevention. This means providing excellent preschool and kindergarten programs; improving curriculum, instruction, and classroom management throughout the grades; assessing students frequently to make sure they are making adequate progress; and establishing cooperative relationships with parents so they can support students' learning at home.

Top-quality curriculum and instruction from age 4 on will ensure the success of most students—but not all of them. The next requirement for the success of all students is intensive early intervention. This means one-to-one tutoring for first graders having reading problems. It means being able to work with parents and social service agencies to be sure that all students attend school, have medical services or eye-glasses if they need them, have help with behavior problems, and so on.

The most important idea in Success for All is that the school must relentlessly stick with every child until that child is succeeding. If prevention is not enough, the child may need tutoring. If this is not enough, he or she may need help with behavior or attendance or eyeglasses. If this is not enough, he or she may need a modified approach to reading or other subjects. The school does not merely provide services to children, it constantly assesses the results of the services it provides and keeps varying or adding services until every child is successful.

Origins of Success for All

The development of the Success for All program began in 1986 as a response to a challenge made to our group at Johns Hopkins University by Baltimore's superintendent of schools, Alice Pinderhughes, its school board president, Robert Embry, and a former Maryland Secretary of Human Resources, Kalman "Buzzy" Hettleman. They asked us what it would take to ensure the success of *every* child in schools serving large numbers of disadvantaged students.

At the time, we were working on a book called *Effective Programs for Students at Risk* (Slavin, Karweit, & Madden, 1989), so we were very interested in this question. After many discussions, the superintendent asked us to go to the next step, to work with Baltimore's Elementary Division to actually plan a pilot program. We met for months with a planning committee and finally produced a plan and selected a school to serve as a site. We began in September 1987 in a school in which all students were African American and approximately 83% qualified for free lunches. Initially, the additional costs needed to fund the program came from a Chapter 2 grant, but the program was soon supported entirely by the same Chapter 1 funds received by all similar schools.

The first-year results were very positive (see Slavin, Madden, Karweit, Livermon, & Dolan, 1990). In comparison to matched control students, Success for All students had much higher reading scores, and retentions and special education placements were substantially reduced.

In 1988-1989, Success for All was expanded in Baltimore to a total of five schools. We also began implementation of Success for All at one of the poorest schools in Philadelphia, in which a majority of the students are Cambodian. This school gave us our first experience in adapting Success for All to meet the needs of limited English proficient students. In 1990-1991, we developed a Spanish version of the Success for All beginning reading program, called *Lee Conmigo,* and began to work in more bilingual schools as well as schools providing English as a Second Language (ESL) instruction (Slavin & Madden, 1999c). In 1992, we received a grant from the New American Schools Development Corporation (NASDC) to develop Roots & Wings, which adds math, science, and social studies to the reading and writing programs of Success for All (Slavin & Madden, 2000). Roots & Wings is currently beginning to be disseminated widely.

Figure 1.1. Numbers of Success for All Schools, 1990-2000

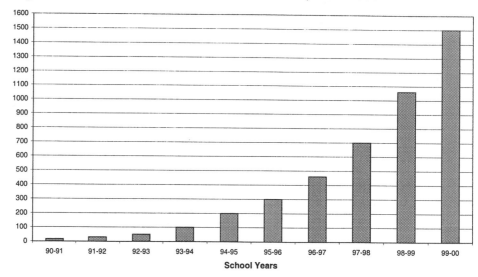

In more recent years, Success for All has grown exponentially. Figure 1.1 shows this growth, which has been from 40% to 100% each year since 1989. As noted earlier, as of fall 2000, it is in about 1800 schools in 700 districts in 48 states throughout the United States. The districts range from some of the largest in the country, such as New York, Houston, Memphis, Los Angeles, Cincinnati, and Miami, to such middle-sized districts as Tuscon, Arizona; Hartford, Connecticut; Columbus, Ohio; Galveston, Texas; Worcester, Massachusetts; Rockford, Illinois; and Modesto, California, to tiny rural districts, including schools on several Indian reservations. Success for All reading curricula in Spanish have been developed and researched and are used in bilingual programs throughout the United States. Almost all Success for All schools are high-poverty Title I schools, and the great majority are schoolwide projects. Otherwise, the schools vary widely.

Overview of Success for All Components

The elements of Success for All are described in detail in the early chapters of this book, but before we get to the particulars, it is useful to see the big picture. Success for All has somewhat different components at different sites, depending on the school's needs and the resources available to implement the program. However, there is a common set of elements characteristic of all.

Reading Program

Success for All uses a reading curriculum based on research and effective practices in beginning reading (e.g., Adams, 1990) and an appropriate use of cooperative learning (Slavin, 1995; Stevens, Madden, Slavin, & Farnish, 1987).

Reading teachers at every grade level begin the reading time by reading children's literature to students and engaging them in a discussion of the story to enhance their understanding of the story, listening and speaking vocabulary, and knowledge of story structure. In kindergarten and first grade, the program emphasizes development of basic language skills with the use of Story Telling and Retelling (STaR), which involves the students in listening to, retelling, and dramatizing children's literature. Big books as well as oral and written composing activities allow students to develop concepts of print as they also develop knowledge of story structure. Specific oral language experiences are used to further develop receptive and expressive language.

Reading Roots (Madden, 1995) is introduced in the second semester of kindergarten. This K-1 beginning reading program uses as its base a series of phonetically regular but meaningful and interesting minibooks and emphasizes repeated oral reading to partners as well as to the teacher. The minibooks begin with a set of "shared stories," in which part of a story is written in small type (read by the teacher) and part is written in large type (read by the students). The student portion uses a phonetically controlled vocabulary. Taken together, the teacher and student portions create interesting, worthwhile stories. Over time, the teacher portion diminishes and the student portion lengthens until students are reading the entire book. This scaffolding allows students to read interesting literature when they only have a few letter sounds. Examples of shared stories appear in Appendices 2.1 and 2.2.

Letters and letter sounds are introduced in an active, engaging set of activities that begins with oral language and moves into written symbols. Individual sounds are integrated into a context of words, sentences, and stories. Instruction is provided in story structure, specific comprehension skills, metacognitive strategies for self-assessment and self-correction, and integration of reading and writing.

Spanish bilingual programs use an adaptation of Reading Roots called *Lee Conmigo* ("Read With Me"). *Lee Conmigo* uses the same instructional strategies as Reading Roots but is built around shared stories written in Spanish.

When students reach the second-grade reading level, they use a program called Reading Wings (Madden, Slavin, Farnish, Livingston, & Calderon, 1996), an adaptation of cooperative integrated reading and composition (CIRC) (Stevens et al., 1987). Reading Wings uses cooperative learning activities built around story structure, prediction, summarization, vocabulary building, decoding practice, and story-related writing. Students engage in partner reading and structured discussion of stories or novels, and in teams they work toward mastery of the vocabulary and content of the story. Story-related writing is also shared within teams. Cooperative learning both increases students' motivation and engages students in cognitive activities known to contribute to reading comprehension, such as elaboration, summarization, and rephrasing (see Slavin, 1995). Research on CIRC has found it to significantly increase students' reading comprehension and language skills (Stevens et al., 1987).

In addition to these story-related activities, teachers provide direct instruction in reading comprehension skills, and students practice these skills in their teams. Classroom libraries of trade books at students' reading levels are provided for each teacher, and students read books of their choice for homework for 20 minutes each night. Home readings are shared via presentations, summaries, puppet shows, and other formats twice a week during "book club" sessions.

Materials to support Reading Wings through the sixth-grade level (and beyond) exist in English and Spanish. The English materials are built around children's literature and around the most widely used basal series and anthologies. Supportive materials have been developed for more than 100 children's novels and for most current basal series (e.g., Houghton Mifflin, Scott Foresman, Holt, HBJ, Macmillan, McGraw-Hill, Silver Burdett-Ginn, Open Court). The upper-elementary Spanish program, Alas Para Leer, is built around Spanish-language novels and basal series.

Beginning in the second semester of program implementation, Success for All schools usually implement a writing and language arts program based primarily on cooperative learning principles (see Slavin, Madden, & Stevens, 1989/1990). The reading and writing/language arts programs are described in more detail in Chapter 2.

Students in Grades 1 to 5 or 6 are regrouped for reading. The students are assigned to heterogeneous, age-grouped classes most of the day, but during a regular 90-minute reading period, they are regrouped by reading performance levels into reading classes of students all at the same level. For example, a reading class taught at the 2-1 level might contain first-, second-, and third-grade students all reading at the same level. The reading classes are smaller than homerooms because tutors and other certificated staff (such as librarians or art teachers) teach reading during this common reading period.

Regrouping allows teachers to teach the whole reading class without having to break the class into reading groups. This greatly reduces the time spent in seat work and increases direct instruction time, eliminating workbooks, dittos, or other follow-up activities that are needed in classes that have multiple reading groups. The regrouping is a form of the Joplin Plan, which has been found to increase reading achievement in the elementary grades (Slavin, 1987).

Eight-Week Reading Assessments

At 8-week intervals, reading teachers assess student progress through the reading program. The results of the assessments are used to determine who is to receive tutoring, change students' reading groups, suggest other adaptations in students' programs, and identify students who need other types of assistance, such as family interventions or screening for vision and hearing problems. This process is described further in Chapter 2.

Reading Tutors

One of the most important elements of the Success for All model is the use of tutors to promote students' success in reading. One-to-one tutoring is the most effective form of instruction known (see Slavin et al., 1989; Wasik & Slavin, 1993). Most tutors are certified teachers with experience teaching Title I, special education, primary reading, or all of these. Often, well-qualified paraprofessionals also tutor children with less severe reading problems. Tutors work one-on-one with students who are having difficulty keeping up with their reading groups. The tutoring occurs in 20-minute sessions during times other than reading or math periods.

In general, tutors support students' success in the regular reading curriculum rather than teaching different objectives. For example, the tutor generally works with a student on the same story and concepts being read and taught in the regular reading class. However, tutors seek to identify learning problems and use different strategies to teach the same skills. They also teach metacognitive skills beyond those taught in the classroom program. Schools may have as many as six or more teachers serving as tutors, depending on school size, need for tutoring, and other factors.

During daily 90-minute reading periods, certified teacher-tutors serve as additional reading teachers to reduce class size for reading. Reading teachers and tutors use brief forms to communicate about students' specific problems and needs and meet at regular times to coordinate their approaches with individual children.

Initial decisions about reading group placement and the need for tutoring are based on informal reading inventories that the tutors give to each child. Subsequent reading group placements and tutoring assignments are made based on curriculum-based assessments given every 8 weeks, which include teacher judgments as well as more formal assessments. First graders receive priority for tutoring, on the assumption that the primary function of the tutors is to help all students be successful in reading the first time, before they fail and become remedial readers. Tutoring procedures are described in more detail in Chapter 3.

Preschool and Kindergarten

Most Success for All schools provide a half-day preschool or a full-day kindergarten or both for eligible students. The preschool and kindergarten programs focus on providing a balanced and developmentally appropriate learning experience for young children. The curriculum emphasizes the development and use of language. It provides a balance of academic readiness and nonacademic music, art, and movement activities in a series of thematic units. Readiness activities include use of language development activities and STaR, in which students retell stories read by the teachers (Karweit & Coleman, 1991). Prereading activities begin during the second semester of kindergarten. Preschool and kindergarten programs are described further in Chapter 4.

Family Support Team

Parents are an essential part of the formula for success in Success for All. A family support team (Haxby, Lasaga-Flister, Madden, Slavin, & Dolan, 1995) works in each school, serving to make families feel comfortable in the school and become active supporters of their child's education as well as providing specific services. The family support team consists of the Title I parent liaison, vice principal (if any), counselor (if any), facilitator, and any other appropriate staff already present in the school or added to the school staff.

The family support team first works toward good relations with parents and to increase involvement in the schools. Family support team members may complete "welcome" visits for new families. They organize many attractive programs in the school, such as parenting skills workshops. Most schools use a program called "Raising Readers," in which parents are given strategies to use in reading with their own children. Family support staff also help introduce a social skills development program called "Getting Along Together," which gives students peaceful strategies for resolving interpersonal conflicts.

The family support team also intervenes to solve problems. For example, they may contact parents whose children are frequently absent to see what resources can be provided to assist the family in getting their child to school. Family support staff, teachers, and parents work together to solve school behavior problems. Also, family support staff are called on to provide assistance when students seem to be working at less than their full potential because of problems at home. Families of students who are not receiving adequate sleep or nutrition, need glasses, are not attending school regularly, or are exhibiting serious behavior problems may receive family support assistance.

The family support team is strongly integrated into the academic program of the school. It receives referrals from teachers and tutors regarding children who are not making adequate academic progress and thereby constitutes an additional stage of intervention for students in need above and beyond that provided by the classroom teacher or tutor. The family support team also encourages and trains parents and other community members to fulfill numerous volunteer roles within the school, ranging from providing a listening ear for emerging readers to helping in the school cafeteria. Family support and integrated services are described further in Chapter 6.

Program Facilitator

A program facilitator works at each school to oversee (with the principal) the operation of the Success for All model. The facilitator helps plan the Success for All program, helps the principal with scheduling, and visits classes and tutoring sessions frequently to help teachers and tutors with individual problems. He or she works directly with the teachers on implementation of the curriculum, classroom management, and other issues; helps teachers and tutors deal with any behavior problems or other special problems; and coordinates the activities of the family support team with those of the instructional staff. The role of the facilitator is described further in Chapter 7.

Teachers and Teacher Training

The teachers and tutors are regular certified teachers. They receive detailed teacher's manuals supplemented by 3 days of inservice at the beginning of the school year, followed by classroom observations and coaching throughout the year. For classroom teachers of Grades 1 and above and for reading tutors, training sessions focus on implementation of the reading program (either Reading Roots or Reading Wings), and their detailed teachers' manuals cover general teaching strategies as well as specific lessons. Preschool and kindergarten teachers and aides are trained in strategies appropriate to their students' preschool and kindergarten models. Tutors later receive 2 additional days of training on tutoring strategies and reading assessment.

Throughout the year, additional inservice presentations are made by the facilitators and other project staff on such topics as classroom management, instructional pace, and cooperative learning. Facilitators also organize many informal sessions to allow teachers to share problems and problem solutions, suggest changes, and discuss individual children. The staff development model used in Success for All emphasizes relatively brief initial training with extensive classroom follow-up, coaching, and group discussion. Training and monitoring procedures are described further in Chapter 7.

Advisory Committee

An advisory committee, composed of the building principal, program facilitator, teacher representatives, parent representatives, and family support staff, meets regularly to review the progress of the program and to identify and solve any problems that arise. In most schools, existing site-based management teams are adapted to fulfill this function. In addition, grade-level or component teams and the family support team meet regularly to discuss common problems and solutions and to make decisions in their areas of responsibility. See Chapter 7 for more on this.

Special Education

Every effort is made to deal with students' learning problems within the context of the regular classroom, as supplemented by tutors. Tutors evaluate students' strengths and weaknesses and develop strategies to teach in the most effective way. In some schools, special education teachers work as tutors and reading teachers with students identified as learning disabled as well as other students experiencing learning problems who are at risk for special education placement. One major goal of Success for All is to keep students with learning problems out of special education if at all possible and to serve any students who do qualify for special education in a way that does not disrupt their regular classroom experience (see Slavin, 1996a). Implications of Success for All for special education are described in Chapter 9.

Roots & Wings

In 1991, we received a grant from New American Schools Development Corporation (NASDC) to create a comprehensive elementary school design for the 21st century. We call the program we designed under NASDC funding Roots & Wings (see Chapter 5). Roots & Wings incorporates revisions of all of the elements of Success for All—reading, writing, and language arts programs, prekindergarten and kindergarten programs, tutoring, family support, and so on—but adds to these a program in mathematics—MathWings—and a program that integrates social studies and science, which we call WorldLab.

WorldLab

WorldLab is an integrated curriculum for science, social studies, and writing, used in Grades 1 through 5. In it, students take on roles as people in history, in other countries, or in various occupations. For example, fifth graders learn about the American Revolution by participating in the writing of their own "declaration of independence" and by serving as delegates to the Constitutional Convention. Fourth graders learn about physics by creating and testing inventions. Third graders learn about the culture of Africa and about simple machines by serving as a council of elders in an African village trying to design a system for irrigating their fields. First and second graders learn scientific method by becoming scientists collecting and integrating information about trees. WorldLab units incorporate writing, reading, math, fine arts, and music, as well as science and social studies. Children work in small, cooperative groups and carry out experiments, investigations, and projects.

MathWings

Roots & Wings schools use a constructivist mathematics program called MathWings (Madden, Slavin, & Simons, 1999) in Grades kindergarten through 6. In this program, based on the standards of the National Council of Teachers of Mathematics, students work in cooperative groups to discover, experiment with, and apply mathematical ideas. The program builds on the practical knowledge base with which all children enter school, helping children build toward formal representations of such familiar ideas as combining and separating, dividing into equal parts, and parts of a whole. It incorporates problem solving in real and simulated situations (including WorldLab), skill practice, calculator use, alternative assessments, writing, and connections to literature and other disciplines. Children learn not only to find the right answer but to explain and apply their new understandings.

Relentlessness

Although the particular elements of Success for All and Roots & Wings may vary from school to school, there is one feature we try to make consistent in all: a relentless focus on the success of every child. It would be entirely possible to have tutoring, curriculum change, family support, and other services, yet still not ensure the success of at-risk children. Success does not come from piling on additional services but from coordinating human resources around a well-defined goal, constantly assessing progress toward that goal, and never giving up until success is achieved.

None of the elements of Success for All or Roots & Wings are completely new or unique. All are based on well-established principles of learning and rigorous instructional research. What is most distinctive about them is their schoolwide, coordinated, and proactive plan for translating positive expectations into concrete success for all children. Every child can complete elementary school a confident, strategic, and joyful learner and can maintain the enthusiasm and positive self-expectations they had when they came to first grade. The purpose of Success for All and Roots & Wings is to see that this vision can become a practical reality in every school.

2

Reading, Writing, and Language Arts Programs

Whereas Success for All and Roots & Wings ultimately incorporate reform in most of the elementary school curriculum and instruction, the heart of the instructional program is reading. The reason for this is obvious; in the early grades, success in school is virtually synonymous with success in reading. Very few primary-grade students are retained or assigned to special education solely on the basis of deficits in math performance, for example. A child who can read is not guaranteed to be a success in elementary school, but a child who cannot is guaranteed to be a failure.

The amount of reading failure in the early grades in schools serving disadvantaged students is shocking. In our studies of Success for All, we found that at the end of first grade, about a quarter of students in our disadvantaged control schools could not read and comprehend the following passage: "I have a little black dog. He has a pink nose. He has a little tail. He can jump and run" (Durrell & Catterson, 1980).

On the 1994 National Assessment of Educational Progress, only 31% of African American fourth graders and 36% of Hispanic fourth graders could read at the "basic" level, compared to 71% of whites (Campell, Donahue, Reese, & Phillips, 1996). In many urban districts, retention rates for first graders topped 20% in the 1980s, and with the new national reaction against social promotion, high retention rates are returning. What these statistics mean is that despite some improvements over the past 20 years, the reading performance of disadvantaged and minority children is still se-

14

riously lacking, and the deficits begin early. The consequences of early reading fail-ure are severe. A child who is not reading adequately by the end of third grade is headed for serious trouble.

The philosophy that guides the development of the reading curriculum in Suc-cess for All emphasizes the need for reading instruction to work for *all* students. We recognize that different children learn to read in different ways, so our approach em-phasizes teaching reading many different ways at the same time. For example, each beginning reading lesson has students reading silently and aloud, singing, tracing letters with their fingers, writing, making visual and auditory discriminations, dis-cussing stories, making predictions, using context clues, and engaging in many other activities. Teaching the same concepts and skills in many different ways both provides reinforcement and allows the curriculum to use to learning strengths of every child.

Grouping

Homeroom classes in Success for All and Roots & Wings are fully heteroge-neous. However, to have enough instructional time to be able to teach reading in many different ways, students are regrouped for reading across grade lines accord-ing to reading level so that all reading classes contain just one level. For example, a reading class working at an early second-grade level might contain first, second, and third graders all reading at the same level. During reading time (90 minutes per day), additional teachers are available to teach reading because certified tutors (and in some schools, media specialists and physical education, special education, or ESL teachers) teach a reading class. This means that reading classes are smaller than homeroom classes. Based on regular curriculum-based assessments given every 8 weeks, reading group assignments are constantly reexamined (see the section to fol-low). Students capable of working in a higher-performing group are accelerated, whereas those who are not performing adequately are given tutoring, family support services, modifications in curriculum or instruction, or other services to help them keep up. Only very rarely would a child repeat a given segment of instruction.

There are many reasons for cross-class and cross-grade grouping for reading in Success for All. First, having all students at one reading level avoids any need for the use of reading groups *within* the class. The problem with reading groups is that when the teacher is working with one group, the other groups are at their desks doing seat work or other independent tasks of little instructional value. To have a full 90 min-utes of active, productive instruction, having only one reading group is essential. Re-search on cross-grade grouping for reading, often called the Joplin Plan, has shown that this method increases student achievement (Slavin, 1987).

In addition, use of cross-class and cross-grade grouping allows the use of tutors and other certified staff as reading teachers. This has many benefits. First, it reduces class size for reading, which has important benefits for achievement in the early grades (Slavin, 1994). Perhaps of equal importance, it gives tutors and other supple-mentary teachers experience in teaching the reading program so that they know exactly what their students are experiencing. When a student is struggling with Lesson 17, the tutor knows what Lesson 17 is, because he or she has taught it.

Eight-Week Assessments

A critical feature of reading instruction in Success for All at all grade levels is assessment of student progress every 8 weeks. These assessments are closely linked to the curriculum. In the early grades, they may include some written and some oral assessments; in the later grades, they use written assessments keyed to novels (if the school uses novels), or they may use "magazine tests" or other assessments provided with basal series. These assessments usually include assessments of skills above students' current level of performance, to facilitate decisions to accelerate students to higher reading groups.

Eight-week assessments are used for three essential purposes. One is to change students' reading groupings, to identify students capable of being accelerated. A second is to decide which students are in the greatest need for tutoring and which no longer need tutoring (see Chapter 3). Last, the 8-week assessments provide an internal check on the progress of every child. They can indicate to school staff that a given student is not making adequate progress and lead them to try other strategies.

The 8-week assessments are given and scored by reading teachers but are collated and interpreted by the facilitator, who uses them to review the progress of all children and to suggest changes in grouping, tutoring assignments, or other approaches to the reading teachers. See Chapter 6 for more on this.

Reading Approaches

The Success for All reading approach is divided into two programs. Reading Roots (Madden, 1999) is usually introduced either in the middle of kindergarten or the beginning of first grade, depending on the district's goals for kindergarten. Reading Roots continues through what would usually be thought of as the first reader and is usually completed by the end of first grade, although a small number of students may not finish Reading Roots until second grade. Reading Roots replaces the usual basals and workbooks with a completely different set of materials. Bilingual schools choosing to teach beginning reading to their Spanish-speaking students in Spanish use Lee Conmigo, which uses the same instructional strategies and processes as Reading Roots but is built around stories and materials in Spanish.

Starting at the second-grade level, students go on to what we call Reading Wings, which continues through the fifth or sixth grade. Reading Wings (Madden, Slavin, Farnish, Livingston, & Calderón, 1999) uses the district's usual basals, anthologies, or novels but replaces workbooks and other supplementary materials with a student-centered cooperative learning process that focuses on developing comprehension skills. Reading Wings involves students in many kinds of active interaction with reading, discussion, and writing. The Reading Wings process, when used with Spanish novels or basals, is called Alas Para Leer.

Reading Roots, *Lee Conmigo,* Reading Wings, and *Alas Para Leer* are described in the following sections.

Reading Roots

There is both magic and method in learning to read. Students come to school knowing that learning to read will be their most important task and that it will be an exciting step in growing up. Taught with effective methods, every child can experience the magic of reading and become a confident, joyful, and strategic reader by the end of first grade.

The Reading Roots program (Madden, 1999) used in Success for All is based on research that points to the need to have students learn to read in meaningful contexts and at the same time to have a systematic presentation of word attack skills (see Adams, 1990). Three basic components—reading of children's literature by the teacher, "shared story" beginning reading lessons, and systematic language development—combine to address the learning needs of first graders in a variety of ways. Teachers read to students every day using children's literature to expose them to the joy and meaning of reading as well as concepts of print.

Building Listening Comprehension

A major principle of Reading Roots is that students need to learn comprehension strategies at a level *above* their current independent reading level. What this means is that the teacher reads children's literature to students and engages students in discussions, retelling of the stories, and writing. The idea is to build reading comprehension skill with material more difficult than that which students could read on their own, because in the early grades, the material children can read independently does not challenge their far more advanced comprehension skills. This process begins in preschool and kindergarten with the STaR program, and STaR continues through first grade. At that point, students begin a Listening Comprehension program in which teachers continue to read to children and teach them to identify characters, settings, problems, and problem solutions in narratives; visualize descriptive elements of stories; identify sequences of events; predict story outcomes; to identify topics and main ideas in expository selections; and so on. The STaR process is described in more detail in Chapter 4.

Building Reading Strategies

Before entering Reading Roots, or early in the program, we expect that students have developed basic concepts about print, are beginning to understand that letters and words represent speech and are meant to communicate a message with meaning, that print progresses from left to right, that spoken and written words are made up of sounds, and so on. These concepts continue to be developed with STaR and are reinforced as students begin to take on the task of reading for themselves in Reading Roots lessons. More specific knowledge of auditory discrimination, hearing sounds within words, knowledge of the sounds associated with specific letters, and blending letter sounds into words are developed in Reading Roots lessons so that students understand the phonetic nature of language and can independently use phonetic synthesis to help them read.

The shared-story beginning reading curriculum emphasizes immediate application of skills to real reading. For example, students read an entire book in the first lesson. Reading Roots lessons are structured and fast paced, involving activities that enable students to learn the new sounds and words introduced in the story thoroughly and quickly. In addition, the lessons develop general strategies for facilitating both word recognition and text comprehension so that students become independent, thinking readers who experience the joy of reading. These strategies include using context and pictures to unlock words and meaning; building knowledge of the purposes for reading; and previewing, self-questioning, and summarizing, which allow students to monitor their own comprehension.

The activities in Reading Roots incorporate the following components:

Shared Stories

Shared stories allow students to read complex, engaging, and interesting stories when they only know a few letter sounds. Each page in a shared story has both a teacher section and a student section. Beginning in Lesson 4, the students' portions of the shared stories use a phonetically regular vocabulary so that the skills students are learning will work in cracking the reading code. The student sections use only the letter sounds and words students have learned, plus a few key sight words and "readles," words represented by pictures. The teacher sections provide a context for the story and include predictive questions that are answered in the student sections. In the earliest stories, the teacher text adds a great deal to the meaning of the stories, but over time, the student sections increase while the teacher sections diminish. This scaffolding method allows children to read meaningful and worthwhile stories from the first weeks of their beginning reading instruction. As they learn systematic strategies for finding the meaning of words, sentences, and stories, students take increasing responsibility for their reading. Soon, they are able to unlock the reading code and join the wacky worlds of Matt and his dog, Sad Sam, the world's most phonetically regular hound dog; Miss Sid, the pesky parrot; Nan and her cat, Pit-Pat; and many other engaging characters. Later, students meet Lana and her huge dog, Fang; and Paco and his mischievous friend, Bob; last, they experience a world of fairy tales and stories from many cultures. During the last quarter of the shared-story sequence, readles, teacher text, and adult text are no longer used. A sample page from a shared story presented in the early part of the sequence and another presented in the latter part are shown in Figures 2.1 and 2.2, and complete shared stories appear in Appendices 2.1 and 2.2 at the end of this chapter.

The shared stories in Reading Roots are organized into four thematically related sections. Level 1, Stories 1 through 15, is built around a first grader named Matt, his dog Sad Sam, and his friends in the neighborhood. Level 2, Stories 16 through 25, describes the experiences of a group of students in Ms. Stanton's first-grade class. Level 3, Stories 26 through 37, focuses around a group of city children and their visits to relatives in the country as the seasons change throughout the year. Level 4,

Figure 2.1

Ms. Tad helped Matt make a card. What do you think was on the card?   **3**

It was Dad.
It was Sad Sam.

Stories 38 through 48, takes students around the world as it introduces both traditional folk and fairy tales and expository text. Expository narratives present information about Sweden, Benin (Nigeria), China, Colombia, and the United States. Each factual story is followed by a tale from that country. Level 4 presents a very challenging reading experience that is designed to make the transition between the carefully sequenced Reading Roots lessons and the novels or basals that students will use in Reading Wings.

Parallel stories are provided for Reading Roots Shared Stories 4 through 37, for use by teachers and tutors to reinforce the skills in the initial story. A parallel story uses the same letters and sight words but introduces additional phonetically regular words in different stories.

Cooperative Learning

Working cooperatively with other students provides children with an opportunity to discuss the concepts and skills they are learning with someone very close to their own level of understanding. In Reading Roots, students confer with their partners as they think of words that begin with a certain sound, as they predict the next event in a story, and as they orally read and reread new and familiar stories. These co-

Figure 2.2

A sea lion teased me one day when Dad and I were fishing. It took my hook. It took my fish. Then it popped up by the boat. It shook its flippers. It seemed to grin at us. What a joke!

operative learning activities provide opportunities for students to explain their understanding to someone else, thus requiring them to organize their own thoughts. Simple peer practice routines are used throughout the lessons as a means of reinforcing and building mastery of basic reading skills. Students read and discuss their stories with partners and work with partners on reading practice activities. These activities increase the amount of time that each student can be actively engaged with text rather than passively listening as other students read. Opportunities for partner discussion of the story and of story-related writing increase the active thinking time for students.

Metacognitive Strategies Instruction

Metacognitive skills are emphasized throughout Reading Roots to help students think about the process of reading, predict what is going to happen in a story, assess their own comprehension, and know how to find meaning when they experience difficulties. Four main strategies used to enhance text comprehension are taught and practiced in the context of the shared stories: (a) understanding the purposes for reading, (b) previewing to prepare for reading, (c) monitoring for meaning to ensure that the text is understood, and (e) summarizing or retelling the main ideas or events of a story.

Choral Response Games

During direct instruction, students are involved in games in which the class responds as a whole to questions. The students have a great deal of fun with these activities and are all involved in thinking and responding. Students need not spend time waiting while others respond one at a time.

Auditory Discrimination and Sound Blending

The activities in these lessons are designed to build auditory discrimination (hearing the separate sounds in words) and sound-blending skills in a developmental sequence so that students will be able to use sound blending as a strategy to aid them in word recognition. With systematic teaching, students become adept at using sound-blending strategies in addition to memory, context, and pictures to unlock the meaning of words and stories. Sound-blending instruction gives a real boost to the many students whose visual memory skills are not strong, a group that often includes students who would fail in reading without this kind of systematic approach to unlocking the reading code.

Writing

Students are encouraged to write to reinforce their learning and to express their response to stories. Writing activities may vary from completing simple letter and word-writing activities that reinforce letter shapes and sounds to answering specific questions about a story, writing personal experiences similar to those in a story, sharing feelings about characters, and summarizing story events. Sound-based spelling is explicitly taught, and teachers are encouraged to respond to the meaning of the ideas students express rather than to errors in spelling or punctuation. Peers assist one another in the writing process as they share their plans and drafts with one another, revise based on peers' suggestions, and celebrate each others' writing.

A Reading Roots Lesson

A 90-minute Reading Roots lesson has three major parts—a STaR or Listening Comprehension unit, the shared story lesson, and a language development unit. Each day begins with a 20-minute STaR lesson, in which the teacher reads and discusses a story. An example of a STaR lesson appears in Chapter 4. The 50-minute shared-story lesson (described in the following section) would be followed by a 20-minute language development lesson, also described in Chapter 4. The activities in a shared-story lesson usually would be completed over 2 or 3 days of reading instruction, depending on the time needed by the particular group to master the story.

The goals for specific activities in Reading Roots are discussed later, along with some specific instructions on effectively implementing the program. As students progress through the sequence, some of the activities described may no longer be used, but the basic parts of the lesson remain. The materials and activities for each lesson are explained in detail in the actual lessons. Lessons are presented over 2 or 3 days, depending on the levels and abilities of the students.

Showtime (Reading Review and Letter Formation Review)

Review and practice are essential elements in acquiring proficiency in any skill area. Review segments are spread throughout the Reading Roots lesson as this structured practice is essential for the development of fluency with letters, sounds, and words.

Reading Rehearsal

In Reading Rehearsal, students reread a familiar story either in pairs or in a whole-class choral reading. The purpose of this Reading Rehearsal is to reinforce the concept that real reading is what reading instruction is all about. Children need to learn early that the essence of reading is the whole act of reading, not a series of unconnected skills. The Reading Rehearsal segment allows students to master reading through repeated practice, to learn words in context rather than through reading word lists, and to master the flow and phrasing of reading necessary to comprehend what is being read.

Letter Formation Review

Introduced in Lesson 2, Letter Formation Review provides practice in sound and name recognition and formation of known letters by using standard cue phrases (e.g., "One stroke down, lift and cross. The sound for 't' is /t/"). This provides the practice needed to assist students in making an automatic association between the formation of the letter and its name and sound. In later lessons, as students become fluent in individual letters, words and even sentences are used as the basis for a brief written review.

Metacognitive Strategies

Thinking About Reading

The focus of Thinking About Reading is to teach students why, when, and how to use metacognitive reading strategies that will help them ask themselves whether they are understanding what they read, recognize if they are not, and know how to find the meaning. Metacognition is the awareness and comprehension of one's own thinking. Successful readers use metacognitive strategies to help them effectively read and comprehend. As noted earlier, the four strategies presented in Reading Roots are (a) understanding the purpose for reading, (b) previewing to prepare for reading, (c) monitoring for meaning, and (d) summarization. These strategies are presented in the context of reading.

Presenting the Story

Setting the Stage

The teacher reads the story to the class as the first presentation of the story. As a part of the initial reading, the teacher provides a broad context for the story by giving background information, adding comments and questions, and requesting predictions to guide students' thoughts about the story.

Sound, Letter, and Word Development Activities

The focus of these activities is to teach students to discriminate sounds in language and to know the shapes of the letters and the sounds that they represent. The lessons are designed to begin with the isolation of specific sounds within the context of meaningful language, then to teach sound and letter correspondence using a wide variety of practice techniques, and last, to apply those techniques directly to the words to be read in the story. Description of the steps involved in the presentation and practice of each sound and letter follow.

Alphabet Song

Sound, letter, and word activities center around a character named Alphie, who brings messages and materials each day to help the class learn letters and sounds. The class sings the alphabet song to entice Alphie, a puppet, to come out of his box each day. The repetition of the alphabet song motivates and gives students an opportunity to hear the names of the letters regularly and thus to become familiar with them and with the order of letters in the alphabet.

Letter Presentation

The following activities are used to present each letter's name and sound.

Two-Picture Game

In this game, students practice hearing the new sound through the use of pictures. Two pictures are presented at once, and students as a group are asked to say the names of the pictures and identify which picture starts with the letter or letter combination being taught. This game again develops the skill of hearing a specific sound in a meaningful word and separating it from other sounds in the word.

Hearing the Sound

Each sound is introduced with a sentence, called the Tongue Twister. It is presented as a message from Alphie, which uses that sound in several words. For instance, the teacher might introduce the /d/ sound by reading Alphie's note: "Today, Alphie has written a silly note about dogs like Sad Sam. Many words begin with the sound /d/: *Dizzy dogs dig doughnuts during December.*"

Students enjoy this procedure and learn that they can use the strategy of saying the word with the first sound separated as a way of hearing how a word starts. It is important to note that sounds are presented as parts of meaningful words so that students use their own knowledge of language as a basis.

Introducing Pictures and Objects

Next, Alphie provides a set of pictures or objects that begin with the sound being taught. For the /d/ sound, Alphie presents the pictures of Dad, dog, duck, and dishes, as well as any actual objects the teacher provides. Students name the pictures or objects and identify the beginning sound for each one.

Making the Sound

The shape of the mouth while producing the sound is identified next. Focusing on the shape of the mouth gives students another cue to help them hear and "see" the separate sounds. As they learn to feel the changes in the shape of their mouths and watch the teacher's mouth, they will more clearly understand the concept that words are made up of groups of sounds. This understanding is crucial for decoding. Later, as they begin to write words, students will be able to use the feeling of change between sounds as an important way to recognize separate sounds.

Introducing the Shape

Last, after many different kinds of practice in hearing and separating the sounds that have been learned, the students are ready for the introduction of the letter shape that identifies the sound. Up to this point, the letter name has not been used. Words have been referred to as having the /d/ sound.

Practicing the Shape

The shape of the letter is practiced using several multisensory routines. Each letter has a verbal pattern associated with it that guides the student through the formation of the letter. For instance, the pattern for the /d/ sound is: "Circle left, way up, back down."

Using a large letter on the board as a model, students use their "magic pencils" (their index fingers) to practice writing the letter in the air, on their desks, and on a partner's hand, arm, or back. The verbal pattern is repeated with each practice.

Letter Games

The following activities present a variety of game formats that focus on the letter sound being taught.

Say-It-Fast

This component gradually introduces the concepts that letters represent sounds, and sounds make words. The objective of this activity, also called *auditory sound blending,* is to sharpen auditory awareness while helping students develop the ability to synthesize the sounds they hear into meaningful words. If a student cannot connect /b/-/e/-/d/ with the familiar word *bed,* then he or she will not be able to blend sounds into recognizable words. The activity has a game format and uses sentence context practice along with a variety of familiar words. It prepares students for future work using sounds for reading and spelling.

Break-It-Down

This activity is the flip side of Say-It-Fast. The teacher says a word and asks students to separate it into individual phonemes. This further develops phonemic awareness and prepares students for both reading and writing.

Students' Words

In this step, students are asked to connect the sound concept they are learning to their own language and experience. Students are asked to select a word they know that starts with the sound they are studying.

Yes-No Game

The Yes-No Game provides a different kind of practice for students in separating sounds within real words. Students are shown a card and asked whether the name of the object on that card begins with the sound being studied. When students have mastered this, they are given a word orally and asked whether the word begins with the letter being studied.

Matching Games

The Matching Games provide practice in sound and letter matching and auditory discrimination. The games begin simply and become more complex as the students gain proficiency. Four levels of games are used in teaching each letter. In each level, three sounds are represented, and pictures or words using those sounds must be matched to them.

Story Activities

Word Presentation

In this segment, story words are introduced. The phonetically regular words are presented using Stretch and Read, and the sight words are presented using repetition or using the context of the sentence in which the word is presented in the story.

Stretch and Read

Students learn that saying the sounds for letters in order (left to right) produces real words. This is done in a slow, exaggerated fashion at first and then, as students become proficient in letter and sound matching, becomes more of a rapid drill activity. Because the words presented in Stretch and Read are the words that students will use to read the story, the skill presented is immediately applicable in a meaningful reading situation. The Stretch and Read strategy will be familiar to them if they need to use a strategy besides memory and context to unlock a word as they read.

Quick Erase

This activity gives students an opportunity for a fun and fast-paced drill using letters and sounds they know from having practiced Stretch and Read. It involves changing one letter of a word at a time to create a new word. Tad becomes mad, mad becomes dad, and so forth. Quick Erase provides a way to explore word patterns and helps students generalize from known words to new words.

Say-Spell-Say

This is simply a repetition procedure to aid in memorization of important sight words. Sight words presented with the Say-Spell-Say process are pronouns, articles, prepositions, and so on.

Using Context

Students use context to unlock the meaning of some nonphonetic story words by analyzing the sentences in which they are found. Sight words commonly presented through context are nouns, verbs, adverbs, and adjectives.

Guided Group Reading

The story has been read to the group before; now, the goal is to assist students in learning to read it by themselves. Students read the story first as a whole class. The teacher reads the story script again to add meaning to the students' text and to keep students focused on understanding what they are reading. Also, metacognitive strategies are reviewed during this segment.

Partner Reading

Students now reread the story with a partner. Each partner reads a page independently, receiving help from his or her partner if it is needed. Students are encouraged to use appropriate expression as they read. Students practice metacognitive strategies in this segment.

Share Sheets

Share sheets are reading and writing activities designed to be used by pairs of students for practice and feedback on their reading and writing. Again, this partner practice increases the opportunities for giving and receiving explanations, as well as for oral reading and writing with feedback. All of the activities are story related. Share sheets are practiced more than once. Eventually, they are taken home to be practiced further with parents and family members.

Spelling

After students have learned to say and read the new letter sound in words, sentences, and the shared story, they learn the correct spelling of the phonetic words.

Stretch and Count

This activity is a preliminary step in the spelling process. After students have had some practice with hearing individual sounds and sound blending, the concept of *auditory* sound and symbol correspondence is introduced. Students are taught to "stretch" simple words into their component sounds and to make a count of the number of sounds in a word.

Stretch and Spell

This lesson segment develops the concept of spelling and using sounds to assist in spelling. Students stretch a word, identify the sounds one at a time, and write the letters they hear.

Celebration

At the end of each day, progress in reading is celebrated by having two students read a portion of a familiar story that they can read with expression.

A teacher's guide to Reading Roots Lesson 18 is included in Appendix 2.3 at the end of this chapter. Lesson 18 would be taught in the second or third month of the program.

Lee Conmigo

Lee Conmigo (Madden, Calderón, & Rice, 1999) is built on the same principles as Reading Roots and uses the same lesson structure and instructional processes. The reading materials used are created according to the same logic as the English materials, except that they follow a sequence of letter presentation appropriate to the Spanish language. The stories are again enhanced by context provided in a teacher-read portion of the story. *Lee Conmigo* lessons built around these stories teach both metacognitive and word attack skills using the same presentations, games, routines, and strategies as Reading Roots.

The one significant difference between Lee Conmigo and Reading Roots lies in the frequent use of syllables (rather than individual letters) as the major unit of sound in Lee Conmigo. Within the Spanish language, words are essentially made up of groups of syllables rather than groups of individual letters. The games and activities in Lee Conmigo have been adapted to take advantage of this. For instance, in Stretch and Spell, words are stretched a syllable at a time (lla-ma) rather than a letter at a time as in English (c-a-t). Lesson 18 of Lee Conmigo is included as Appendix 2.4 at the end of the chapter.

Reading Wings

Reading Wings (Madden, Slavin, Farnish, et al., 1999) is the reading approach used in Success for All and Roots & Wings from the second-grade level to the end of elementary school. It is an adaptation of CIRC, a cooperative learning program that encompasses both reading and writing and language arts. Studies of CIRC have shown it to be effective in increasing students' reading, writing, and language achievement (Stevens et al., 1987).

The curricular focus of Reading Wings is primarily on building comprehension and thinking skills, fluency, and pleasure in reading. Reading Wings assumes that students coming out of Reading Roots have solid word attack skills but need to build on this foundation to learn to understand and enjoy increasingly complex material.

As in Reading Roots, students in Reading Wings are regrouped for reading across grade lines, so a 3-1 reading class could be composed of second, third, and fourth graders. In addition, students are assigned to four-member or five-member learning teams that are heterogeneous in performance level, sex, and age. These teams choose team names and sit together at most times. The teams have a responsibility to see that all team members are learning the material being taught in class. Each week, students take a set of quizzes. These contribute to a team score, and the teams can earn certificates and other recognition based on the team's average quiz scores. Students also contribute points to their teams by completing book reports and writing assignments and by returning completed parent forms indicating that they have been reading at home each evening. Figure 2.3 shows a sample score sheet.

The main activities of Reading Wings are described in the following section.

Story-Related Activities

Students use their regular basal readers, novels, anthologies, or whatever materials are available in the school. Guides, called Treasure Hunts, have been developed to accompany a large number of current basals and novels, including Spanish basals and novels.

Stories are introduced and discussed by the teacher. During these lessons, teachers elicit and provide background knowledge, set a purpose for reading, introduce new vocabulary, review old vocabulary, discuss the story after students have read it, and so on. Presentation methods for each segment of the lesson are structured. For example, teachers are taught to use a vocabulary presentation procedure that requires a demonstration of understanding of word meaning by each individual, a review of methods of word attack, repetitive oral reading of vocabulary to achieve automaticity, and use of the meanings of the vocabulary words to help introduce the content of the story. Story discussions are structured to emphasize such skills as making and supporting predictions about the story and understanding major structural components of the story (e.g., problem and solution in a narrative).

After stories are introduced, students are given a series of six activities to do in their teams when they are not working with the teacher in a reading group. The sequence of activities is as follows:

1. Partner Reading. Students read the story silently first and then take turns reading the story aloud with their partners, alternating readers after each paragraph. As their partner reads, the listener follows along and corrects any errors the reader makes.

2. Story Structure and Story-Related Writing. Students are given questions related to each narrative story emphasizing the story structure (characters, setting, problem, and problem solution). Halfway through the story, they are instructed to stop reading and to identify the characters, the setting, and the problem in the story and to predict how the problem will be resolved. At the end of the story, students respond to the story as a whole and write a few paragraphs on a topic related to the story (for example, they might be asked to write a different ending to the story).

3. Words Out Loud. Students are given a list of new or difficult words used in the story that they must be able to read correctly in any order. These words are presented by the teacher in the reading group, and then students practice their lists with their partners or other teammates until they can read them smoothly.

4. Word Meaning. Students are given a list of story words that are new in their speaking vocabularies and asked to write a sentence for each that shows the meaning of the word (i.e., "An *octopus* grabbed the swimmer with its eight long legs," not "I have an *octopus*"). At higher grade levels, students are asked to look some of the words up in the dictionary and paraphrase the definition.

5. Story Retell. After reading the story and discussing it in their reading groups, students summarize the main points of the story to their partners. The partners have a list of essential story elements that they use to check the completeness of the story summaries.

6. Spelling. Students pretest one another on a list of spelling words each week and then work over the course of the week to help one another master the list. Stu-

Figure 2.3 Sample Team Score Sheet

SAMPLE TEAM SCORE SHEET

TEAM SCORE SHEET

TEAM: _Reading Champs_ STORY TITLE: _Jumanji_ WEEK OF: _February 6-10_

Team Members	Words Out Loud Test	Story Test	Mean-ingful Sentence Test	Reading Comp. Test	Adven-tures in Writing	Team Work Points	Book Re-sponse 1	Book Re-sponse 2	Read & Respond Form*	Total	Aver-age
Mary	100	100	95	90	90	90	95			660	(660÷7) 94.3
Juan	100	90	90	85	95	90	100			650	(650÷7) 92.9
Tamika	100	80	85	90	90	95	(95+20) 115		20	765	(765÷8) 95.6
Roger	80	85	100	95	100	90	100		20	670	(670÷7) 95.7

*Do not count this column of bonus points when determining the number of columns to divide by.

TEAM TOTAL **378.5**

TEAM SCORE (378.5÷4) **94.6**

RW-TSS 4/98

Superteam!

TEAM COOPERATION POINTS

Day 1	Day 2	Day 3	Day 4	Day 5
20	20	10	20	20

30

Copyright © 2000 by Success for All Foundation. Reprinted with permission.

dents use a "disappearing list" strategy in which they make new lists of missed words after each assessment until the list disappears and they can go back to the full list, repeating the process as many times as necessary.

Partner Checking

After students complete each of the activities listed previously, their partners initial a student assignment record form indicating that they have completed or achieved the criterion on that task. Students are given daily expectations as to the number of activities to be completed, but they can go at their own rate and complete the activities earlier if they wish, creating additional time for independent reading (see later description).

Tests

At the end of three class periods, students are given a comprehension test on the story, asked to write meaningful sentences for certain vocabulary words, and asked to read the word list aloud to the teacher. Students are not permitted to help one another on these tests. The test scores and evaluations of the story-related writing are major components of student's weekly team scores.

The energy and excitement in Reading Wings comes from the teamwork. Students become very involved with their team members and want to ensure that they are all succeeding. As students become more skilled, the discussions between partners and among team members become rich and challenging. Students no longer simply look for the right answer, they demand reasons and evidence to support answers. Books and stories come alive for students as they engage in meaningful discussion with their peers about their responses to their reading. Their enjoyment of reading grows at the same time as their skill and fluency with more and more complex material.

The teacher's edition of a sample Treasure Hunt for the story *Jumanji* is included in Appendix 2.5. The student edition and test are included in this manual. The Reading Wings process for students reading in Spanish, called *Alas Para Leer,* is the same as for students reading in English. The teacher's edition of a sample Spanish Treasure Hunt for Chapter 1 of a novel titled *Un Hatillo de Cerezas* is included in Appendix 2.6.

Listening Comprehension

Listening comprehension provides an additional opportunity to stretch students' ability to understand more and more complex language in a variety of texts. Each day, the teacher reads to students from a novel, anthology, newspaper, magazine, or other source of text at students' interest level but above their current reading level. The teacher then uses the reading as an opportunity to present a lesson focusing on comprehension skills, such as visualization of story characters and settings, identification of problems and attempts to solve problems, story mapping, or sequence of events in narratives. More advanced lessons deal with aspects of authors' craft, such as similes and metaphors, the creation of mood, character development, and using information from expository texts.

Direct Instruction in Reading Comprehension

Students receive direct instruction from the teacher in reading comprehension skills, such as identifying main ideas, drawing conclusions, and comparing and contrasting ideas. A special curriculum was designed for this purpose. After each lesson, students work on reading comprehension worksheets or games (or both) as a whole team, first gaining consensus on one set of worksheet items, then practicing independently, assessing one another's work, and discussing any remaining problems on a second set of items.

Independent Reading

Every evening, students are asked to read a trade book of their choice for at least 20 minutes. In most schools, classroom libraries of paperback books are established for this purpose. Parents initial forms indicating that students have read for the required time, and students contribute points to their teams if they submit a completed form each week. In a twice-weekly "book club," students discuss the books they have been reading and present more formal book reports, trying to entice others to take home the same book. "Book reports" can take many forms, from the completion of a brief summary form to an oral summary, advertisement, puppet show, or whatever other form the reader and teacher wish to use. Independent reading and book reports replace all other homework in reading and language arts. If students complete their story-related activities or other activities early, they may also read their independent reading books in class.

Writing and Language Arts

Writing and language arts are critical elements of the Success for All and Roots & Wings programs, particularly because writing is the opposite side of the reading coin. In prekindergarten, kindergarten, and first grade, emergent literacy strategies, such as journal writing, shared writing, and sound-based spelling are used to build students' interest in expressing their ideas in writing. In Reading Roots and Lee Conmigo, students regularly write to respond in some way to the story or to give their answers to questions about the story. In Reading Wings, students exercise their writing skills in responses to Treasure Hunt questions and in creative story-related writing activities.

All of these activities use writing to support the learning of reading while providing opportunities to write. However, students also need specific instruction in how to improve their writing. A formal writing and language arts instructional program is usually introduced in Success for All when most teachers are comfortable with the reading program. In practice, this usually means that the writing and language arts program is introduced in the spring of the first implementation year or in the fall of the second year.

Writing and language arts instruction in Success for All and Roots & Wings is usually provided to students in their heterogeneous homerooms, not in their reading groups. The basic philosophy behind the writing and language arts programs is that writing should be given the main emphasis and that language arts, especially mechanics and usage, should be taught in the context of writing, not as separate topics.

There are two levels in the Success for All and Roots & Wings writing and language arts approach. Both are based on the ideas of writing process (Calkins, 1983; Graves, 1983), which emphasizes writing for a real audience, writing for revision, and gradually building spelling and mechanics in the context of writing. Writing From the Heart, used in Grades 1 and 2, uses an informal version of writing process, whereas CIRC Writing Wings, used in Grades 3 through 6, uses a more formal writing process model with regular four-member peer response groups and students working compositions through from plan to draft to revision to editing to publication. Descriptions of these programs follow.

Writing From the Heart

Young children think of writing as an extension of oral communication. Most, given the undivided attention of an audience, will talk endlessly about their experiences. Young authors rarely have a problem of too little to say; their problem is overcoming the barriers they perceive to putting their ideas down on paper.

The goal of Writing From the Heart (Madden, Wasik, & Petza, 1989), the writing and language arts program used in Grades 1 and 2 in Success for All, is to tap students' innate desire, energy, and enthusiasm for communication and to move them to the next step of sharing their ideas with others through writing. When writing is seen as mastery of spelling and mechanics, it is a formidable task. Students will ultimately need to master these skills, but first, they need to develop pleasure and fluency in putting their thoughts on paper. Most important, students need to see writing as a personal expression, not an ordinary school task. They must put their hearts into their writing, not just their minds.

Writing From the Heart uses a writing-process model, which means that students write for a real audience and learn to revise their writing until it is ready for "publication." Students do not work in formal writing teams (that will come in third grade), but they do work informally with partners while they are writing.

The seven main elements of Writing From the Heart are as follows:

1. Modeling and Motivating Writing. At the beginning of each lesson, the teacher provides a model or motivator for writing. For example, the teacher may read a story that is like what students will be writing or may ask students to describe experiences that relate to a particular kind of writing. The teacher may introduce formats to help students plan their writing. For example, in writing about "myself," students are given a set of questions to answer about themselves that they then use to put into a story.

2. *Writing a "Sloppy Copy."* Students are encouraged to write a sloppy copy, a first draft of their compositions. They are taught to use "sound spelling" (invented spelling) if they cannot spell a word. For example, DINASR is a way a student might write dinosaur.

3. *Partner Sharing.* At several points in the writing process, students share their writing with partners and receive feedback and ideas from them.

4. *Revision.* Students learn to revise their compositions using feedback from partners and from the teacher. Specific revision skills are taught and modeled in the lessons. Students learn to add the information necessary to help their audience follow and enjoy their stories.

5. *Editing.* In preparation for publication, the teacher helps each child prepare a perfect draft of his or her composition, complete with pictures. This is when DINASR becomes "dinosaur."

6. *Publication.* Final drafts of students' writings are "published" in a class book, read to the class, and recognized in as many ways as the teacher can think of.

7. *Sharing and Celebration.* At many points in the writing process, students have opportunities to share their writing with the class. The teacher sets up a special "author's chair" from which the authors present their latest works. Authors are taught to ask three questions of their audience:

- What did you hear? Can you tell me about my story?
- What did you like about my story?
- What else would you like to know about my story?

The teacher models use of the author's chair by presenting his or her own writing and models answers to the author's questions.

Writing From the Heart prepares students for the Writing Wings program starting in Grade 3 by convincing students that they are authors and have something to say; teaching them that writing is a process of thinking, drafting, revising, and polishing ideas; and letting them know that writing is fun. They are then ready to learn more about the craft of writing with more formal instruction in tricks of the trade, style, mechanics, and usage.

Writing Wings

The writing and language arts program used in the upper-elementary grades is one developed earlier as part of CIRC for Grades 3 and up (Madden, Farnish, Slavin, Stevens, & Sauer, 1999). In this program, students are assigned to four-member or five-member heterogeneous writing teams. Writing Wings has two major instructional formats. About 3 days each week are used for writing process activities and 2 for language arts instruction.

Writing-Process Activities

Writing-Concept Lessons

Each writing-process day begins with a brief lesson on a writing concept. For example, the first lesson is on "mind movies," visualization of events in a narrative to see where additional detail or description is needed. Other lessons include organizing imaginative narratives, using observation to add life to descriptions, writing personal narratives, mysteries, persuasive arguments, explanatory writing, and so on. The writing-concept lessons are meant to spark ideas and help students expand on their writing and evaluate their own and others' compositions.

Writing Process

Most of the writing and language arts period is spent with students writing their own compositions while the teacher circulates among the teams and confers with individual students. Students draft many compositions and then choose a smaller number they would like to carry all the way through the five steps to publication. The steps are as follows.

1. *Prewriting.* Students discuss with their teammates a topic they would like to address and an audience for their writing. They then draft a plan, using a "skeleton planning form," an "idea net," or other forms to organize their thinking.

2. *Drafting.* After the student prepares a plan in consultation with teammates, he or she writes a first draft, focusing on getting ideas on paper rather than on spelling and mechanics (they will come later).

3. *Team Response and Revision.* Students read their drafts to their teammates. The teammates are taught to rephrase the main idea of the story in their own words, mention two things they liked about the story, and note two things they'd like to hear more about. The teacher may also confer with students at the revision stage to applaud students' ideas and suggest additions and changes. Specific revision guides for specific categories of writing assist students in responding usefully to their teammates' writing. For instance, as students learn to enrich their narratives with rich description, they use a team response guide that asks them to tell the author (their

teammate) their favorite descriptive words. As they look at the writing of their team-mates, they learn to look for those features in their own writing. Students make revisions based on their teammates' responses.

4. Editing.   Once the author is satisfied with the content of the writing, he or she is ready to correct the mechanics, usage, and spelling. Students work with a partner to go through an editing checklist. The checklist starts with a small number of goals (e.g., correct capitalization and end punctuation) but then adds goals as students complete language arts lessons. For example, after a lesson on subject-verb agreement or run-on sentences, these skills may be added to the checklist. The author first checks the composition against the checklist, then a teammate does so, and last, the teacher checks it.

5. Publication.   Publication involves the creation of the final draft and celebration of the author's writing. Students carefully rewrite their work incorporating all final corrections made by the teacher. They then present their compositions to the class from a fancy author's chair and may then contribute their writing to a team book or a team section of a class book. These books are proudly displayed in the class or library. In addition, students may be asked to read their compositions to other classes or to otherwise celebrate and disseminate their masterpieces!

A sample presentation guide for a writing lesson focusing on rich expression in a personal narrative is included in Appendix 2.7. This guide covers the development of the concept and the planning, drafting, and team response sections of the writing process. The other steps would be completed later.

Revision and Editing Skills Lessons

About 2 days each week, the teacher teaches structured lessons on language mechanics skills. These are presented as skills for revision and editing, because their purpose is to directly support students' writing. The teacher determines the order of lessons according to problems students are experiencing and skills they will need for upcoming writing. For example, the teacher may notice that many students are having problems with incomplete sentences, or the teacher may anticipate that because students are about to write dialogue, they may need to learn how to use quotation marks.

Students work in their four-member writing teams to help one another master the skills taught by the teacher. The students work on examples, compare answers with each other, resolve discrepancies, explain ideas to each other, and so on. Ultimately, students are quizzed on the skill, and the teams can earn certificates or other recognition based on the average performance of all team members. As noted earlier, immediately after a revision and editing skills lesson, the new skill is added to the editing checklist so that language arts skills are immediately put into practice in students' writing.

CHAPTER 2 APPENDICES

Appendix 2.1.
Reading Roots Shared Story 18:
Fang

Scott and Tanya practice kicking her ball during recess. Lana joins them. What will
happen to the ball?   **1**

Scott rolls the ball.

BAM!

Tanya kicks it.

She *runs* fast.

Lana says, "The ball is off the field!"

2   Scott and Tanya look for the ball in the bushes, while Lana looks on the other side of the
playground. Suddenly, Scott sees something. What is it?

"Look, Tanya!" gasps Scott.

Tanya looks.

She sees a big fat dog.

The dog *runs* fast.

It bumps into Tanya.

She sits in the mud.

Poor Tanya! How do you think she feels about being pushed into the mud?   3

"ICK!" says Tanya, "Mud is not fun.
Go, dog!"
The big dog sits.
He pants.

4   Abid starts to shake. He turns pale. What has Abid seen that has scared him?

Abid says, "See the dog's fangs!"
"FANGS!!" says Tanya.
The big dog says, "RUFF!"
The kids climb up the [jungle gym].
"Can we fit?" asks Abid.

5

Lana fast.
runs
"Fang!" Lana says.

She skids to a stop.

"Fang is not bad," says Lana.

6   Lana explains that Fang is her St. Bernard. He is gentle, even though he has big teeth. He follows her to school when he gets lonely. What will the other children do now?

Lana says, "Fang is a fun dog.

He likes kids."

The kids get off the [jungle gym].

All of a sudden, Derrick has an idea. What do you think it is?   7

Derrick says, "Dogs can sniff.
Can Fang sniff the ball?"
Lana nods.
"Get the ball, Fang," says Lana.

8   Fang puts his nose to the ground. Do you think he can find the ball?

Fang runs.
He sniffs.
He digs fast in a stack of leaves.
The kids say, "Fang got the ball back!"

Fang is a hero. He has found the missing ball!

Lesson 18

Letter Sound: /f/ as in fit, fat, fun

Green Words (Phonetic):

fit	fast	fun	sniff	bam
fat	fangs	off	stack	bumps
				dog

Red Words (Sight):

rolls   field   go

Story

Story by Laura Barton Rice
Illustrations by Jennifer Clark

Slavin, R.E., & Madden, N.A., *One Million Children: Success for All.* © Corwin Press Inc.

Appendix 2.2.
Reading Roots Shared Story 42:
A Farm in China

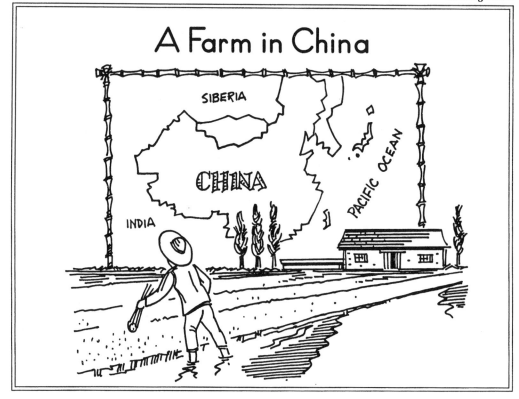

Chen May Woo lives in the north of China. In China they say the last name first.

Chen May Woo's dad's name is Chen Ji Ling. Her mom's name is Chen Ling Ha. Her grandma's name is Chen Eu Fong.

May Woo lives on a big, big farm. Many families share the work on this farm. They plant wheat and rice. They raise this food to eat and to sell. May Woo's family has a pig, a duck, and a goose.

Most of the food May Woo eats is raised on the farm. Her mom
makes meals. She chops small bits of meat and vegetables. May Woo
helps chop the food. May Woo does not need a fork. She picks up
her food with a spoon and chopsticks. She drinks tea, instead of milk,
with meals.

May Woo has a big class at school. Fifty children are in her
room. She goes to school six days a week. The children are learning
to read and write.

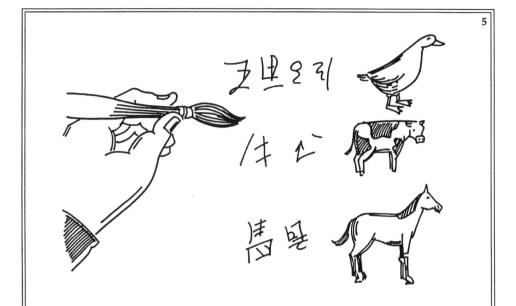

5

It is hard to read and write Chinese. In China, a picture stands for every idea. The Chinese alphabet has more than 5,000 pictures! May Woo and her classmates must learn to write all of these pictures.

6

Once, May Woo's class went to the zoo. May Woo liked to see the pandas. Wild pandas live in the west of China. They stay in the big bamboo forests. Pandas like to eat bamboo.

May Woo and her class also visited the Great Wall of China.
It is tall and made of thick stone. It is very, very long. It swoops up hills
deep into China. It is so long, it could stretch from New York to California!
It is so big, it can be seen from space!

May Woo does fun things after school with her classmates.
They eat lunch by the goldfish pool. Then, they play Chinese jump rope,
ping pong, five stones, and hopscotch. They like to kick a small bean bag,
too. They must try to keep it in the air.

9

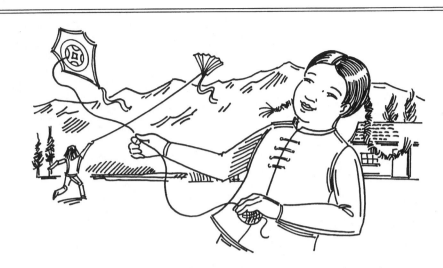

May Woo also likes to fly kites. Kites were invented in China! They are made of silk and paper in all shapes and sizes.

Some big kites are 16 feet high. More than one person is needed to fly them. Soft-wing kites have wings that flap. In China, most kite sticks are made of bamboo.

10

Lots of other things were invented in China. Paper-cut pictures were invented there. Some paper-cut pictures are red for good luck.

Last year, May Woo made a paper-cut picture for the New Year feast. She cut a long dragon out of red paper. Then she looped it in the room where all the farm families celebrated.

After the New Year feast, there were fireworks. Fireworks were invented in China, too! May Woo held her grandmother's hand as she looked up at the bright fireworks. At the end of the display, a big red dragon lit up the sky. Everyone cheered and clapped.

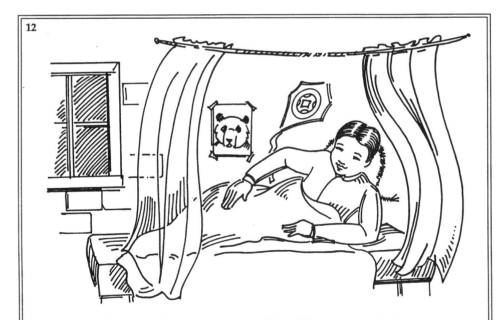

When the fireworks were finished, May Woo went to bed. She dreamed about the Chinese New Year, the bright fireworks, and her paper-cut dragon. It was a very good dream!

Lesson 42

Word Mastery List

This is the list of new story words that children are expected to practice.

The letter sound introduced in this lesson is long **"oo"** as in **scoops, food, pool**.

Plain words are Phonetic Words (Green Words) that children can sound out.

The underlined words are Challenge Words (Brown Words). Children can memorize some parts and sound out other parts of the words.

The boxed words are Sight Words (Red Words) that children can memorize by saying, spelling, then saying the word again.

Have your child tell you how the starred words are used in the story.

looped	goose	celebrated	<u>fork</u>
swoops	food	*display	<u>hard</u>
*spoon	chopsticks	*invented	<u>north</u>
pool	stretch	<u>family</u>	six
	dragon	<u>farm</u>	instead
			also

Story by Wendie Old
Illustration by Scott Mattern
Copyright © 2000 by Success for All Foundation. Reprinted with permission.

Slavin, R.E., & Madden, N.A., *One Million Children: Success for All.* © Corwin Press Inc.

Appendix 2.3.
Reading Roots Lesson 18

LESSON 18: *FANG*

OBJECTIVES

1. **Reinforce:** Monitoring for Meaning strategy. (See **Guided Group Reading**.)
2. **Letter/Sound:** "f".
3. **Special Story Skill:** Identify and describe new story characters. (See **Story Discussion**.)
4. **Review:** Using context to find meaning. (See **Guided Group Reading**.)

PREPARATION

1. **Tongue Twister:** Fang found five fat fish by the fence.
2. **Objects and Pictures:** Fang, feet, fish, five
3. **Student Picture Cards:** Have one Student Picture Card for each student.
4. **Key Picture:** feet
5. **Two-Picture Game:** football [fork]-dog, feather-bus, firefighter [foxes]-tiger, five-six
6. **Yes-No Game Pictures:** fish-bug, fan-cat, fire-tie, five-door
7. **Matching Games:** (Letter Cards) **"f"**, **"b"**, **"s"**
   (Key Picture Cards) feet, balloon, sun
   (Picture Cards) fan, bed, feet, soap, fire, sun, sock, book
8. **Readles:** runs, jungle gym, leaves
9. **Stretch and Spell:** fun, fast, fit, fat
10. **Letter and Word Formation Review:** (Letter Cards) **"s"**, **"u"**, **"b"**
11. **Characters:** Scott, Tanya, Lana, Fang, Paco

A. SHOWTIME

1. Reading Rehearsal. Have students read from a familiar story using whole-group choral reading or partner reading. Be sure to motivate students and allow time to scan the story and do a "word check" before beginning. Every student should have a copy of the book. Focus students on reading with expression and for fluency. (It is not necessary to read the whole story.)

2. Letter and Word Formation Review. Using the Letter Cards for the last three letters learned, **"s"**, **"u"**, and **"b"**, have students quickly make each letter in the air, and on a paper or slate, three times, saying the cue phrase as they do so. Review one or two additional Letter Cards if necessary. Review letters and the Word Wall on a daily basis, at appropriate times during the lesson.

On Days 2 and 3, also review the current letter and practice stretching and spelling the spelling words you have chosen for the week. Quickly review the Word Wall.

B. SETTING THE STAGE

1. Introduction. Use the enlarged text or distribute the Shared Story. Say: *"We are going to read another story about the school friends we have already met. This time, we will meet a new friend, Lana, who causes a commotion during recess."*

PREVIEW the story. Say: *"Let's Preview the story by looking at the title and the cover picture. Remember, we learned that this way we will understand the story better when we read it. The title of this story is **Fang**. What is a **fang**?"* (Use Think/Pair/Share to discuss students' responses.) *"A **fang** is a very long and sharp tooth. Wolves have **fangs**. Why do you suppose this story is called*

18 - 1

Fang?" (Use Think/Pair/Share to discuss students' responses.) *"Let's look at the picture on the front cover. What do you see?"* (Use Think/Pair/Share to discuss students' responses.) *"The picture shows a very large dog. Could this be why the story is called* **Fang**?"* (Use Think/Pair/Share to discuss students' responses.)

Allow one minute for students to look through the book to enjoy and become familiar with the pictures.

    2. Background Questions. Say: *"Do you have a pet? What other stories have we read about pets?"* (Use Think/Pair/Share to discuss students' responses.)

    3. Predictive Question. Ask: *"What will the big dog do?"* (Use Think/Pair/Share to discuss students' responses.)

    4. Teacher Script. Read to page 4. Ask the Predictive Question and have students respond. Encourage students to support their predictions. Then finish reading the story. Read slowly, with expression. Stop to comment and question (see the Teacher Script below for a model). Model the Monitoring for Meaning strategy as you read by stopping at the end of each page and asking aloud, "Did I understand what I read?" Then briefly paraphrase aloud what you just read. Stop to comment and question (see the Teacher Script below for a model, but do **not** use the "Think out loud" dialogues in parentheses during this first reading).

NOTE: Underlined words are context words. Listen as students read along with you during Guided Group Reading. Use the suggested comments in parentheses to quickly model how to figure out these words only if you notice students having trouble with a word.

---

1   Scott and Tanya practice kicking her ball during recess. Lana joins them. What will happen to the ball?
    Scott rolls the ball.
    BAM!
    Tanya kicks it.
    She **runs** fast.
    Lana says, "The ball is off the field!"

---

2   Scott and Tanya look for the ball in the bushes, while Lana looks on the other side of the playground. Suddenly, Scott sees something. What is it?
    "Look, Tanya!" gasps Scott.
    Tanya looks.
    She sees a big fat dog.
    The dog **runs** fast.
    It bumps into Tanya.
    She sits in the mud.

---

3   Poor Tanya! How do you think she feels about being pushed into the mud?
    "Ick!" says Tanya. "Mud is not fun.
    Go, dog!"
    The big dog sits.
    He pants.

---

18 - 2

4   Paco starts to shake. He turns pale. What has Paco seen that has scared him?
Paco says, "See the dog's fangs!"
"FANGS!!" says Tanya.
The big dog says, "RUFF!"
(Think out loud: "The big dog says,...I don't know that word. I can sound out the last part, ŭŭŭfff. A dog might say **Ruff**.")
The kids climb up the **jungle gym.**
(Think out loud: "The kids...I don't know that word. Maybe if I read on, it would help. How would the kids get up the jungle gym. They might **climb**.")
"Can we fit?" asks Paco.

MAKE A PREDICTION: *What will the dog do? Will the children be all right?* (Use Think/Pair/Share to discuss students' predictions. Encourage them to support predictions.)

5   Lana **runs** fast.
"Fang!" Lana says.
She skids to a stop.
"Fang is not bad," says Lana.

6   Lana explains that Fang is her St. Bernard. He is gentle, even though he has big teeth. He follows her to school when he gets lonely. What will the other children do now?
Lana says, "Fang is a fun dog.
He likes kids."
The kids get off the **jungle gym.**

7   All of a sudden, Derrick has an idea. What do you think it is?
Derrick says, "Dogs can sniff.
Can Fang sniff the ball?"
Lana nods.
"Get the ball, Fang," says Lana.

8   Fang puts his nose to the ground. Do you think he can find the ball?
Fang **runs.**
He sniffs.
He digs fast in a stack of **leaves.**
The kids say, "Fang got the ball back!"
Fang is a hero. He has found the missing ball!

5. Story Discussion. Direct students to identify and describe new characters introduced in the story. Have them think about and discuss how the children changed the way they felt about Fang in this story. Encourage them to focus on what they think the Purpose for Reading the story was. Collect the Shared Stories (or have students put them away). Then, tell students that they are going to learn all the sounds, letters, and words they will need to read this story by themselves.

C. LETTER ACTIVITIES

1. Alphabet Song. Have students sing an alphabet song to invite Alphie to come out.

18 - 3

Slavin, R.E., & Madden, N.A., *One Million Children: Success for All.* © Corwin Press Inc.

2. Letter Presentation.

a. Hearing the Sound. Introduce the Tongue Twister by reading today's "note" from Alphie: *"Many words contain the sound /f/. Pretend that you are detectives so that you can discover where you hear this sound in words as you listen to Alphie's note about Fang."* Read Alphie's tongue twister with as much expression as you can:

Fang found five fat fish by the fence.

Say the first /f/ word and have students repeat it. Then, say the word again, stretching the beginning sound. Have students repeat it. Repeat this process for each /f/ word in the Tongue Twister.

Note: This is an auditory activity. The Tongue Twister should not be posted or written on the board.

b. Introducing /f/ Objects and Pictures. Tell students that now Alphie wants to show them some things that start with /f/. Name each object or picture as you pull it from Alphie's box, and have students repeat the name. Stretch the /f/ sound in the word as you say it. Show each one again, asking, *"What sound can you hear at the beginning of ___?"* Have the group respond by stretching the /f/ sound.

Fang	feet	fish	five

c. Two-Picture Game. Explain to students that you will show them two pictures and they will have to find the one that begins with /f/. Show the top two pictures from the pile. Name each picture, and then have your students name it. Give them five seconds to think, and then have them signal which picture starts with /f/ by pointing to the correct picture. If the students make an error, name the correct picture and have them repeat it. If needed, check a few students quickly for understanding after the group seems to have achieved fluency with the game.

football [fork]	feather	firefighter [foxes]	five
dog	bus	tiger	six

d. Making the /f/ Sound. Say: *"Our Key Picture for /f/ is feet."* Have everyone in the group make the /f/ sound. Ask: *"How do your mouths move to make the /f/ sound?"* Discuss the sound like this: *"What moves when you say /f/? Is it your lip or your tongue?"* (Lip) *"Which one moves, the bottom or the top?"* (Bottom) *"Do your teeth work, too, or just your lips?"* (Teeth, too) *"Right, the top teeth touch the bottom lip. What do I hear? Is it my voice or just air coming out?"* (Just air) *"Right, your voice box is off. /f/ is just air. Is your bottom lip getting really hot or really cool when you blow that air over it? Right, really cool."* Have students stretch the /fff/ sound again together. It should not be bounced.

e. Introducing the Shape. Pull Alphie's pennant out of his box and introduce the letter's name: *"The letter that goes with /fffff/ is 'f'. Let's go over our letter's objects and pictures."*

Display the **"f"** objects or pictures you presented, one at a time. (Try to choose items that are related to the story. Alternatively, use the pictures named.) As students name them, write each one on the board in a vertical list, emphasizing the sound/letter match. Say the cue phrase, *"If we hear it with our ears, we'll see it with our eyes."*

Fang	feet	fish	five

18 - 4

f. Practicing the "f" Shape. Write the upper- and lowercase "f" on the chalkboard. Use Think/Pair/Share to discuss their similarities and differences with the students.

Introduce the verbal pattern for "f": *"Curve left, straight down, lift and cross."*

Have students use the lower case "f" on the board for a model as they make an "f" in the air and say the cue phrase. Have them make the letter, repeating the cue phrase in unison each time:

> on their desks, as big as they can.
> on their desks, as small as they can.
> on a partner's hand, arm, back, etc.

When students have practiced the shape four or five times, add the sound to the cue phrase: *"Curve left, straight down, lift and cross. The sound for 'f' is /f/."* Then have students practice "f" several more times as they say the entire cue phrase.

Optional: Instruct students to trace the letter with you several times on their Letter Practice Sheet (Appendix 6) while they say the cue phrase in unison.

3. Letter Games.

a. Students' /f/ Words. Give students 30 seconds to tell their partners all the /f/ words they can think of. Highlight the theme of school friends playing together at recess in *Fang*. Challenge them to think of "f" words related to the story or their own experiences. Allow all students to share their favorite word with a partner. Have all partnerships share their favorite word. As they respond, write their words on the board. All students should receive a Student Picture Card as a reward.

b. Say–It–Fast (Optional). Remind students that Alphie speaks a special language that is helpful to them as they are learning to read because he says words so slowly that they can hear all the parts. Tell them that they are going to hear some words in Alphie's special language, and then say them in our language. Say: *"I am going to say some words in Alphie's special language. I want you to listen to all the sounds as I say each word, think for a few seconds, and when I signal to you, I want you to Say–It–Fast!"* Say each word in the list below, stretching each sound. (If students still need clarification, you may give a sentence for words they have trouble understanding as real words, but try to limit the sentences so that they can focus on auditory sound blending.) Signal two seconds for Think Time, then signal the group to respond together as you say the word quickly with them. Have students respond as a group. Keep the pace rapid.

2 Phonemes	3 Phonemes	4 Phonemes	5 Phonemes
g–o	f–u–n	s–n–i–ff	b–u–m–p–s
o–ff	b–a–m	f–a–s–t	T–a–n–y–a
		L–a–n–a	
		F–a–ng–s	

c. Break–It–Down (Optional). Remind students that Alphie's special language is helpful to them as they are learning to read. Tell them that now Alphie needs their help to understand some words, so they need to say these words in his special language. Say: *"I am going to say some words in our language. Listen to each word. When I give you the signal to Break–It–Down, I want you to say the word in Alphie's special language so he can hear all the*

18 - 5

sounds." Say each word quickly in the list below. Signal two seconds for Think Time, then signal the group to respond together as you stretch the sounds of the word with them. Students should say the word and Break–It–Down when you give the signal to begin. Have students respond as a group, and keep the pace rapid.

2 Phonemes	3 Phonemes	4 Phonemes	5 Phonemes
th–e	b–a–ck	s–o–b–s	g–a–s–p–s
ou–t	b–u–g	s–n–u–g	s–m–a–ck–s
	b–a–ck	S–c–o–tt	c–a–nn–o–t

Ask students why they think it is important to say things in Alphie's special language. (It will help them to put sounds together as they learn to read.) Then tell them that they are going to use Alphie's special language as they learn to read the story's new words.

d. (Visual) Yes-No Game. Show the pictures to your students one at a time. When you show each, say the name of the picture, and have students repeat it. Then have them think for five seconds about the sound with which the word starts, and then point to *Yes* or *No* to show whether or not it starts with */f/*. Have them say *"Yes"* or *"No"* as they point. If needed, check a few students quickly for understanding after the group seems to have achieved fluency with the game.

fish	**fan**	**fire**	**five**
bug	**cat**	**tie**	**door**

e. (Auditory) Yes-No Game. Say each of the words in the list below, one at a time. After saying each one, have your students repeat it. Give them five seconds to think, and then have them point to *Yes* or *No* to indicate whether the word begins with */f/*. If needed, check a few students quickly for understanding after the group seems to have achieved fluency with the game.

fat	**fold**	**fawn**	**fox**
bucket	**jacket**	**hat**	**lamb**

f. Matching Games. Use pictures selected during the lesson preparation that begin with the sounds */f/*, */b/*, and */s/*. Have students identify the key picture, letter name, and sound.

ACTIVITY 1.   **Have students match pictures of objects with Letter Cards *accompanied by* Key Picture Cards. (Use a pocket chart or a chalkboard ledge.)**

Name each picture and have students repeat the name. Give your students a few seconds to think, and then, at your signal, have them say the beginning sound, point to the side of the board that indicates the letter with which the word starts, and say the name of the letter. Continue until students are fluent.

fan	**bed**	**feet**	**soap**

ACTIVITY 2.   **Have students match spoken words with Letter Cards *accompanied by* Key Picture Cards.**

18 - 6

Say the words below one at a time. Give your students a few seconds to think, and then, at your signal, have them say the beginning sound, point to the side of the board that indicates the letter with which the word starts, and say the name of the letter. Continue until students are fluent.

big	fat	fast	back

ACTIVITY 3.   **Have students match pictures of objects with Letter Cards (no Key Picture Cards).**

Remove the Key Picture Cards. Go through the set of pictures, one at a time. Name each picture and have students name it. Following Think Time, have students say the beginning sound, point to the Letter Card only, and say the name of the letter. Continue until students are fluent.

fire	sun	sock	book

ACTIVITY 4.   **Have students match spoken words with Letter Cards (no Key Picture Cards).**

Say the following words to the class, one at a time. Following Think Time have students say the beginning sound, point to the correct beginning letter, and say the name of the letter. Continue until students are fluent.

sick	fun	bin	fist

D. STORY ACTIVITIES

1. Word Presentation.

a. Stretch and Read. Have the students Stretch and Read the story's new phonetic words with you.

fit	*fast	fun	*sniff	bam
fat	*fangs	off	*stack	*bumps
				dog

On Day 1, stretch each of the story's new phonetic words twice and "say-it-fast" once. On Day 2, stretch each word once and "say-it-fast" once. On Day 3, review the words and stretch only as needed. On Day 1, the teacher should provide sentences using the starred word(s) in the context of the story. On Days 2 and 3, have students orally create a sentence with their partners. Call on partnerships to share their sentences with the class.

b. Quick Erase. Start with **fat,** finish with **sun,** changing one letter at a time. Help students Stretch and Read as needed. Use the words in sentences as needed to make sure that students recognize them as words they know.

fat ✿ fast ✿ fist ✿ fit ✿ fin ✿ fun ✿ sun

c. Say-Spell-Say. Say-Spell-Say the story's new sight words, **rolls, field,** and **go.** You will need to make red word cards for **rolls** and **field.** Have students say each word, soft-clap it by letter, and say it again. Say-Spell-Say each word three times on Day 1, twice on Day 2, and once on Day 3.

18 - 7

Slavin, R.E., & Madden, N.A., *One Million Children: Success for All.* © Corwin Press Inc.

Introduce the story's readles, **runs, jungle gym,** and **leaves.** Show the readle pictures and use the words for the readles in sentences.

         d. Word Wall. Use the Word Wall to post green and red words from the previous two stories. Keep high-frequency words even longer. (Some of the words may start out as red words and may become green words as new letters are learned.) Taking 30 to 60 seconds each time, chorally review the words, in order and out of order, very rapidly three to four times during a lesson.

         2. Guided Group Reading. Now, tell students that they are going to read the story for themselves. Remind them that it has many words that contain or start with the /b/ sound. Ask them to put on their listening ears so they can hear this special new sound in the story. Distribute the Shared Stories. Use the enlarged text to demonstrate while students use their Shared Stories.

         a. Modeling Use of Context Clues. Write the sentence(s) below on the board or on sentence strip(s) with the context word(s) covered. Be sure that the Word Strategies Chart (see Appendix) is posted. Say: *"Let's think about what to do when we come to a word that we do not know and we cannot sound out."* When presenting each sentence, ask: *"What word could go in the space that is covered so that the sentence would make sense?"* (Have students discuss possibilities with their partners. List possibilities. If there are several words that would make sense, tell the students the first letter, or uncover the first letter, and have them talk with their partners about which words beginning with that sound/letter would make sense in the sentence.) *"What other strategies from the Word Strategies Chart could we use to figure out the word? Does reading on help? Does thinking about the story help? Does the picture help? If none of these strategies help, what else can we do?"* (First, ask your partner. If your partner doesn't know, ask the teacher.) Have students look in their books to see what word the author chose to use.

      Page 4.   *The big dog says "_____(RUFF)!"*

                    The kids _____(climb) up the jungle gym.

         b. Teacher/Student Reading. Review the story's characters. Review how to use the Previewing strategy. Then, read the teacher text and the story again (see the Teacher Script for the Story Presentation) with expression, while students read their part at the same time in a low voice. Read each story sentence twice with the students to help them build fluency. If a sentence contains an underlined context word, listen to be sure students are getting the word. If not, use the suggested comments in parentheses to quickly help students figure out the word. Continue to ask questions to reinforce comprehension of the story. Tailor your questions to monitor students' levels of comprehension.

Model the Monitoring for Meaning strategy as you read by stopping at the end of each page and asking aloud, *"Did I understand what I read?"* Then briefly paraphrase aloud what you just read. For example:

      Page 1.   Say: *"Did I understand what I read? Yes, Scott, Tanya, and Lana kick a soccer ball off the field."*

On page 3, remind students that they can use context to figure out word meaning and usage. They have already learned to read **pants** as an article of clothing. Present it as a verb:

      Page 3.   *The big dog sits. He **pants.***

                         18 - 8

3. Partner Reading. Direct students to take turns with their partner to read alternate pages of the story aloud, with expression, and to help each other use appropriate strategies for green words, red words, and context words.

> Circulate around the room to assist as needed. You may need to continue to model helping or taking turns within a partnership. Observe the progress of each student as you circulate. Use the Class Record Form, page A8-1, to record fluency and expression.

When students have finished the partner reading, read the questions aloud. Use Think-Pair-Share to discuss the answers. Encourage them to use the book to find specific clues to the answers.

a. Monitoring for Meaning. Reinforce the importance of using the Monitoring for Meaning strategy. Have students read each page and then ask, *"Did I understand what I read?"* Have them explain what they read to their partner before going on to the next page.

b. Story Comprehension. Oral discussion of the Comprehension Questions promotes a better understanding of the story. After Partner Reading, lead an oral discussion of the Comprehension Questions below. Use Think-Pair-Share to discuss the answers. Encourage students to use the book to find specific clues to the answers.

a. **How did the ball get lost?**
b. **Why did the children climb up the jungle gym?**
c. **Why did the dog bark at the children when they yelled "FANGS!"?**
d. **Who found the ball?**
e. **What happened to change how the children felt about Fang?**

4. Stretch and Spell. This Shared Treasure focuses on story comprehension and sentence-reading practice. Be sure to do a teacher-directed review of sides one and two of the Shared Treasure before partner practice. Before students complete the Comprehension section on page 2, be sure to model the process for writing an answer to the following question on the board. (Have students Think-Pair-Share to come up with possible answers to the question.)

fun   **fast**   **fit**   **fat**

5. Shared Treasure. This Shared Treasure focuses on story comprehension and sentence-reading practice. Be sure to do a teacher-directed review of sides one and two of the Shared Treasure before partner practice. Before students complete the Comprehension section on page 2, be sure to model the process for writing an answer to the following question on the board. (Have students Think-Pair-Share to come up with possible answers to the question.)

*Did Fang bump Tanya? (**Fang did bump Tanya.**)*

Remember that the goal of the Shared Treasure is to provide repeated practice for fluency. The goal is not to simply fill it out. Allow students to color in a star for each successful reading they accomplish with their partner. Have students read and respond to the Shared Treasure with their partner, and have partners share with the group.

Have students use some of their partner practice time to practice spelling words.

6. Story Related Writing. Story Related Writing focuses on writing about a topic generated by the story that relates to students' own experiences. Be sure to direct a discussion of the writing prompt. Then, have students plan their writing with their partners but do their writing individually. Have partners share their writing with each other, and have some students share with the group. Allow students to take home their writing to share with as many people as they can.

E. CELEBRATION

1. Performance. At the end of each day, have two students read, with expression, a page or two from a story they have practiced. Be sure to let students know at least one day in advance that they have been selected for the Reading Celebration Performance so that they can take home a story of their choice to practice. Have the entire class provide applause and praise, and present the student with a Reading Celebration Certificate. **Enjoy your Celebration and remember to do it every day!**

For the Spelling Celebration on Fridays, give students a piece of paper and have them number it. Tell the children that you will give them a chance to show you all that they have learned about the new sounds by spelling some words that contain these sounds. Say each spelling word you have chosen, use it in a sentence, and repeat the word before moving on to the next word. Be sure to provide plenty of praise for all attempts and celebrate progress for each student. You can give students stickers for their tests, and post them in your room until the next test.

2. Sound/Word Review. Summarize the day's lesson by reviewing all sounds quickly, using the pennants under the sequenced alphabet or your Letter Cards. Use group response to review the words on the Word Wall, in order and out of order, very rapidly.

> TEACHERS, PLEASE REMEMBER: Using the Word Wall and the current list of green and red words, work in three to four quick reviews during the 90-minute reading block. Frequent, but brief, reviews of words and sounds will increase your students' reading fluency, as will repeated readings of stories, Shared Treasure sheets, and Story Related Writing.

F. HOMEWORK

Let students take their Shared Treasure Sheets and current or familiar Shared Stories home to read to as many people as they can. Listeners can initial in the boxes at the bottom of the Shared Treasure Sheet or sign the "***Reading Roots*** Homework Bookmark" or the "Please Read With Me Signature Sheet" after listening to the child read from the Shared Story (see the Appendix for samples). Have students return the Share Sheet or form. At the end of the first day of the lesson, ask students to look for and think about lots of "**f**" words for the next day's lesson. Give students a copy of the five spelling words on a Stretch, Trace, and Write form (see sample in the Appendix) to take home and practice once or twice during the week.

18 - 10

LESSON 18
Shared Treasure

Word Reading. *Have students take turns reading aloud the phonetic words with their partner.*

fit	fast	fun	sniff	bam fat
fangs	off	stack	bumps	
				dog

Have students take turns reading aloud the sight word with their partner.

go

Sentence Reading. *Have students take turns reading aloud the sentences with their partner. Encourage them to read with expression.*

Tanya kicks the ball off the field.

A big, fat dog bumps into Tanya.

Paco says, "The dog has fangs!"

It is Lana's dog, Fang.

Fang is a fun dog.

Fang gets the ball.

Have a few students read out loud to the class with expression.

TSS-18-1

LESSON 18
Shared Treasure

Comprehension. *Ask the question:* **"Whom does Tanya meet when she is playing ball?"** *Then, review with students how to answer a question with a complete sentence. Have students take turns reading the questions and having their partners answer orally in a complete sentence. Have them write the answer to the last question in a complete sentence. They may draw readles for the words they cannot write.*

Did the dog have fangs?

_____

_____

Was the dog big and fat?

_____

_____

Did the kids like Fang?

_____

_____

Did Fang like the kids?

_____

_____

_____

_____

Practicing Concepts. *Have students color a star every time they read the words or sentences or share their ideas for answers with their partner. Once Shared Treasures have been mastered, have students take them home. Tell students to read their Shared Treasures to as many people as possible. Each listener should write their initials and the date in the designated box.*

TSS-18-2

LESSON 18
Story Related Writing

Letter Writing. *Have students stretch and read the letter, then write it three times.*

f

Stretch and Spell. *Have students take turns with their partner stretching the word for each picture. After they have said the word, direct students to write the first letter of the picture in the box.*

Fang _____	fan _____

Writing Ideas. *Say: "At first, the kids were scared of Fang. They thought he was big and that he had very large teeth. They found out that Fang was a friendly dog when he helped them find their lost ball. Have you ever been scared of anything before? Why? Take turns with your partner to read the sentence below. Plan with your partner to write about something that scared you. Then, write!" Present* **scared** *as a sight word.*

I was scared!

_____

_____

_____

_____

Have students share their writing with their partners, and have a few students share with the class.

TSS-18-3

Slavin, R.E., & Madden, N.A., *One Million Children: Success for All.* © Corwin Press Inc.

Appendix 2.4.
Lee Conmigo Lesson 18

LESSON 18: *LAS GOTITAS*

OBJECTIVES

1. **Introduce:** Closed syllables with **"d"** at the end of a word. (See **Stop and Read** and **Quick Erase.**)
2. **Letter/Sound:** (voiced) **"g"**.
3. **Review:** Monitoring for Meaning. (See **Teacher Script.**)

PREPARATION

1. **Tongue Twister:** *Gaby Gomez ganó golosinas.*
2. **Pictures and Objects:** *gato, gotitas, gusano*
3. **Student Picture Cards:** Have one Student Picture Card for each student.
4. **Key Pictures:** *gato* (/ga/), *gotitas* (/go/), and *gusano* (/gu/)
5. **Two-Picture Game:** *galleta-jirafa, gotitas-yeso, gusano-bigote*
6. **Yes-No Game Pictures:** *gallina-zeta, gorila-burro, gusano-sopa*
7. **Matching Games:** *radio, rosa, gallina, ñandú, gotitas, ñisñil, gusano, rubí, gorila, remo*
8. **Readles:** *escuela, comer/come, enfermera, aplaude*
9. **Tap and Spell:** *mago, miga, dedo*
10. **Letter Formation Review:** (Letter Cards) **"n"**, **"r"**, **"ñ"**

> In this lesson, the sound /g/ is followed by the cue **(voiced)**. This cue indicates how the sound is to be made. It is not intended as a description of the sound when discussing it with students.

A. SHOWTIME

1. Reading Rehearsal. Have students re-read a familiar story with whole group choral reading or partner reading. Be sure to motivate students and allow time to scan and do a "word check" before beginning. Every student should have a copy of the book. Focus students on reading with expression and for fluency. (It is not necessary to read the whole story.)

2. Letter Formation Review. Using the Letter Cue Cards for the last three letters learned, **"n"**, **"r"**, and **"ñ"**, have students quickly make each letter in the air and on a paper or slate three times, saying the cue phrase as they do so. Review one or two additional Letter Cards if necessary. On Days 2 and 3, also review the current letter and practice how to Tap and Spell the spelling words you have chosen for the week. Quickly review the Word Wall.

B. SETTING THE STAGE

1. Introduction. Use the enlarged text or distribute the Shared Story. Allow one minute for students to look through the book to enjoy and become familiar with the pictures. Say: *"Hoy vamos a leer un cuento que se trata de la amiga de Ema, Ada. Ada tiene que tomarse unas gotitas de medicina. ¿Por qué tiene que tomarse las gotitas de medicina? ¿Cuál puede ser nuestro propósito de la lerctura?"* (Use Think-Pair-Share to discuss students' responses.)

Preview the story. Say: *"Vamos a hacer un Reconocimiento Previo del cuento leyendo el título y observando el dibujo de la portada."* (Read it aloud as your students repeat or read along in

18-1

AUTHORS' NOTE: The page numbers referred to in the text are from *Osito, Osito* published in 1987.

Slavin, R.E., & Madden, N.A., *One Million Children: Success for All.* © Corwin Press Inc.

unison if they are able.) *"Se llama **Las gotitas**. ¿Qué clase de gotitas son?"* (Use Think-Pair-Share to discuss students' responses.) *"Veamos el dibujo de la portada. Es posible que nos ayude a entender por qué Ada tiene que tomarse estas gotitas."* (Discuss the cover illustration with the class.)

2. Background Questions. Ask: *"¿Alguno de ustedes ha tomado gotitas de medicina? ¿Qué clase de gotitas tomaron? ¿Por qué?"* (Use Think-Pair-Share to discuss students' responses.)

3. Predictive Questions. Ask: *"¿Qué pasa con Ada? ¿Por qué necesita tomar gotitas de medicina?"* (Use Think-Pair-Share to discuss students' responses.)

4. Teacher Script. Model the Monitoring for Meaning strategy as you present the story by stopping at the end of each page and asking aloud, *"¿Entendí lo que leí?"* Then briefly paraphrase aloud what you just read. Ask the predictive question after page 7 and have students respond. Encourage students to support their predictions. Then finish reading the story.

---

1   *Es la hora del almuerzo. Los niños de la clase de Ema están en la cafetería. Están muy entusiasmados. Algo muy especial ocurrirá después del almuerzo. ¿Qué crees que sea?*
Ese día, un mago está en la **escuela**.
¡A los niños les gusta ese mago!
No pueden **comer**.
Ada dice, "No tengo apetito."

---

2   *Los niños están tan agitados que no pueden comer, pero lo tienen que hacer.*
La señorita Sara dice, "Niños, tienen que **comer**.
Después, pueden ver al mago."
Ada **come** su guiso.
Come su postre de mango.

---

3   *Algo le pasa a Ada. ¿Qué es?*
Ada **come** con demasiada prisa.
"Ada, ¿qué te pasa?" pregunta Ema.
"¡Ay! ¡Mi estómago!" dice Ada.
"Trata de tomar algo," dice la señorita Sara.

---

4   *¿Qué hará Ada?*
Ada no tiene ganas de nada.
"¿Te sientes mal?" pregunta la señorita Sara.
"Sí. Tengo algo en el estómago," dice Ada.
"Toma agua," insiste la señorita.
Ada dice, "No puedo tragar ni una gota."

MAKE A PREDICTION: *¿Qué le pasa a Ada? ¿Cómo sanará?* (Pause for students' predictions. Have students discuss predictions. Encourage them to support predictions.)

18-2

5 *El dolor de estómago aumenta. Ada va a la enfermería a ver si la señora Ágata, la enfermera, le puede ayudar. Los otros niños van a ver al mago.*
"¿Qué te pasa, Ada?" pregunta la **enfermera**.
Ada dice, "¡Ay! Es mi estómago."
"Siéntate," dice la señora Ágata.
"Yo tengo un remedio.
Tengo unas gotitas que sanan todo."

6 *La enfermera atiende a Ada.*
La señora Ágata le da tres gotitas a Ada.
Ada no las traga.
Las **huele**.
Dice, "¡Ay! ¡Qué amargas!"
"Tómalas, tómalas," dice la señora Ágata.

7 *¿Qué hace Ada?*
Ada se sienta y espera.
Está triste.
"No estés triste, Ada," dice la señora Ágata.
"Estoy triste por el mago.
Lo puedo oír en el patio," dice Ada.

8 *Oyen unos ruidos en el pasillo. ¿Qué está pasando?*
"¡Señora Ágata! ¡Señora Ágata!"
Entra el mago.
"¿Qué pasó?" pregunta la señora Ágata.
"¡Me apreté el dedo con la puerta!" dice el mago.

9 *La enfermera atiende al mago. Él se sienta junto a Ada.*
La señora Ágata pone gotitas en el dedo del mago.
El mago espera.
Sonríe a Ada.

10 *Muy pronto, el estómago de Ada sana, y también el dedo del mago. ¿Qué pasa ahora?*
El mago dice, "Señora Ágata,
¡USTED sí es una maga! Nos sanó rápidamente. . .
Este regalo es para usted."
¡De su galera el mago saca tres gardenias!
Ada **aplaude** y **aplaude**.
Ada está muy contenta. El mago le ha dado una demostración privada de magia.

18-3

Slavin, R.E., & Madden, N.A., *One Million Children: Success for All.* © Corwin Press Inc.

5. Story Discussion. Have students think about and discuss the story. Encourage them to focus on what they think the purpose for reading the story was. Ask: *"¿Qué pasó en el cuento? ¿Cuál fue nuestro propósito de la lectura? ¿Aprendimos lo que queríamos aprender?"* Have them compare their predictions about the story with what they learned after reading it. Ask them how the story showed why Ada needed the drops. Then, tell students that they are going to learn all the sounds, letters, and words they will need to read this story by themselves. Collect the Shared Stories (or have students put them away).

C. SOUND ACTIVITIES

1. Alphabet Song. Have students sing an alphabet song to invite Alphie to come out.

2. Letter Presentation.

a. Hearing the (voiced) "g" Sound. Introduce the tongue twister. Pull a note from Alphie's box and say: *"Hoy Alfi ha escrito una nota chistosa sobre las gotitas de Ada. En esta nota, muchas palabras empiezan con /g/ (sonora)."* Read Alphie's tongue twister with as much expression as you can.

Gaby Gómez ganó golosinas.

Say each word that starts with (voiced) **"g"**, then rapidly repeat the first syllable three or four times. Have students repeat after you each time.

Note: This is an auditory activity. The tongue twister should not be posted or written on the board.

b. Introducing (voiced) "g" Pictures and Objects. Tell students that now Alphie wants to show things that start with (voiced) /g/. Name each Key Picture as you pull it from Alphie's box and have students repeat the name. Emphasize the (voiced) **"g"** sound as you rapidly repeat the first syllable of the word before you say it. Show each picture again, asking, *"¿Qué sonido escuchan al principio de _____ ?"* Have the group respond by rapidly repeating the syllable, then naming the picture.

gato	*gotitas*	*gusano*

c. Two-Picture Game. Explain to students that you will show them two pictures, and they will have to find the one that begins with (voiced) /g/. Show the top two pictures from the pile. Name each picture, and then have your students name it. Give them five seconds to think, and then have them signal which picture starts with (voiced) /g/ by pointing to the correct picture. If needed check a few students quickly for understanding after the group seems to have achieved fluency with the game.

galleta	*gotitas*	*gusano*
jirafa	*yeso*	*bigote*

d. Making the (voiced) "g" Sound. Show the Key Picture for *gotitas* and say: *"Digan* **gotitas**. *¿Se mueve su lengua o sus labios cuando empiezan a decir* **gotitas***?"* (Lengua). *"¿Dónde está trabajando, en la parte de en frente o atrás de la boca? Si no están seguros, pongan el dedo en la parte de arriba de la boca y vean dónde toca su lengua cuando dicen el sonido."* (En frente). *"Sí, su lengua empuja en la parte de en frente y toca la parte de abajo de su boca. ¿Se queda ahí o se mueve? ¿Lo pueden decir sin mover la lengua?"* (No) *"Cuando mueven la lengua,* *qué sale de la garganta?"* (Aire) *"Vamos a ver si su voz está prendida o apagada."* (Prendida) *"Sientan la vibración en la garganta cuando hacen el sonido. Se para cuando dejan que se baje la lengua."* Have all practice feeling how their mouths make the (voiced) **"g"** sound.

e. **Introducing the "g" Shape.** Pull Alphie's pennant out of his box and introduce the letter's name. Say: *"La letra que va con el sonido /g/ (sonora) es la 'g'."*

Display the **"g"** pictures or objects you presented, one at a time. As students name them, write each one on the board in a vertical list, emphasizing the sound/letter match. Say the cue phrase, *"Si lo puedes oír, lo puedes ver."*

gato   *gotitas*   *gusano*

f. **Practicing the "g" Shape.** Write the upper- and lowercase **"g"** on the chalkboard. Use Think-Pair-Share to discuss their similarities and differences with the students.

Introduce the actual writing of **"g"**. Say: *"Ahora vamos a practicar la 'g' para que podamos escribirla."* Point to the lowercase **"g"** and continue: *"Ésta se usa más seguido y es por eso que la vamos a aprender primero."*

Introduce the verbal pattern for **"g"**: *"Círculo con un ganchito. (Encorvando hacia abajo, hacia arriba, hacia abajo, con un ganchito en el agua.)"*

Have students use the lower case **"g"** on the board for a model as they make a **"g"** in the air and say the cue phrase. Have them make the letter, repeating the cue phrase in unison each time:

    on their desks, as big as they can.
    on their desks, as small as they can.
    on a partner's hand, arm, back, etc.

When students have practiced the shape four or five times, add the sound to the cue phrase: *"Círculo con un ganchito. (Encorvando hacia abajo, hacia arriba, hacia abajo, con un ganchito en el agua.) El sonido de la 'g' es /g/ (sonora)."* Then have students practice **"g"** several more times as they say the cue phrase.

Optional: Instruct students to trace the letter with you several times on their Letter Practice Sheet while they say the cue phrase for the letter shape in unison.

g. **Syllable Sounds.** Present the Syllable Wheel for (voiced) **"g"**. Then say: *"Vamos a juntar la 'g' con /a/, /o/, y /u/. Recuerden cómo colocaron los labios cuando hicieron el sonido /g/ (sonora). Preparen la boca para decir /g/ (sonora)."* (Point to **"g"**.) *"Ahora añadan /o/."* After students say the syllable sound, use it in a word, then say the word again, repeating the first syllable several times. Continue putting together (voiced) **"g"** with the other vowels.

go	**ga**	**gu**
*como **go**titas*	*como **ga**to*	*como **gu**sano*
***gogogogo**titas*	***gagagaga**to*	***gugugugu**sano*

Review the cue phrase for the letter shape, and add the syllable sounds to complete the cue phrase. *"Círculo con un ganchito. (Encorvando hacia abajo, hacia arriba, hacia abajo, con un ganchito en el agua.) El sonido de la 'g' es /g/ (sonora). /Ga/, /go/, /gu/."*

Review the syllables rapidly, using the Syllable Wheel.

3. Syllable Games.

a. Student's (voiced) "g" Words. Give students 30 seconds to tell their partners all the /ga/, /go/, and /gu/ words they know. Highlight the story's theme of taking medicine to get better. Challenge them to think of **"g"** words related to the story or to their own experiences. Allow all students to share their favorite word with a partner. Have all partnerships share their favorite word with the group. As they respond, write their words on the board, and give each student a Student Picture Card as a reward.

b. Say-It-Fast. Remind students that Alfi speaks a special language that is helpful to them as they are learning to read because he says words so slowly that they can hear all the parts. Tell them that they are going to hear some words in Alfi's special language, and then say them in our language. Say each word in the list below, pausing between each syllable. (If students still need clarification, you may give a sentence for words they have trouble understanding as real words, but try to limit the sentences so that they can focus on auditory sound blending.) Signal two seconds for "Think Time," then signal the group to respond together as you say the word quickly with them. Have students respond as a group. Keep the pace rapid.

(2 Syllables)	(3 Syllables)
ga-na	*ga-ra-je*
go-ma	*go-mi-ta*
gu-la	*gu-sa-no*

c. Break-It-Down. Remind students that Alfi's special language is helpful to them as they are learning to read. Tell them that now Alfi needs their help to understand some words, so they need to say these words in his special language. Say each word quickly in the list below. Signal two seconds for "Think Time" then signal the group to respond together as you say the parts of the word with them. Students should be able to think of the word and Break-It-Down when you give the signal to begin. (Students may clap or tap lightly as they say each syllable when they Break-it-Down.) Have students respond as a group, and keep the pace rapid.

(2 Syllables)	(3 Syllables)
mago	*gotitas*
miga	*amargas*
usted	*ganamos*

Ask students why they think it is important to say things in Alfi's special language. (It will help them to put sounds together as they learn to read.) Then tell them that they are going to use Alfi's special language as they learn to read the story's new words.

d. (Visual) Yes-No Game. Tell students that you are going to show them more pictures on cards. Show the pictures to your students, one at a time. When you show each picture, say the name, and have students repeat it. Then, have them think for five seconds, and point to the sign *(Sí* or *No)* to show whether or not it starts with **/ga/, /go/,** or **/gu/.** Check individual students quickly for understanding after the group has achieved fluency with the game.

gallina	*gorila*	*gusano*
zeta	*burro*	*sopa*

e. (Auditory) Yes-No Game. Say each of the words in the list below, one at a time. After saying each one, have your students repeat it. Give them five seconds to think, and then have them point to *(Sí* or *No)* to indicate whether the word begins with **/ga/, /go/,** or **/gu/.** Assess individual students, as needed, in order to determine whether children need additional practice.

gato	*gota*	*gusano*
muñeca	*tenedor*	*silla*

f. Matching Games. Use pictures selected during the lesson preparation that begin with the letters **"ñ", "r",** and **(voiced) "g".**

Activity 1. **Have students match pictures of objects with Syllable Wheels <u>accompanied by</u> Key Pictures. (Use a pocket chart or chalkboard ledge.)**

radio	*rosa*	*gallina*	*ñandú*	*gotitas*

Activity 2. **Have students match spoken words with Syllable Wheels <u>accompanied by</u> Key Pictures.**

guiso	*ñu*	*ropa*	*galleta*	*Rosa*

Activity 3. **Have students match pictures of objects with Syllable Wheels (no Key Pictures.)**

ñisñil	*gusano*	*rubí*	*gorila*	*remo*

Activity 4. **Have students match spoken words with Syllable Wheels (no Key Pictures.)**

rama	*gusto*	*ñoña*	*resta*	*goma*

D. STORY ACTIVITIES

1. Word Presentation.

a. Stop and Read. Quickly flash the Syllable Cards for all known sounds, and have students give the sound only. Introduce the story's new words by sharing Alfi's whispered message: *"Cuando aprenden a hacer sonidos, están listos para aprender algunas palabras."* As you present each word, Stop and Read it with your students by parts. (See the first example below for an introductory method to model pausing between each of the parts.) Allow students to blend the parts as they become familiar with the words through repeated reading. Use your judgement to decide if they are ready to blend the parts during the first reading, or if they should continue to

18-7

pause between the parts until they are comfortable with blending. (For examples of methods to blend the parts, see the Teacher's Page, *Working with Syllable Sounds*.)

Model how to Stop and Read the story's new words. For example:

(1) (Read the first part.)	*es*	■		
(2) (Read this and add the next.)	*es*	*tó*	■	
(3) (Read these and add the next.)	*es*	*tó*	*ma*	■
(4) (Read these and add the next.)	*es*	*tó*	*ma*	*go*
(5) (Read the word.)	*estómago*			
(6) (Say a sentence.)	*A la niña le duele el estómago.*			

Have students Stop and Read the following as you did *estómago**. Point out that the **"u"** in *guiso* is silent.

mago	*amargas*	*gotitas*	*apreté*	*tomar**
miga	*pregunta**	*traga*	*dedo**	*guiso*
ganas	*insiste*	*trata*	*sanan*	

Then tell students they are going to read a word with a new tag-along letter. Say: *"A veces a la 'd' le gusta pegarse al final de una palabra. Por ejemplo, vamos a decir esta palabra por partes como la pronunciamos."* Have children say *usted* with you, pausing between the parts, then have them say it fast. Next, show students how to Stop and Read *usted*.

(1) (Read the first part.)	*us*	■
(2) (Read this and add the next.)	*us*	*ted*
(3) (Read the word.)	*usted*	
(4) (Say a sentence.)	*Usted es el*	
	presidente.	

Remind students how to use the parts of *agua** (a word with two vowels together) to make it easier to read.

(1) (Read the first part.)	*a*	■	
(2) (Read this and add the next.)	*a*	*gu*	■
(3) (Read these and add the next.)	*a*	*gua*	
(4) (Read the word.)	*agua*		
(5) (Say a sentence.)	*Tomé un vaso agua*		
	fresca.		

Have students Stop and Read *gardenias* and *remedio* as you did *agua**.

Remind students that we will call the words we can figure out by using sounds **"green"** words. On Day 1 provide sentences using starred words in the context of the story. On Day 2, students can orally create a sentence for these words with their partners. Call on partnerships to share their sentences.

   b. Quick Erase. Tell students that you are going to play the Tag-Along Quick Erase Game, starting with some nonsense rhymes. Have children quickly repeat the tag-along **"d"** syllable patterns after you.

18-8

Slavin, R.E., & Madden, N.A., *One Million Children: Success for All.* © Corwin Press Inc.

dad-sad-rad
ded-sed-red
did-sid-rid
dod-sod-rod
dud-sud-rud

Tell children that now they will make some real words from these sounds with the tag-along **"d"**. Play Quick Erase by starting with **poned** and ending with **edad**, changing one letter at a time. Have students Stop and Read as needed. Use the words in sentences as needed to make sure that students recognize them as words they know. (Note to the teacher: The following imperative verbs, ending with **"d"**, use the *vosotros* form: *pongan/poned, puedan/poded, usen/usad, den/dad.* Students may not be familiar with the usage of the pronoun *vosotros*. Do not explain the usage of the pronoun to students, instead, show them through example. When you use the verbs in sentences, make it clear in your example that *vosotros* is another way of saying *ustedes*: **Poned** *los libros sobre la mesa. Me refiero a vosotros, es decir, a ustedes.*)

poned→poded→pared→red→sed→usad→dad→edad

Quickly review by presenting the Tag-Along Syllable Wheel for **"d"** and having the children say the tag-along syllables again.

        c. Say-Spell-Say. Say-Spell-Say the story's Sight Word, *algo*. Have students say the word, soft-clap it by letter, and say it again. Say-Spell-Say the word three times on Day 1, twice on Day 2, and once on Day 3. Remember to color the Sight Word red.

Introduce the story's Readles, *escuela*, *comer/come*, *enfermera*, and *aplaude*. Use the Readles in a sentence.

        d. Word Wall. Use the Word Wall for red and green words from the previous two stories. Keep high frequency words even longer. (Some of the words may start out as red words and may become green words as new letters are learned.) Three or four times during a lesson, take 30 to 60 seconds for a rapid choral review of the words in order and out of order.

        2. Guided Group Reading. Review how to use the Previewing strategy. Redistribute the Shared Story, or have students take out their Shared Story. Use the enlarged text to demonstrate while students use their Shared Stories. Now, tell students that they are going to read the story for themselves. Remind them that it has many words that contain or start with /ga/, /go/, or /gu/. Ask them to put on their listening ears so they can hear these special new sounds in the story.

        a. Modeling Use of Context Clues. Read the sentence(s) below you have written on the board or on sentence strip(s). (Keep the context word(s) covered.) Ask: *"¿Qué palabra podría ir en el espacio cubierto para que la oración tuviera sentido?"* Have students use Think-Pair-Share, then list their suggestions. If several make sense, say, or uncover, the first letter of the context word, and have them use Think-Pair-Share to figure it out. If this does not work, remind students of the other strategies on the posted Word Strategies Chart (Looking in the book to read what comes after the sentence with the context word, looking at the illustrations, asking their partner, and finally, asking you.)

        Page 2.   *"Come su postre de _____(mango)."*

        Page 4.   *"¿Te sientes _____(mal)?" pregunta la señorita Sara."*

18-9

Page 10.   *"Este _____(regalo) es para usted."*

Page 10.   *"¡De su _____(galera) saca tres gardenias."*

b. Teacher/Student Reading. Go over the names of the story's characters. Then, read the introductory script and the story again (see **Setting the Stage**) with expression. Have students listen as you read the teacher's text at the top of the page, then have them read along in a low voice as you read the student's text. Read each story sentence twice to help students build fluency. Continue to ask questions to reinforce comprehension of the story.

3. Partner Reading. Encourage students to use the Previewing strategy. Direct students to take turns with their partner to read alternate pages of the story aloud, with expression, and to help each other. Use appropriate strategies for green words, red words, and context words.

> Circulate around the room as students read to assist as needed. You may need to continue to model how to help or take turns within a partnership. Observe the progress of each student as you circulate. Use the Class Record Form, page A11-1, to record fluency and expression.

a. Monitoring for Meaning. Reinforce the importance of using the Monitoring for Meaning strategy. Have students read each page and then ask, *"¿Entendí lo que acabo de leer?"* Have students explain what they have read to their partner before before going on to the next page.

b. Story Comprehension. When students have finished the partner reading, read the questions below aloud, then lead an oral discussion. Have students use Think-Pair-Share to discuss the answers. Encourage them to use the book to find specific clues to the answers. Encourage partners to give each other feedback.

a.   *¿Qué le pasa a Ada?*
b.   *¿Por qué no quiere ir Ada a la enfermería?*
c.   *¿Por qué no quiere Ada tomar las gotitas?*
d.   *¿Cómo se siente Ada cuando el mago va a la enfermería? ¿Por qué?*

4. Tap and Spell. Tap and Spell the words orally with the group as in Lesson 6, or distribute scrap paper and have students spell and write the words as you help them Tap and Spell, as in Lesson 11.

mago   *miga*   *dedo*

5. Shared Treasure. This Share Sheet focuses on story comprehension and sentence reading practice. Be sure to do a teacher directed review of sides one and two of the Shared Treasure before partner practice. Before students complete the Comprehension section on page 2, be sure to model the process for writing an answer to the following question on the board. (Have students use Think-Pair-Share to come up with possible answers to the question.) Challenge students to write a complete sentence.

¿Tiene Ada apetito?

Remember that the goal of the Shared Treasure is to provide repeated practice for fluency. The goal is not to simply fill it out. Allow the students to color in a star for each successful reading they accomplish with their partner. Have students read and respond to the Shared Treasure with their partner, and have partners share with the group. Have students use some of their partner practice time to practice spelling words.

6. Story Related Writing. This Share Sheet focuses on writing about a topic suggested by the story that relates to students' own experiences. Have students plan their writing with their partner and then write individually. Have partners share their writing with each other, then have some students share with the group.

E. CELEBRATION

1. Performance. At the end of each day, have two students read, with expression, a page or more from a story they have mastered. Be sure to let students know at least one day in advance that they have been selected for the Reading Celebration Performance so that they can take home a story of their choice to practice. Have the entire class provide applause and praise, and present the student with a Reading Celebration Certificate. **Enjoy your celebration and remember to do it every day!**

For the Spelling Celebration on Fridays, give students a piece of paper and have them number it. Tell the children that you will give them a chance to show you all that they have learned about the new sounds by spelling some words that contain these sounds. Say each spelling word you have chosen, use it in a sentence, and repeat the word before moving on to the next word. Be sure to provide plenty of praise for all attempts and to celebrate the progress of each student. You can give students stickers for their tests, and post them in your room until the next test.

2. Syllable Sound Review. Summarize the day's lesson by quickly using Syllable Wheels to review all syllables. Use two quick reviews. The first time, have students say only the syllable sound. The second time, have students say the sound, and then spell the syllable. Keep the pace very rapid. Use group response to review all the words on the Word Wall, in order and out of order, very rapidly.

> TEACHERS, PLEASE REMEMBER: Using the Word Wall and the current list of green and red words, work in three to four quick reviews during the 90-minute reading block. Frequent but brief reviews of words and syllables will increase your students' reading fluency, as will repeated readings of stories and Shared Treasure sheets.

F. HOMEWORK

At the end of the first day of the lesson, ask students to look for and think about lots of /ga/, /go/, /gu/ words for tomorrow's lesson. Let students take their completed Shared Treasure sheets, Story Related Writing and current or familiar Shared Stories home to read to parents and other family members. Listeners can initial in the boxes at the bottom of the Shared Treasure sheet and sign one of the signature sheets (*Señalador de Tareas de Lee Conmigo* or *Por Favor, ¡Lee Conmigo!*) after listening to the child read from the Shared Story (see the Appendix for samples). Have students return the Shared Treasure and signature sheet. Give students a copy of the spelling words on an *Aplaudir, Trazar y Escribir* form (included in the Appendix) to take home and practice once or twice during the week.

18-11

LESSON 18
Shared Treasure

Word Reading. *Have students take turns reading aloud the phonetic words with their partner.*

guiso	dedo	traga	amargas	estómago
mago	remedio	ganas	tomar	insiste
miga	apreté	gotitas	pregunta	sanan
agua	trata	gardenias		

usted

Have students take turns reading the Sight Word with their partner.

algo

Sentence Reading. *Have students take turns reading aloud the sentences with their partner. Encourage them to read with expression.*

El mago está en la escuela .

Pero Ada no lo puede ver.

Tiene un dolor en el estómago.

La señora Ágata le da unas gotitas.

El mago entra.

Se dañó el dedo.

La señora Ágata sana al mago y a Ada.

Have a few students read out loud with expression to the class.

TSS-18-1

LESSON 18
Shared Treasure

Comprehension. Ask: ¿Quiere ver Ada al mago? Have students take turns reading each question, then have them orally answer with a complete sentence. Have students write a complete sentence to answer the last two questions. They may make their own Readles for those words that they cannot write.

¿Tiene Ada apetito? _____

¿Tiene Ada un dolor en el estómago? _____

¿Sana la Señora Ágata a Ada? _____

¿Está Ada triste por no ver el mago? _____

¿ Aplaude Ada? _____

Practicing Concepts. Have students color a star every time they read the letters or share their ideas with their partner. Once Share Sheets have been mastered, have students take them home. Tell students to read their Share Sheets to as many people as possible. Each listener should write their initials and the date in the designated box.

TSS-18-2

LESSON 18
Story Related Writing

Letter Writing. *Have students say the sound of the letter, then write it three times.*

g			

Tap and Spell. *Have students take turns with their partner saying the word for each picture. Then have students write the letter that they can hear at the beginning of each word. Challenge students to write* ***gotitas.***

gotitas _____   gato _____

Writing Ideas. *Have students think about and discuss how Ada's stomach ache was cured. Then, read the prompt: "Ada toma gotitas. Su estómago sana. [Yo] Tomo..." Have students read it after you. Tell them to remember a time when they were sick and had to take medicine. Then have them describe what happened. Tell them to plan their writing with their partner. Encourage them to describe what they did.*

Ada toma gotitas.

Su estómago sana.

Tomo _____

_____

_____

_____

_____

Have students share their writing with their partner, and have a few students share their writing with the class.

TSS-18-3

Slavin, R.E., & Madden, N.A., *One Million Children: Success for All.* © Corwin Press Inc.

Appendix 2.5.
Teacher's Guide to a Treasure Hunt for *Jumanji*

Reading Wings™

JUMANJI
BY
CHRIS VAN ALLSBURG

TH4-36   HOUGHTON MIFFLIN COMPANY   01231

Success for All™
Roots and Wings™

© 1998 SUCCESS FOR ALL FOUNDATION, INC.

Reading Wings™

TEACHER EDITION

JUMANJI

BY

CHRIS VAN ALLSBURG

TH4-36   HOUGHTON MIFFLIN COMPANY   01231

Production Team:
Anna Marie Farnish
Pamela Cantrell

Slavin, R.E., & Madden, N.A., *One Million Children: Success for All.* © Corwin Press Inc.

JUMANJI TEACHER EDITION CHRIS VAN ALLSBURG

STORY SUMMARY: *Jumanji* tells how two children, out looking for adventure, find a mysterious board game in the park. After Peter and Judy's parents leave for the opera, the children tire of playing their old games and messing up the house. Looking for excitement, they journey to the park where they find a game called Jumanji under a tree. They take the game home and read the instructions that explicitly state that once the game is started, it must be finished. They soon find out what this direction means, as everything that is happening in the game also happens in real life. Soon Peter and Judy are sitting in their living room with monsoon rains pouring down, a lion in the bedroom, and monkeys making a mess in the kitchen. Anxious to finish the game, they are relieved when Judy finally reaches Jumanji, a city of golden buildings and towers, and all of the animals and confusion disappears into a cloud. The two children quickly return the game to the park. When the parents return home from the opera, they do not believe the story of the day's adventures. However, Peter and Judy know that the trouble isn't over when they see two of their friends running through the park, carrying Jumanji.

✍ ABOUT THE AUTHOR: Chris Van Allsburg received his Bachelor of Fine Arts from the University of Michigan and his Master of Fine Arts from Rhode Island School of Design. Currently, he lives in Providence, Rhode Island with his wife Lisa, and his cat Cecil. He has received numerous awards for his illustrations and is praised for his off-beat stories, loved by both children and adults. Van Allsburg likes to include a drawing of a dog in each of his books and he describes himself as "a writer who is motivated by the images that I see in my mind."

LISTENING COMPREHENSION / READ ALOUD CONNECTIONS

Every author has a unique style and students can learn about that style by studying story elements and the craft used by the author. *Jumanji* has many examples of **foreshadowing,** or hints and clues that certain events will occur later. Select a book or story that has examples of foreshadowing for examination during the Listening Comprehension. Call attention to how these techniques support the author's style and reinforce the students' ability to construct meaning while reading. Examples of other stories with foreshadowing include: *Night Noises* by Mem Fox, *The Snow Queen* retold by Joan Collins, *The Firebird* by Selina Hastings, and *The Headless Horseman* by Washington Irving.

1

JUMANJI   TEACHER EDITION   CHRIS VAN ALLSBURG

BUILDING BACKGROUND: In order to prepare students for reading *Jumanji*, discuss the following topics with them.

- ○ *Jumanji* is a fantasy. Ask students if they know what a fantasy is. What are the differences between a fantasy and realistic fiction?

- ○ Ask the students how a board game is played. What are some examples of board games? What makes a board game fun? Do you ever get 'bored' with board games? Why?

- ○ Jumanji is an African game that brings the wild animals of Africa into Peter and Judy's house. Using the K-W-L learning model, make a list of what the students already know about the wild areas of Africa. What is an African safari like? What kinds of animals live there? What kinds of animals live in African jungles? Make another list of the things that students might like to find out about these places. As students learn about Africa while reading the book, create a third list of what they have learned. Ask students to include in their lists, the things that they might see, hear and do in a jungle.

- ○ It has been speculated that the adventures of the board game Jumanji are related to the opera "Aïda." The opera is set in Africa and while the parents were seeing it, the children have an African adventure of their own. Consult with the music teacher and play a selection from this opera for the class. Ask the class what images the music gives them and, later, discuss how this relates to the tone of the story. *Aïda* by Leontyne Price tells the story of the opera and may be used to compare illustrations, setting, and tone with *Jumanji*.

? PREVIEW/PREDICT/PURPOSE: Have students read and think about the title of the book, look at the illustrations and read the first two pages. Have students predict what might happen in the story. Then have them use their predictions to set a purpose for reading such as, **"I'm going to read to find out what happens when the children play the game."**

JUMANJI MAY BE COUPLED WITH THE FOLLOWING READING/ LISTENING COMPREHENSION/STUDY SKILLS EXERCISES:

✔Drawing Conclusions (RC)   ✔Fact and Fantasy (RC)

✔Character Traits (RC/LC)   ✔Cause and Effect (RC/LC)

✔Following Directions (SS)   ✔Problem Solving with Failed Attempts (LC)

✔Foreshadowing (LC)   ✔Mood (LC)

READ THE FIRST THREE PAGES ALOUD TO STUDENTS

2

JUMANJI   TEACHER EDITION   CHRIS VAN ALLSBURG

✦ WORD MASTERY LIST ✦

* agreed 3	opera 1	laughter 1	silence 1
* revealing 5	slouched 1	sweater 3	board 5
* gasping 9	horror 7	piano 7	whisker 9
* instant 11	stampede 17	rumble 17	interrupted 25
* relief 23	exhaustion 23	lava 21	erupts 21
volcano 21	guide 15		

TREASURE HUNT

SECTION I. Read through page 13. Discuss the answers to the questions with your partner. Then write your answers, while your partner answers separately.

1. Describe the main characters in this story. Peter and Judy were the main characters in this story. Judy was a determined, bossy older sister. Peter was a follower.

2. What did the children do when their parents left? Why? Peter and Judy made a mess in the house and then went looking in the park for adventure. They were bored with their games at home.
•How is this different from what you would have done?

3. What did the children find in the park? Peter and Judy found a game called Jumanji. The mysterious way that they found the game, the fact that the game is designed for the bored and restless, the phrase "Fun for some but not for all," and the direction that states that the game, once started, must be finished, all indicate that playing Jumanji will be an adventure.
•What clues did the author give to help you predict that Jumanji will be an exciting game?

4. Explain how the game, Jumanji, is special. When Peter landed on a square, the animal appeared, just like the game said. The events of the game were occuring in real life.

5. Why do you think that the author wrote the words for instruction D in capital letters? Why must the children continue playing the game? Instruction D was written in capital letters to show that it was the most important instruction. The game's directions stated that the game would not end until someone reached the city of Jumanji and won the game. The animals wouldn't go away until then.

3

Make a Prediction

What has happened in the story so far? How is that different from what you expected? What will happen next? Will Peter and Judy be able to finish playing Jumanji? Give reasons for your answers. (Discuss students' predictions. Have students give support for their predictions.)

SECTION II. Finish reading the story. Discuss the answers to the following questions with your partner. Then each of you should write your answers separately.

1. **What has happened in the story that lets you know that this story is a fantasy and not realistic fiction?** Each time that Peter or Judy landed on a new space, whatever was written in that game square would happen in real life.

2. **How do you think the children felt as they played the game? How do you know?** Peter and Judy were probably very scared that something bad would happen to them. They rushed to try to finish the game quickly. Judy begged to roll a twelve so the game would be over.

3. **What did the children do with the game when they were finished?** They rushed it back to the park so it wouldn't be in their house anymore.
•*What would you have done in their situation? Why?*

4. **Why did the adults laugh when the children tried to tell them about their day?** The adults didn't believe Peter's story. They thought that the children were playing make believe.
•*How might Peter and Judy have tried to convince them that they were telling the truth?*

5. **What do you think the children learned?** The children learned to read directions carefully. They also decided that their ordinary games weren't so boring after all.

6. **What do you think the game maker meant by, "Free game. Fun for some but not for all." Did Peter and Judy have fun playing Jumanji? Why?** (Answers may vary. Accept those that are supported.)   The game is only fun if the players follow the directions. Otherwise, the animals will never leave. The game maker may also mean that the game is more scary than fun. Peter and Judy did not enjoy the game because they were very scared. They rushed through the game and wanted it to be over quickly, even though it had been an exciting experience to remember.

4

JUMANJI   TEACHER EDITION   CHRIS VAN ALLSBURG

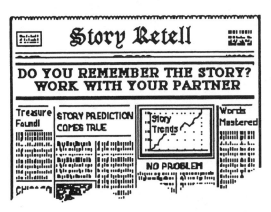

1. How did Peter and Judy feel at the beginning of the story? The two children were bored. They were tired of playing their games and making a mess in the house. They wanted to do something exciting.

2. Explain what happened when the children played Jumanji. Each time they landed on a space, something new would happen. Whatever was written in the game square happened in real life. Peter and Judy had to finish the game so that the wild animals would disappear and their house would return to normal.

3. Compare how Peter and Judy felt about their old games at the start of the story to how they felt at the end. At the beginning of the story, Peter and Judy were very bored with their old games and were anxious to find some excitement. After playing Jumanji, they were more appreciative of their old games.

4. What conclusion did Peter and Judy's parents draw about Peter's tale of adventure? Why did they make this conclusion? The parents laughed at the story, assuming that Peter was imagining the adventure. The parents had found Peter and Judy soundly asleep on the couch and probably could not imagine that such confusion could have taken place that evening in their own home.

Adventures in Writing!

<u>Choose one of the following:</u>

1. At the end of the story, Daniel and Walter Budwing had found the game in the park. Mrs. Budwing said that the two boys did not read directions carefully. Write several paragraphs about Daniel and Walter. What will happen when they play Jumanji? What clues from the story let you know that this might happen? Will they finish the game? Describe their exciting adventures as they play Jumanji. Include a picture of the scene that Mr. and Mrs. Budwing might find if they arrive home in the middle of the game.

2. Imagine that Peter and Judy's parents arrived home in the middle of the Jumanji game. What would their parents have done? Would Judy and Peter have gotten in

5

JUMANJI   TEACHER EDITION   CHRIS VAN ALLSBURG

trouble? Would the game ever be finished? Pretending that you are Peter or Judy, write several paragraphs persuading your parents that the game must be finished.

✦ STORY TEST ANSWERS ✦

1. **Why did Peter and Judy go to the park?** Peter and Judy were bored. They wanted to play in the park since it would surely be more exciting than their games at home.

2. **Why did Judy read the directions to Jumanji carefully?** There was a note taped to the box that said that they should read the directions carefully.

3. **What happened when Judy and Peter played Jumanji?** Everything that happened in the game happened in real life. There were wild animals all over the house.

4. **How did the adults react to Peter's story?** The adults laughed because they thought that he was making it all up.

5. **What was the new problem at the end of the story?** Walter and Daniel had found the game and they usually did not follow directions carefully. They might get hurt playing the game.

 EXTENSION ACTIVITIES

1. **What's Your Game?** Using the game Jumanji as a model, create your own game in which you pretend that the things you include in the game really happen. Think about the rules that Van Allsburg used for Jumanji. Use things or places that interest you. How about a game about outer space, or about deep sea travel?

2. **African Experience:** The game of Jumanji takes place in an African jungle, but not all of Africa is a jungle like the one in the story. Africa has large cities, deserts, coastline and grasslands. Research the continent of Africa. Once you have found enough information on the continent, create a tour brochure that highlights the important facts about Africa and describes major points of interest.

3. **Van Allsburg Illustrations:** Chris Van Allsburg's books are all well known for their exceptional illustrations. Pick another book of Van Allsburg and compare and contrast those illustrations to the ones found in *Jumanji*. Pick your favorite illustration from each book and write, along with your comparison, why you like those drawings the most. What does the author do to contribute to suspense through his illustrations?

6

JUMANJI   **TEACHER EDITION**   **CHRIS VAN ALLSBURG**

4. **Volcano:** Research volcanoes. How are they formed? Where are major ones located? What are some famous volcanic eruptions? Why are they considered to be dangerous? Write a report on your findings to present to your class, along with a diagram of a volcano.

5. **Games Alive!** Pick your favorite board game and imagine what would happen if that game came to life while you were playing, as they did in *Jumanji*. Are you alone or are you playing with a partner? Write several paragraphs telling what happens and how you react. How does the game end?

6. **Allsburg Interview:** Pretend that you will have the opportunity to interview Chris Van Allsburg. Write five questions for the author/illustrator about his life, his stories or his illustrations. Then, exchange your questions with a partner and, pretending that you are Van Allsburg, answer the questions as you think that he would.

❋ So, You Want to Read More ❋

- ... by Van Allsburg? Look for *The Garden of Abdul Gasazi, The Polar Express, The Mysteries of Harris Burdick,* or *Ben's Dream.*

- ... fantasy books? Try *James and the Giant Peach* by Roald Dahl, *Mufaro's Beautiful Daughters* by John Steptoe, or *The Secret Garden* by Frances Hodgson Burnett.

7

Reading Wings™

STUDENT EDITION

JUMANJI
BY
CHRIS VAN ALLSBURG

TH4-36   HOUGHTON MIFFLIN COMPANY   01231

Production Team:
Anna Marie Farnish
Pamela Cantrell

✦ WORD MASTERY LIST ✦

* agreed	opera	laughter	silence
* revealing	slouched	sweater	board
* gasping	horror	piano	whisker
* instant	stampede	rumble	interrupted
* relief	exhaustion	lava	erupts
volcano	guide		

TREASURE HUNT

SECTION I. Read through page 13. Discuss the answers to the questions with your partner. Then write your answers, while your partner answers separately.

1. **Describe the main characters in this story.**

2. **What did the children do when their parents left? Why?**

3. **What did the children find in the park?**

4. **Explain how the game, Jumanji, is special.**

5. **Why do you think that the author wrote the words for instruction D in capital letters? Why must the children continue playing the game?**

1

Slavin, R.E., & Madden, N.A., *One Million Children: Success for All.* © Corwin Press Inc.

Make a Prediction

What has happened in the story so far? How is that different from what you expected? What will happen next? Will Peter and Judy be able to finish playing Jumanji? Give reasons for your answers.

SECTION II. Finish reading the story. Discuss the answers to the following questions with your partner. Then each of you should write your answers separately.

1. **What has happened in the story that lets you know that this story is a fantasy and not realistic fiction?**

2. **How do you think the children felt as they played the game? How do you know?**

3. **What did the children do with the game when they were finished?**

4. **Why did the adults laugh when the children tried to tell them about their day?**

5. **What do you think the children learned?**

6. **What do you think the game maker meant by, "Free game. Fun for some but not for all." Did Peter and Judy have fun playing Jumanji? Why?**

1. How did Peter and Judy feel at the beginning of the story? The two children were. bored. They were tired of playing their games and making a mess in the house. They wanted to do something exciting.

2. Explain what happened when the children played Jumanji. Each time they landed on a space, something new would happen. Whatever was written in the game square happened in real life. Peter and Judy had to finish the game so that the wild animals would disappear and their house would return to normal.

3. Compare how Peter and Judy felt about their old games at the start of the story to how they felt at the end. At the beginning of the story, Peter and Judy were very bored with their old games and were anxious to find some excitement. After playing Jumanji, they were more appreciative of their old games.

4. What conclusion did Peter and Judy's parents draw about Peter's tale of adventure? Why did they make this conclusion? The parents laughed at the story, assuming that Peter was imagining the adventure. The parents had found Peter and Judy soundly asleep on the couch and probably could not imagine that such confusion could have taken place that evening in their own home.

3

Slavin, R.E., & Madden, N.A., *One Million Children: Success for All.* © Corwin Press Inc.

Adventures in Writing!

Choose one of the following:

1. At the end of the story, Daniel and Walter Budwing had found the game in the park. Mrs. Budwing said that the two boys did not read directions carefully. Write several paragraphs about Daniel and Walter. What will happen when they play Jumanji? What clues from the story let you know that this might happen? Will they finish the game? Describe their exciting adventures as they play Jumanji. Include a picture of the scene that Mr. and Mrs. Budwing might find if they arrive home in the middle of the game.

2. Imagine that Peter and Judy's parents arrived home in the middle of the Jumanji game. What would their parents have done? Would Judy and Peter have gotten into trouble? Would the game ever be finished? Pretending that you are Peter or Judy, write several paragraphs persuading your parents that the game must be finished.

4

Slavin, R.E., & Madden, N.A., *One Million Children: Success for All.* © Corwin Press Inc.

EXTENSION ACTIVITIES ✎

1. **What's Your Game?** Using the game Jumanji as a model, create your own game in which you pretend that the things you include in the game really happen. Think about the rules that Van Allsburg used for Jumanji. Use things or places that interest you. How about a game about outer space, or about deep sea travel?

2. **African Experience:** The game of Jumanji takes place in an African jungle, but not all of Africa is a jungle like the one in the story. Africa has large cities, deserts, coastline and grasslands. Research the continent of Africa. Once you have found enough information on the continent, create a tour brochure that highlights the important facts about Africa and describes major points of interest.

3. **Van Allsburg Illustrations:** Chris Van Allsburg's books are all well known for their exceptional illustrations. Pick another book of Van Allsburg and compare and contrast those illustrations to the ones found in *Jumanji*. Pick your favorite illustration from each book and write, along with your comparison, why you like those drawings the most. What does the author do to contribute to the feelings of suspense through his illustrations?

4. **Volcano:** Research volcanoes. How are they formed? Where are major ones located? What are some famous volcanic eruptions? Why are they considered to be dangerous? Write a report on your findings to present to your class, along with a diagram of a volcano.

5. **Games Alive!** Pick your favorite board game and imagine what would happen if that game came to life while you were playing, as they did in *Jumanji*. Are you alone or are you playing with a partner? Write several paragraphs telling what happens and how you react. How does the game end?

6. **Allsburg Interview:** Pretend that you will have the opportunity to interview Chris Van Allsburg. Write five questions for the author/illustrator about his life, his stories or his illustrations. Then, exchange your questions with a partner and, pretending that you are Van Allsburg, answer the questions as you think that he would.

❋ SO, YOU WANT TO READ MORE ❋

- . . . by Van Allsburg? Look for *The Garden of Abdul Gasazi, The Polar Express, The Mysteries of Harris Burdick,* or *Ben's Dream.*

- . . . fantasy books? Try *James and the Giant Peach* by Roald Dahl, *Mufaro's Beautiful Daughters* by John Steptoe, or *The Secret Garden* by Frances Hodgson Burnett.

Appendix 2.6.

Reading Wings™

TEST

JUMANJI

BY

CHRIS VAN ALLSBURG

TH4-36   HOUGHTON MIFFLIN COMPANY   01231

Production Team:
      Anna Marie Farnish
      Pamela Cantrell

JUMANJI	**TEST**	**CHRIS VAN ALLSBURG**

STORY TEST

NAME:_____

1. **Why did Peter and Judy go to the park?**

_____

_____

_____

2. **Why did Judy read the directions to Jumanji carefully?**

_____

_____

_____

3. **What happened when Peter and Judy played Jumanji?**

_____

_____

_____

4. **How did the adults react to Peter's story?**

_____

_____

_____

5. **What was the new problem at the end of the story?**

_____

_____

_____

JUMANJI   **TEST**   CHRIS VAN ALLSBURG

WORD MEANING TEST

Write a sentence for each one of these words.

agreed   revealing

gasping   instant

relief

_____

_____

_____

_____

_____

_____

_____

_____

_____

_____

_____

_____

_____

_____

_____

_____

_____

_____

Appendix 2.7.
Treasure Hunt for Chapter 1 of
Un Natillo de Cerezas

Reading Wings™
Alas para Leer™

EDICIÓN DEL MAESTRO

UN HATILLO DE CEREZAS

DE
MARÍA PUNCEL

TH2-1S   01133

 *UN HATILLO DE CEREZAS*   MARÍA PUNCEL

EDICIÓN DEL MAESTRO

RESUMEN DEL CUENTO: Tema y enfoque de la selección
El cuento se desarrolla en un valle donde Antonio es ayudante de panadero. Un día al llevar el pan a vender al mercado se encuentra al tío Curro que le regala un hatillo de cerezas. A Antonio le encantaban las cerezas pero decidió llevárselas a la abuela Francisca porque sólo podía comer cosas blandas y jugosas. La abuela Francisca decidió dárselas a su hermana María. El hatillo de cerezas fue pasando de mano en mano hasta que llegó de nuevo a las manos de Antonio que se sorprendió de como fue que el hatillo de cerezas llegó de nuevo hasta él. Antonio disfrutó mucho de las cerezas pero le pidió a su madre que investigara porque le habían regresado las cerezas.

SOBRE LA AUTORA   Conozcamos a María Puncel.

CONSTRUYENDO CONOCIMIENTO: Estrategias previas a la lectura
Explíqueles que *Un hatillo de cerezas* es el relato de un grupo de campesinos que se demuestran afecto y cariño haciéndose un regalo singular. Luego escriba en el pizarrón "Es mejor dar que recibir" y anime a los estudiantes a intercambiar ideas sobre lo que esa frase significa para ellos. Pídales que mencionen ocasiones en que le hayan dado un regalo singular a alguien o hayan compartido algo excepcional con otros. Pídales que expliquen cómo se sintieron y que discutan por qué los regalos hacen que una persona se sienta bien.
Muestre como se hace un hatillo:
- con un cuadro de tela se forma un hatillo
- un hatillo se puede formar con una servilleta
- las cerezas pueden ir dentro de un hatillo

COMPRENSIÓN AUDITIVA/ CONEXIONES DE LECTURA EN VOZ ALTA: Todos los autores tienen un estilo único. Los estudiantes pueden aprender ese estilo al estudiar los elementos del cuento y la habilidad del autor. *Un hatillo de cerezas* es un **cuento de ficción.** Escoja otro **cuento de ficción** para leer en voz alta a los estudiantes. Asegúrese que los estudiantes se den cuenta de cómo las técnicas de los **cuentos de ficción** apoyan al estilo del autor y refuerzan la habilidad del lector para construir el significado   mientras lee. Unos ejemplos de otros **cuentos de ficción** son: *Jugo de pecas* y *La princesa de papel.*

PREVISIÓN/PREDICCIÓN/PROPÓSITO: Pídales a los estudiantes que lean y mediten sobre el título del cuento, que miren el dibujo de la portada, y que lean las primeras dos páginas. Haga que los estudiantes predigan lo que pueda pasar en el cuento. Después, pídale que se propongan un propósito para leer, tal como, **"Voy a leer para saber quien se comerá las cerezas."**

LEA LAS PÁGINAS 1-3 EN VOZ ALTA A LOS ESTUDIANTES

1

UN HATILLO DE CEREZAS   MARÍA PUNCEL

EDICIÓN DEL MAESTRO

❖ PALABRAS RETADORAS ❖

*hogosas	*hatillo	*destacar	exquisito
serenos	*hundida	bobalicón	atascado

Búsqueda de Tesoros

SECCIÓN I. Lee las páginas 1 a 5. Discute las respuestas a las preguntas con tu compañero. Luego, escribe tus respuestas, mientras que tu compañero contesta por separado.

1. ¿Por qué trabajaba Antonio desde la noche hasta el amanecer? Antonio trabajaba desde la noche hasta el amanecer porque era ayudante de panadero.

• *¿Por qué tendría que llevar Antonio el pan que hacía en la panadería al mercado?*

2. ¿Por qué marchaba Antonio a los caseríos del valle? Las respuestas varían.

3. ¿Por qué crees que el caballo se espantó? Las respuestas varían.

4. ¿Cómo crees que le hicieron Antonio y Farina para quitar el carro del atolladero? Las respuestas varían.

5. ¿Por qué le dio las cerezas el tío Curro a Antonio? Antonio le ayudó al tío con su carro.

6. Explica por qué se hacía la boca de Antonio agua sólo de pensar en las cerezas. Las respuestas varían.

• *¿Por qué se dice que se le hace uno "agua la boca" cuando piensa en algo sabroso?*

2

UN HATILLO DE CEREZAS

MARÍA PUNCEL

EDICIÓN DEL MAESTRO

Haz una Predicción

¿Qué va a hacer Antonio con las cerezas?
Justifica tus respuestas. (Discuta las
predicciones de los estudiantes. Pídales que
apoyen sus predicciones con el texto.)

SECCIÓN II. Lee hasta la página 10. Discute las respuestas a las preguntas con tu compañero. Luego, escribe tus respuestas, mientras tu compañero contesta por separado.

1. **¿Por qué le dio Antonio a su abuela las cerezas?** Las respuestas varían.

*   *Discute lo que tú hubieras hecho con las cerezas.*

2. **¿Por qué no se comió la abuela Francisca las cerezas para el almuerzo?** La abuela se las quería dar a su hermana María.

3. **¿Por qué iba ser mejor que María se comiera las cerezas, según la abuela?** María dice siempre tener un sabor amargo en la boca.

*   *¿Cómo es que tiñen las madejas de lana?*

4. **¿Por qué crees que María quería dar las cerezas a Pedro?** Las respuestas varían.

5. **¿Por qué crees que Anita tuvo que ir a llevarle a Pedro las cerezas?** Las respuestas varían.

6. **¿Crees que Pedro va a comerse las cerezas?** Las respuestas varían.

3

EDICIÓN DEL MAESTRO

Contar el Cuento

¿Recuerdas el Cuento?
Trabaja con tu Compañero

Tesoro Encontrado	La Predicción de la Historia Sale Verdadera	Dirección de la Historia	Palabras Aprendidas
		Sin Problema	

1. **¿Cuál era el trabajo de Antonio?** Antonio era ayudante de panadero. Trabajaba cada noche hasta el amanecer: preparaba la masa, calentaba el horno y cocía las hogazas. Antonio ponía los panes en grandes cestos y los llevaba por los caseríos del valle, para repartir el pan.

2. **¿Qué pasó una mañana?** Antonio encontró el carro del tío Curro atascado. El caballo del tío Curro se asustó y el carro se hundió en un hoyo. Antonio de muy buena voluntad le ayudó a sacar el carro del atolladero.

3. **¿Cómo recompensó el tío a Antonio?** El tío Curro le dio a Antonio unas cerezas. El tío Curro tomó una servilleta e hizo un hatillo para que se las llevara. A Antonio se le hacía agua la boca sólo de pensar en ellas.

¡Aventuras con la Escritura!

Escoge una de las siguientes opciones:

1. Antonio y Farina ayudaron a su tío Curro en el carro. ¿Qué crees que tenían que hacer para sacar la rueda del hoyo? Descríbelo en dos o tres palabras.

2. ¿Te gustan las cerezas? ¿Qué fruta te gusta mejor? ¿Por qué? Imagina que tienes un amigo que nunca ha probado esa fruta. Escribe dos o tres palabras que tratan de persuadirlo a probar la fruta.

3. ¿Has recibido un regalo especial que alguien más quería? ¿Has compartido un regalo con un amigo para poder gozar juntos? Escribe un párrafo sobre cuando compartiste un regalo con alguien importante.

4

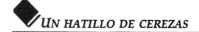 *UN HATILLO DE CEREZAS*   MARÍA PUNCEL

EDICIÓN DEL MAESTRO

✳ RESPUESTAS DEL EXAMEN DEL CUENTO ✳

1. **¿Por qué trabajaba Antonio de la noche a la mañana?** Antonio trabajaba de la noche a la mañana porque era ayudante de panadero.

2. **¿Por qué marchaba Antonio a los caseríos del valle?** Las respuestas varían.

3. **¿Por qué le dio las cerezas a Antonio el tío Curro?** Las respuestas varían.

4. **¿Por qué no se comió Antonio las cerezas?** Las respuestas varían.

5. **¿Por qué no se comió la abuela las cerezas?** Las respuestas varían.

6. **¿Por qué no se comió María las cerezas?** Las respuestas varían.

5

Slavin, R.E., & Madden, N.A., *One Million Children: Success for All.* © Corwin Press Inc.

Appendix 2.8.
Teacher Presentation Guide for
Activity 1 of Writing Wings Lesson 1

Training Lesson

Unit 1: CREATING MIND MOVIES

OBJECTIVE: In this lesson, you will help students become familiar with the writing process from prewriting to publication while learning how to develop enough detail in their narrative writing to keep readers interested.

LESSON OUTLINE:

1) Short Overview: The Writing Process
2) Writing Activity #1 — "_____ Made Me Furious"
   a) Prewriting
   b) Drafting
   c) Responding and Revising
   d) Editing
   e) Scoring
   f) Final Drafting
   g) Publication in team books entitled, "I was Furious" or a title of the team's choice.

PREPARATION AND MATERIALS:

Skeleton Planning Form. Have enough copies of this form for each of your students. A full page-sized copy of this form is included at the end of the lesson. You will also need a copy for the overhead or to put up on the board.

Team Response Guide. A Team Response Guide appears at the end of the lesson too. Have copies to pass out to each student before the Responding segment of the lesson. You will also need a copy for the overhead or to put up on the board.

Editing Checklist. Each student will need a copy of the Editing Checklist when they begin the editing process. You will also need a copy for he over head or to put up on the board. This form is included at the end of this lesson.

Sample Passage Overheads. Overheads of the sample passages used in this unit are included at the end of this lesson.

Team Score Sheets. You will need one copy of the Team Score Sheet for each team.

Sample Team Publication. Have one or two samples of a team pubication to show to your class.

A Copy of the Book *Anastasia Krupnik* to give students a vivid sample of a character who is angry.

1

TEACHER PRESENTATION:

Give an overview of the writing process. Explain, saying something like this: "Today we are going to continue learning about what authors do and how they work so that you will grow as an author. I say grow because you're already authors. You started writing long before you came to this class. However, in this class you will have many more chances to write about topics that are important to you, to share your writing with others, and to publish your work.

All authors go through a number of steps when they write. Let me read a portion of a book entitled, If You Were a Writer... by Joan Lowery Nixon. I want you to listen to find out one or two things that a writer has to do."

(Read pages 11 to 16. After school Melia sat with her mother on the porch... "We'd still need some honey, but we'd have a good idea for a story, Mother answered.)

Say: Melia has led us to the first of five steps that all authors use to help them create a great piece of writing. That first step is called prewriting and its the step where we begin to plan what we are going to write.

Tell students that all authors go through a number of steps as they develop a piece of writing. The author of *Charlotte's Web*, the author of *The Mouse and the Motorcycle*, in fact, every author has gone through the same process that they will go through as they become authors.

There are five steps that authors use to help them to create a great piece of writing. Explain to your students that these steps will give them guidelines to follow when they are writing and will take some of the frustration out of getting their ideas on paper. Explain the steps like this.

> **PREWRITING:** This is when you begin to plan what you are going to write. Think about what your topic will be and decide who the audience is. Also think about what form your writing will take. Will it be a paragraph? A poem? A letter? A story?
>
> **DRAFTING:** Drafting is getting your ideas down on paper. Write down all of the ideas you have. Don't worry about if you've spelled every word correctly. Don't worry about capitalization or punctuation. Just be creative and write down your great ideas before you forget them! (You might call this your "sloppy copy").
>
> **RESPONDING & REVISING:** You will all work with your teams to make your writing better. Your teammates will respond to what you've written, ask questions about things in your writing that they didn't understand, and

2

CREATING MIND MOVIES

encourage you to write more about the things that you liked. You will revise your work based on your team conference.

EDITING: When you are happy with what you've said in your writing, you are ready to check to see if the spelling, punctuation, and grammar are correct. We will have checklists to help you with editing and your partner will help you here too.

PUBLICATION:. You've done great work, and it's time to celebrate. Writing is for people to read, of course, so you will make a final GREAT copy of your writing and publish it in a team book like this one (show a copy of a student booklet), or post it on the wall, put it on the internet, mail it to a friend or read it to someone..

(OVERHEAD 1.1)

We will use these steps to help us every time we write. During this lesson cycle we are going to practice these steps as we learn how to write with enough detail to keep a reader interested.

Introduce the lesson, saying something like the following: "One of the best things about reading something that is written very well is that you can picture it in your mind as you read it. Read each of the phrases silently as I uncover them up on the overhead."

(Show the students the following phrases one at a time on the overhead. Read each of them aloud after students have read them to themselves.)

> a train
> a toy train
> a toy circus train

(OVERHEAD 1.2)

Discuss with students how the pictures in their minds change as they read each phase that added a detail to the description of the train.

Then, read the following personal narrative or share a story of your own.

"How My Sister Made Me Furious"

Can you imagine how furious I was when my sister, Joan, broke my new train? Aunt Mary gave it to me for Christmas. I had wanted a train ever since I could remember. It was a circus train with a car for each circus animal. It was my most prized possession. Joan wanted to play with it and kept asking me for it. I showed her how to use the control box and told her to be very careful. Then she pushed the wrong button. The train went off the tracks and crashed into the wall. Now the control box doesn't work, the

3

tracks are bent out of shape, and the train is smashed. I'm so mad at Joan I haven't talked to her since she broke the train last Monday.

(OVERHEAD 1.3)

Ask your students what they found interesting about the story and discuss those things that they wanted to know more about or didn't understand. Explain that readers often like to read about personal experiences that writers have—things that happened in their lives. Explain that in this lesson, they will be writing about experiences from their lives that they think will interest their audience, which will be their classmates.

PREWRITING. Pass out copies of the Skeleton Planning Form that you have made for the students and put a copy of the form on the board or overhead. Explain to students that the Skeleton Planning Form will help them to organize their thoughts as they begin to write.

Go over the TAP-F section on the skeleton form, clarifying what each prompt means. Tell your students that in this assignment, you want them to share with their classmates an event that made them so angry they could feel the steam coming out of their ears. Have the students look at their copies of the Skeleton Plan.

Explain that the first blank, **"Topic,"** is what they are going to write about. Since they already know that their topic is "an event that made them furious," have the students fill in this first blank on their planning sheets as you fill it out on the overhead sample.

When students have finished, ask them if they know who the **audience** is for their writing. You may need to explain to younger students that an audience is the person or people who will be reading their publications. Ask students if they remember for whom you said they would be writing. When a student has answered, "classmates" demonstrate on the overhead how to fill in the blank next to the audience prompt as the students fill in their own planning forms.

Discuss with students the **purpose** of writing. Sometimes people write just to tell a story. Sometime people write to explain how to do something, or to describe something. They may write to tell something about themselves or to persuade. Have students think about their **purpose** for writing about a time when they were furious and discuss it as a class. They should arrive at the conclusion that they are writing to tell a story, then fill in the blank next to the word "purpose" on their forms.

Explain that the last blank in the first section is for the **form** their writing will take. Tell students that sometimes the format will be a letter, a list of instructions, or a journal entry, but for this assignment, you want them to write a paragraph. Fill in the blank next to "format" on your overhead sample as students do so on their planning forms.

4

SKELETON PLAN		
Topic?	Something that made me furious	
Audience?	Classmates	
Purpose?	To tell my story to my friends	
Format?	A paragraph	
QUESTIONS	ANSWERS	DETAILS
What happened first?		
second?		
next?		
What happened last?		
Teammate Initials _____		

(OVERHEAD 1.4)

Reiterate that every time that they write something, they will use a planning form to help them identify what the topic, audience, purpose, and format of their writing will be. Tell students that they can remember these four important planning tools by the mnemonic TAP-F.

Say: Now I'd like to read a short selection from the book *Anastasia Krupnik* to give you an excellent exampple of a character talking about events that have made her furious.

Read *Anastasia Krupnik*, page 20 to the end of the first sentence at the top of page 21. With feedback from your students, list the events that made Anastasia angry. Then have students think about some of the things that have made them angry. Finally, chart ideas realated to events that have made students angry. If you need some warm-ups, try some starters, like:

★ The day I got a new video game and my brother wouldn't let me use the TV.

★ The day I missed the opening of a movie with my friends because I had to clean my room.

★ The day I stole second base during a play-off game, but the umpire called me out.

★ In the car on our trip to the beach, my brother kept hitting me, but I kept getting in trouble for it.

Discuss how to keep a reader interested. Point out that readers will stay interested in a piece of writing if the author includes enough information to let the reader share the experience. Explain, "Sometimes if the author has written his story very well, we can see a movie of the story in our minds while we read it. This is what we're going to call a MIND MOVIE. If the author includes lots of clear detail, the reader will be able to see a mind movie of the story. If the reader has to guess about the details, the movie won't get rolling. Remember how the picture in your head got a little better each time we added details to the description of the train? You can do the same with your writing by adding details. Your job as an author in this unit is to treat your classmates to great mind movies by writing with vivid details."

Use the following story to illustrate how the movie begins to roll as the details are filled in. (This story provides an illustration of developing a mind movie.) Show each passage on the overhead and ask the subsequent questions.

> I had been playing with my friend Paul and went inside to get my glove.
> Ruth was in my room. My desk drawer was open. She said that she was
> helping Mom put away my clothes. I was furious.
>
> (OVERHEAD 1.5)

Ask the class: "Can you see a movie in your mind or do you have to guess what happened?" Obviously, they have to guess. Ask the students the following questions to help them see what was missing from their mind movies:

- Do you know what the author and Paul are playing?
- Do you know what kind of glove the author went inside to get?
- Do you know who Ruth is?
- Do you know why the author is furious?

For this example, you have to write your own script if you're going to picture the experience in your minds." Now try this story:

> I had been playing marbles with my friend Paul. Jeff came by and asked
> us if we wanted to play baseball, so I went inside and got my baseball
> glove. When I went in my room, my sister Ruth was there. My desk drawer
> was open, and she was looking under some of the papers that were on
> top. When Ruth saw I was there, she said she had just come in with the
> laundry and was putting it away for mom. Ruth knows that I don't have
> clothes in my desk drawers. She was snooping and I was furious!
>
> (OVERHEAD 1.6)

Ask your students what additional information helped them to see a movie in their minds. Ask them what they still need to guess. They now know that the author was playing marbles with his friend. They know that he went inside to get his baseball glove because

6

Jeff asked them if they wanted to play. We now know that Ruth is his sister and she was snooping in his desk drawers. Now try this story:

> I had been playing marbles out in front of my house with my best friend Paul. Jeff came by on his bike and said there were a bunch of kids in the park who were starting a game of baseball. He asked us if we wanted to play. We both said "Super!" and I went inside to get my baseball glove. When I went in my room, my sister Ruth was there. She didn't see me come in. My desk drawer was open, and she was looking under some of the papers that were on top. Then Ruth noticed I was in the room. She looked startled to see me and her face turned red. I'm sure she could tell I was angry that she was looking in my desk. She tried to make an excuse, saying she was helping Mom with the laundry and had just come in my room to put my clothes away. Ruth knows that I don't have clothes in my desk drawers. I can't believe she expected me to believe her! She was snooping in my room, and I was furious!
>
> (OVERHEAD 1.7)

Ask your students what additional information helped them see a movie in their minds. Ask them if they still need to guess as much as they had to when they read the first two examples. Point out that the story and the mind movie were improved with each draft as the details were filled in so that the reader did not have to guess.

Complete a planning form for one of the topics you brainstormed as a class to demonstrate how the form is used. A sample is given below.

SKELETON PLAN		
Topic?	Something that made me furious-my mom was snooping	
Audience?	Classmates	
Purpose?	To tell my story to my friends	
Format?	A paragraph	
QUESTIONS	ANSWERS	DETAILS
What happened first?	I was playing with Paul	we were playing marbles in front of my house
second?	Jeff asked if we wanted to play baseball	he was on his bike we both wanted to play I needed my glove

7

Slavin, R.E., & Madden, N.A., *One Million Children: Success for All.* © Corwin Press Inc.

next?	I went inside to get my glove	Went in my room Saw Ruth snooping in my desk.
What happened last?	Ruth said she was putting away my laundry	Ruth knows I don't have clothes in my desk drawer Ruth was snooping in my room. I was furious

Teammate Initials _____

Teammate feedback on planning. Students should brainstorm and talk with teammates about things that have made them angry. Have students select something that made them furious and complete their planning forms.

When some students have completed their planning forms, ask for a volunteer to discuss his or her plan with the class. Model with that student for the class how to help the author develop the plan by asking for more information about things they have to guess to fill in their mind movie.

Now have all your students present what they wish to write about to a teammate. Have the teammates try to visualize a mind movie, and ask for more details if they find they have to guess. HAVE THE RESPONDING TEAMMATE WRITE HIS OR HER INITIALS IN THE LOWER RIGHT CORNER OF THE PLANNING FORM.

DRAFTING. Have your students write their first draft on every other line so that they can make additions and changes as their story develops. Emphasize to students that during the drafting stage, their goal is simply to get their ideas down. They need not worry about correct spelling or mechanics, or even if they have expressed their ideas as well as possible. (Sometimes students like to call this their "sloppy copy" to emphasize that their focus is on what they are saying, not on correctness or tidiness.) You may wish to have your students complete their draft during class or for homework. If you have time to allow drafting during class time, confer briefly (1 to 2 minutes) with as many students as possible, helping them to develop their mind movie.

Review the Team Response Guide. Before having students read their stories to their team, review the Team Response Guide below. Explain to students that this guide will help them learn how to provide one another with useful feedback. Using the Team Response Guide, they will:

8

A) Restate, in one sentence, what the author had to say. This gives important feedback to the author about whether his or her basic message got across.

B) State what they liked or found interesting. This provides encouragement.

C) Ask questions to find out more about the topic presented. These questions will tell the author what else the audience would like to know, and may point out things that are not clear.

It is very important to encourage students to identify and share what they like about a piece of writing with the author. This kind of feedback is often very effective in developing an author's confidence.

TEAM RESPONSE GUIDE
CREATING MIND MOVIES — ACTIVITY #1

AUTHOR:

READ your paper with expression.
   2) Take notes about your teammates' suggestions.

ASK each of the questions below. Make sure ALL of your teammates respond to your story.

   1) What was the story about? What was the main idea?

   2) What did you like most about the story?

   3) Picture your mind movie. Do you have to guess about details? What details are missing? Is there anything you want to ask me?

NOTES ON TEAMMATES SUGGESTIONS:

_____
_____
_____
_____

TEAMMATES: Be thoughtful and aware of your teammates' feelings. Share your ideas, especially those that will help the author.

(OVERHEAD 1.8)

9

Model Use of Team Response Guide. Have all students practice reading their compositions out loud (in a murmur) before the class responding begins to help them read smoothly and clearly. Then have one student from each team read his or her writing to the class, and have the class respond by using the Team Response Guide. The author takes the role of the discussion leader, asking the group questions about his or her story so that the group can provide useful feedback. (This will let the author maintain some control over the discussion as it may be very stressful for some authors to receive feedback from their teams.) Model the way you want students to respond to questions, especially how to provide positive comments, and even how to phrase somewhat critical comments. Ask the author for more details about the parts you don't understand and always have students comment on the writing, not on the author. Keep the tone very encouraging. Enjoy the readings with the class.

After the discussion, have the author write a brief note summarizing the responses and noting things the readers had to guess at the end of the draft. Help the first author or two to again provide a model for the class.

TEAM RESPONSE. Have the students read their pieces one at a time to their teams. Tell students that they will help their teammates using the Team Response Guide.

Your role during this time is to move around the room, listening and helping students respond usefully to their teammates' responses. Remind the authors to allow some discussion of each question and then to move on to the next question. Remind students to write a note about their teammates' responses at the bottom of the draft.

REVISION. Have your students revise their drafts with a particular focus on developing the ideas (the mind movie) presented in their writing so that their audience can have a more thorough understanding of what they are writing about. Have them use the feedback they have received from the class or their teammates, as well as their own response to their writing at this point. Hold brief conferences with as many students as you can, focusing on the development of the ideas in the writing to provide additional feedback.

Team Response. Have the author read the new drafts to the team and point out what was changed and why. Have the teammates comment on the revision, particularly noting what they liked. You may want to have a student volunteer to read his/her new draft to the class and assisting in noting changes to provide a model.

EDITING. Note: As you present the Editing Checklist to your students you will need to have a copy of the checklist for each student and a copy of the story you will edit on the board or an overhead projector.

Present the Editing Checklist on the next page to your students:

10

CREATING MIND MOVIES

....

NAME: _____   EDITOR'S NAME: _____

EDITING CHECKLIST

Sentence Sense

Read each sentence to a teammate.
Ask the following questions about each sentence:
      1. Does the sentence make sense?
      2. Is the sentence complete?

With your teammate's help, rewrite any sentences that need work. Check below when you have read each sentence and answered the questions about each one.

	Author	Teammate	Teacher
Each sentence has been checked.	_____	_____	_____

Author: Check and correct errors in grammar and mechanics (especially capitalization and punctuation) and spelling. Then give your paper to your teammate to check. Make sure you go over with your teammate any problems he or she finds.

Grammar and Mechanics

	Author	Teammate	Teacher
1. Does each sentence end in a period, question mark, or exclamation point?	_____	_____	_____
2. Are the first words in the sentence capitalized?	_____	_____	_____
3. Are proper names capitalized?	_____	_____	_____
4. Are the paragraphs indented?	_____	_____	_____
5. Are the commas in the right places?	_____	_____	_____
6. _____	_____	_____	_____

Spelling

Read your writing to check your spelling by STARTING AT THE LAST LINE AND GOING UP TO THE FIRST LINE. Circle words if you are not sure they are spelled correctly. Ask a teammate to help you spell a word or look it up in the dictionary.

	Author	Teammate	Teacher
Spelling errors have been corrected.	_____	_____	_____

[OVERHEAD 1.9]

As they edit, they will follow these steps:

11

1) They will read their compositions to a teammate to check for sentence sense, using the first section of the Editing Checklist as a guide.

2) They will check their own papers for errors in capitalization, punctuation, sentence sense, and spelling.

3) They will have a teammate check their papers for errors in capitalization, punctuation, sentence sense, and spelling.

The Editing Checklist is given below:
Model using the checklist with your class by using the following paragraph.

BEGINNING LEVEL

"My Guinea Pig Had Fleas"
I woke up yesterday morning with brite red itchy spots all over my left arm and leg. I even had some bites. Under my arm. Itching like crazey. I went to give my guinea pig his breakfast. he was scratching himself. Like crazy too! I found what was biting us. There were dozens of black specks on his skin under his fur. they were Fleas. I gave him a bath that morning to get rid of the Fleas.

(OVERHEAD 1.10)

INTERMEDIATE AND ADVANCED LEVELS

"My Guinea Pig Had Fleas"
I woke up yesterday morning with brite red, itchy spots all over my left arm and leg. I even had some Bites under my arm. Itching like crazey. So much I could not stop scratching them. When I finally did stop scraching for a minute, I want to give my guinea pig his breakfast. he was scratching himself like crazy too! I pushed back his fur, and found what was biting us dozens of tiny wiggling black specs on his skin under his fir. they were Fleas. I have him a bath that morning to get rid of the Fleas.

(OVERHEAD 1.11)

Sentence Sense. As you read each sentence with your students, you will find several incomplete sentences. There is also a sentence that does not make sense. Have your students help you correct these sentences.

Capitalization and Punctuation. Your students will discover that several extra words are capitalized although they do not begin sentences or represent proper names be sure that the first word in every sentence begins with a capital letter.

12

Spelling. The reason for reading the composition from bottom to top is that misspellings are easier to identify out of context.

Add objectives to the Editing Checklist that your students have mastered. Add objectives one at a time, making sure your students have the instruction they need to recognize and correct errors.

Now have your students begin to edit their revised writing with a teammate. This may be a good time for you to work with individual students who need assistance with mechanics. You may set individual mechanics objectives that are either above or below class objectives for individual students. Have the students note specific objectives on their Editing Checklists. Also, write the specific objectives on the inside back cover of the student's writing folder, and have students put a star next to an objective when you hand back a paper that has no errors related to that objective.

Evaluating and Scoring Content. Have students turn in their planning form, first draft, revised and edited draft, and editing form for the composition they are planning to publish. Let them know that you will score and comment on both mind movies and mechanics. They can use your comments to make revisions for the FINAL, PUBLISHED DRAFT which will come next.

Give two scores on the final draft: One for creating a good mind movie and one for mechanics. Give scores indicated below:

MIND MOVIE (Content)		MECHANICS	
Complete	80 points	Perfect or almost	20 points
Almost complete	75 points	A few errors	15 points
Still needs more detail	70 points	Several errors	10 points
Just a skeleton of a draft	65 points	Not well edited	5 points

Remember that some students will make mechanics errors when they try to use sentences more difficult than those they have already mastered. Since you want to encourage this type of experimentation, do not penalize students for errors they make when this occurs. Do not count errors on mechanics objectives you have not yet taught. Also, the scores you give should reflect your judgment of the writing the student has done compared to his past performance. If a student who has great difficulty writing makes a significant improvement in either content or mechanics, you may give that student the highest score even though the writing may not be perfect.

Final Drafting. Have your students write a final draft to go in their team books or they may be published in another way. They may illustrate their compositions with a drawing if they wish.

13

PUBLICATION & CELEBRATION. Completing this publication has taken lots of time and effort from your students, and it is something of which they should be proud. Reading publications to the class in the Author's Chair with suitable fanfare (no critical comments, just appreciation), placing their writing in the team books, finding opportunities to read from the team books to other classes, allowing the books to be checked out from the class library to go home at night, and so on, will emphasize the importance of the work your students have done. Allow teams time to choose a title for their books and to bind them. The names of all the authors and the date of publication should go on the cover of the book.

(OVERHEAD 1.12)

THE WRITING PROCESS

PREWRITING: This is when you begin to plan what you are going to write. Think about what your topic will be and decide who the audience is. Also think about what form your writing will take. Will it be a paragraph? A poem? A letter? A story?

DRAFTING: Drafting is getting your ideas down on paper. Write down all of the ideas you have. Don't worry about if you've spelled every word correctly. Don't worry about capitalization or punctuation. Just be creative and write down your great ideas before you forget them!

RESPONDING & REVISING: You will all work with your teams to make your writing better. Your teammates will respond to what you've written, ask questions about things in your writing that they didn't understand, and encourage you to write more about the things that you liked. You will revise your work based on your team conference.

EDITING: When you are happy with what you've said in your writing, you are ready to check to see if the spelling, punctuation, and grammar are correct. We will have checklists to help you with editing and your partner will help you here too.

PUBLICATION:. You've done great work, and it's time to celebrate. Writing is for people to read, of course, so you will make a final GREAT copy of your writing and publish it in a team book, post it on the wall, put it on the internet, mail it to a friend, or read it to someone.

15

Slavin, R.E., & Madden, N.A., *One Million Children: Success for All.* © Corwin Press Inc.

a train

a toy train

a toy circus train

16

"How My Sister Made Me Furious"

Can you imagine how furious I was when my sister, Joan, broke my new train? Aunt Mary gave it to me for Christmas. I had wanted a train ever since I could remember. It was a circus train with a car for each circus animal. It was my most prized possession. Joan wanted to play with it and kept asking me for it. I showed her how to use the control box and told her to be very careful. Then she pushed the wrong button. The train went off the tracks and crashed into the wall. Now the control box doesn't work, the tracks are bent out of shape, and the train is smashed. I'm so mad at Joan I haven't talked to her since she broke the train last Monday.

17

Slavin, R.E., & Madden, N.A., *One Million Children: Success for All.* © Corwin Press Inc.

(OVERHEAD 1.15)

SKELETON PLAN

Topic?	
Audience?	
Purpose?	
Format?	

QUESTIONS	ANSWERS	DETAILS
What happened first?		
second?		
next?		
?		
What happened last?		

Teammate Initials   _____

I had been playing with my friend Paul and went inside to get my glove. Ruth was in my room. My desk drawer was open. She said that she was helping Mom put away my clothes. I was furious.

(OVERHEAD 1.17)

I had been playing marbles with my friend Paul. Jeff came by and asked us if we wanted to play baseball, so I went inside and got my baseball glove. When I went in my room, my sister Ruth was there. My desk drawer was open and she was looking under some of the papers that were on top. When Ruth saw I was there, she said she had just come in with the laundry and was putting it away for mom. Ruth knows that I don't have clothes in my desk drawers. She was snooping and I was furious!

20

I had been playing marbles out in front of my house with my best friend Paul. Jeff came by on his bike and said there were a bunch of kids in the park who were starting a game of baseball. He asked us if we wanted to play. We both said "Super!" and I went inside to get my baseball glove. When I went in my room, my sister Ruth was there. She didn't see me come in. My desk drawer was open, and she was looking under some of the papers that were on top. Then Ruth noticed I was in the room. She looked startled to see me and her face turned red. I'm sure she could tell I was angry that she was looking in my desk. She tried to make an excuse, saying she was helping Mom with the laundry and had just come into my room to put my clothes away. Ruth knows that I don't have clothes in my desk drawers. I can't believe she expected me to believe her! She was snooping in my room, and I was furious!

21

Slavin, R.E., & Madden, N.A., *One Million Children: Success for All.* © Corwin Press Inc.

;;

TEAM RESPONSE GUIDE
CREATING MIND MOVIES — ACTIVITY #1

AUTHOR:

READ your paper with expression.

ASK each of the questions below. Make sure ALL of your
  teammates respond to your story.

  1) What was the story about? What was the main idea?

  2) What did you like most about the story?

  3) Picture your mind movie. Do you have to guess about
     details? What details are missing? Is there anything you
     want to ask me?

  NOTES ON TEAMMATES SUGGESTIONS:

  _____

  _____

  _____

  _____

TEAMMATES: Be thoughtful and aware of your teammates'
             feelings. Share your ideas, especially those
             that will help the author.

;;

22

Slavin, R.E., & Madden, N.A., *One Million Children: Success for All.* © Corwin Press Inc.

CREATING MIND MOVIES

(OVERHEAD 1.20)

::

NAME: _____   **EDITOR'S NAME:** _____

EDITING CHECKLIST

Sentence Sense

Read each sentence to a teammate.
Ask the following questions about each sentence:
  1. Does the sentence make sense?
  2. Is the sentence complete?

With your teammate's help, rewrite any sentences that need work. Check below when you have read each sentence and answered the questions about each one.

	Author	Teammate	Teacher
Each sentence has been checked.	_____	_____	_____

Author: Check and correct errors in grammar and mechanics (especially capitalization and punctuation) and spelling. Then give your paper to your teammate to check. Make sure you go over with your teammate any problems he or she finds.

Grammar and Mechanics

	Author	Teammate	Teacher
1. Does each sentence end in a period, question mark, or exclamation point?	_____	_____	_____
2. Are the first words in the sentence capitalized?	_____	_____	_____
3. Are proper names capitalized?	_____	_____	_____
4. Are the paragraphs indented?	_____	_____	_____
5. Are the commas in the right places?	_____	_____	_____
6. _____	_____	_____	_____

Spelling

Read your writing to check your spelling by STARTING AT THE LAST LINE AND GOING UP TO THE FIRST LINE. Circle words if you are not sure they are spelled correctly. Ask a teammate to help you spell a word or look it up in the dictionary.

	Author	Teammate	Teacher
Spelling errors have been corrected.	_____	_____	_____

23

"My Guinea Pig Had Fleas"

I woke up yesterday morning with brite red itchy spots all over my left arm and leg. I even had some bites. Under my arm. Itching like crazey. I went to give my guinea pig his breakfast. he was scratching himself. Like crazy too!   There were dozens of black specks on his skin under his fur. they were Fleas. I gave him a bath that morning to get rid of the Fleas.

24

CREATING MIND MOVIES

(OVERHEAD 1.22)

INTERMEDIATE AND ADVANCED LEVELS

"My Guinea Pig Had Fleas"

I woke up yesterday morning with brite red, itchy spots all over my left arm and leg. I even had some Bites under my arm. Itching like crazey. So much I could not stop scratching them. When I finally did stop scraching for a minute, I want to give my guinea pig his breakfast. he was scratching himself like crazy too! I pushed back his fur, and found what was biting us dozens of tiny wiggling black specs on his skin under his fir. they were Fleas. I have him a bath that morning to get rid of the Fleas.

25

3

Tutoring Programs

Tutoring is the most important means by which Success for All ensures that *all* students will succeed in reading. It is the most expensive element of the program but also probably one of the most cost-effective, because it is tutoring, more than any other feature, that enables the school to reduce retentions and special education placements (see Chapters 8 and 9).

Tutors in Success for All are usually certified teachers with backgrounds in reading or early childhood education. In most schools, highly trained paraprofessionals are also used, and volunteers may provide some supplementary tutoring. In many schools moving away from traditional Title I pullout models, tutors were once the Title I remedial teachers. Some tutors are special education teachers, in which case they primarily tutor special education students or students at risk for special education placement. Some are bilingual or ESL teachers and would specialize in English language learners.

Tutors have a dual role. During reading period (usually 90 minutes per day), certified teachers teach a reading class, both to reduce class sizes for reading and to give them a thorough idea of what the regular reading program is. The rest of the day,

AUTHORS' NOTE: Barbara Wasik and Martha French contributed to this chapter.

tutors work one on one with children who are having the greatest difficulties learning to read.

Decisions about which students need tutoring are made based on students' scores on 8-week assessments (see Chapter 2) plus teacher recommendations. First graders receive priority for tutoring, although second and third graders can be tutored if enough tutoring services are available. In high-poverty schools, we recommend providing enough tutoring for 30% of first graders, 20% of second graders, and 10% of third graders. A number of first-, second-, and third-grade tutoring "slots" are set aside based on the number of tutors available and scheduling constraints, and then the lowest-achieving students at each grade level are assigned tutors. Students leave tutoring when their performance no longer places them among the lowest achievers in their grade. The average student who receives any tutoring will meet with a tutor every day for a semester (18 weeks), but some first graders have stayed in tutoring for as long as $1\frac{1}{2}$ years, into mid-second grade.

Tutors meet with children 20 minutes each day. The school's schedule is set up so that tutors can work all day without ever taking students from reading, language arts, or math periods. Many schools reorganize their days to add 20 minutes each day to social studies, and then those students who receive tutoring are taken from social studies. In this arrangement, social studies periods are placed at different times for different classes and grades. Some schools have special resource periods or find other ways to schedule tutoring with minimum impact on students' other subjects. Before-school and after-school tutoring can sometimes extend the hours available for tutoring when transportation is not a problem.

Basic Principles of Tutoring in Success for All and Roots & Wings

The tutoring program in Success for All and Roots & Wings is based on a set of fundamental principles. These are as follows (adapted from Madden, Wasik, & French, 1999).

Tutoring Is One to One

One-to-one tutoring is the most effective form of instruction, especially for students with reading problems (Slavin, 1994; Wasik & Slavin, 1993). One reason for the effectiveness of one-to-one tutoring is that it allows tutors to teach to the individual student's needs. Tutors can make individual learning plans that fit the student's needs and can spend as much time as needed to teach a particular sound-blending or comprehension strategy.

Also, in one-to-one tutoring, a tutor has the opportunity to give constant, immediate feedback to a student. If a student makes an error when reading, immediate corrective feedback can be provided, along with the instruction needed to prevent further errors. This on-line diagnostic assessment and feedback is not possible when working with an entire class or even a small group.

Because tutors have the opportunity to provide intensive instruction to each student, they learn a lot about the students' strengths and weaknesses and what approaches work best with each. Tutors capitalize on this knowledge and use it in presenting material in the best way that will help students learn and remember the information.

One-to-one tutoring increases the opportunity for reading. When it is just one tutor and one student, the student can read and reread until he or she has mastered words, comprehended the story, and can read fluently. These opportunities are typically limited for poor readers during group instruction.

Tutoring Supports Classroom Instruction

Tutoring is closely coordinated with classroom instruction. The tutor works to support student success on the material that is presented in class, rather than teaching a separate program. For example, if the consonant sound /n/ is being taught in the student's reading class, then the tutor works on words and stories using this sound during tutoring. This helps students keep up with class instruction and helps accelerate their learning. The repeated practice with and exposure to the material presented in the classroom helps students solidify their reading knowledge.

Students Learn to Read by Reading

Students learn to read by reading. Reading is a complex process that involves decoding of words, tracking of words across the page, and constructing meaning from individual words as well as sentences and paragraphs. Success in reading requires the coordination of these complex activities. Therefore, teaching each of these activities in isolation will not teach a student to read and comprehend text. Reading connected text helps develop decoding skills, helps with fluency, and facilitates reading comprehension. Tutoring provides an opportunity for students to read and get on-line feedback on their reading.

Communication Between Tutors and Classroom Reading Teachers Is Essential

Tutors must communicate with the reading teacher of the students they are tutoring. It is essential that the tutors know how the students they are tutoring are performing in the classroom. They need to adapt each tutoring plan to the specific areas in which the student is having problems. The teacher also needs to be informed of the student's progress and other specific information that the tutor can provide that would help the teacher work better with the student.

The Tutoring Process
in Reading Roots

Tutoring Goals

The primary focus of tutoring is to help the student learn to create meaning from the printed word. The tutor reinforces the Reading Roots lessons presented in the reading classroom, providing students with a number of strategies to figure out unknown words and to understand the meaning of sentences and paragraphs. These strategies include

- Mastering letter and sound relationships and using phonics to sound out unknown words
- Using pictures and context to figure out unknown words
- Using pictures and context to add meaningful information about what is happening in the story to promote comprehension
- Using comprehension-monitoring strategies to improve comprehension

Assessment Checklist

Before the tutor begins working with a student, he or she administers the Assessment Checklist (see Appendix 3.1). The Assessment Checklist helps the tutor determine the specific problems and strengths of a student and to tailor the tutoring session to meet the specific needs of the student. The tutor can determine if the student is having problems with phonemic awareness, sounding out words, recognizing specific letter sounds, or understanding connected text or has more basic problems with concepts about print or tracking. The Assessment Checklist also identifies children's strengths, which become a basis for tutoring interventions.

A tutoring plan tailored to the needs of the particular student is made based on the information gained from the Assessment Checklist. The assessment may show that a student has difficulty understanding basic concepts about print and tracking from left to right as well as sounding out words. The tutor would then integrate opportunities to review and reinforce basic concepts about print into the basic tutoring activities, such as rereading a familiar story, and would ensure that as the student read, he or she used a finger or other support strategy to assist in tracking. Another student might have difficulties with memory, sound blending, or comprehension strategies. Many strategies are used in the basic tutoring model to address these difficulties, but the tutor's plan would set the priorities and specific strategies helpful in focusing on the specific student's difficulties. For example, the tutor may decide to use the opportunity for rereading a familiar story as a time to allow the student to become fluent enough with a single story to allow that story to be read to a special audience, such as a group of kindergarten students or a special adult, to highlight fluency and expression and to celebrate a successful reading experience.

As the plan is developed, the tutor identifies backup strategies to implement if the initial strategies are not successful. The tutor also plans a timetable for evaluation of progress to determine if the plan needs to be changed.

A second assessment, Analysis of Strategy Use, allows tutors to better understand students' strengths and weaknesses in using specific strategies for reading by observing the student reading a new text. The tutor can assess whether a student recognizes errors in reading, identifies the strategies attempted to fix the errors, and notes whether the strategy attempted was successful. Specific interventions designed to enhance the student's effective use of strategies are described in detail.

Activities for Tutoring in Reading Roots

The following is a list of specific activities that are typically included in a 20-minute Reading Roots tutoring session, followed by an explanation of these activities.

- Rereading familiar stories
- Quick review of letter sounds, phonetic words, and sound blending
- Reading current stories
- Skill-focused writing

Rereading Familiar Stories

Familiar stories are those that the student has read several times in class or in tutoring and has mastered fairly well. Rereading familiar stories helps the student develop rapid word recognition, expression in oral reading, and comprehension skills. When reading a story for the first time, a student focuses mainly on the individual words. In doing this, considerable effort is put into sounding the words out, so the student is not attending as well to the meaning of the individual words and sentences. When reading a story a second or third time, the student will have practiced pronouncing the words and will be better able to direct his or her attention to understanding the story. The tutor plays an important role in this activity, asking the student questions about what he or she has read, teaching understanding of the message communicated in the story, and teaching metacognitive strategies to facilitate finding of the story's meaning (see the discussion to follow).

Rereading a familiar story also helps develop fluency and confidence in reading and gives the child a sense of pride and accomplishment. It helps the student practice familiar words and familiar sentence patterns and gives the student repeated opportunities to comprehend the material. Being able to read fluently and with expression indicates that the student comprehends what he or she is reading. It may take three or four or more readings of the same story before the student reads it with appropriate intonations and expression. However, each time the student reads the story, he or she focuses on different parts of the reading process, which reinforces word recognition strategies and comprehension skills.

Students' rereading of familiar stories provides an opportunity for tutors to teach metacognitive comprehension monitoring skills, "tricks of the trade" that effective readers use to monitor their own reading and help make sense of it.

The purpose of this activity is to teach the student how to read for meaning and monitor comprehension at the same time. Often, a student will read the words in a story but not understand the message being communicated in the text. For students with reading problems, comprehension monitoring is not a skill that comes automatically with reading. The tutor needs to teach this skill.

There are two parts to teaching comprehension-monitoring skills. One is to help the student know whether he or she understood the text. The second is to teach the student what to do when he or she does not understand.

The tutor begins by teaching the student to ask questions that determine if he or she is understanding what is being read. First, the tutor models these self-monitoring strategies. After the student has read a section of a story, the tutor may ask a question that will assess his or her understanding, such as "Does what you have just read make sense to you; do you understand what happened in the story?" The student is asked to summarize in his or her own words what he or she just read.

The idea is to get students into a routine of asking themselves comprehension check questions. After the student reads a section of the text, the tutor continues to ask, "Did that make sense to you?" The student gets to the point where he or she knows what question to ask. As the student reads a section of the text, the tutor may ask, "What question do you ask yourself?" and the student will respond, "Did what I read make sense?" Early on, the tutor asks comprehension check questions very frequently, after the student has read only one or two sentences. As the student progresses, these questions are asked only after key paragraphs or at critical points in the story.

As the student learns to ask general comprehension check questions, the tutor may teach him or her to ask more specific questions to check comprehension. These questions can be either explicit ("What did you find out from that sentence or paragraph?") or inferential ("Why do you think the main character did what he did?").

If the student cannot answer the comprehension check questions correctly or does not provide information to show that he or she understands the reading, the tutor demonstrates how to find the answer. The tutor may begin by instructing the student to reread the section that he or she has just read out loud, explaining that rereading the story will improve understanding so the student will be able to tell if what he or she read makes sense.

After the student has reread the section of a story, the tutor may ask the comprehension check question again, "Does what you have read make sense?" If the student is still unable to answer the question, he or she may assess other obstacles that might be interfering with comprehension, such as inadequate vocabulary knowledge, word recognition skills, or background knowledge, and may help the student with any of these. Appendix 3.2 shows a section of the Roots & Wings *Tutoring Manual* that illustrates reading a familiar story.

Quick Review of Letter Sounds and Words

Students need to get to the point where knowledge of the letter sounds is automatic so that their attention can be free to focus on comprehension. Repeated practice of the letter sounds or phonetically regular words during a quick review helps the student overlearn these sounds. Important sight words are also briefly practiced. This activity should take no more than 1 minute. See Appendix 3.3 for sample dialogue as given in the Tutoring Manual.

Reading New Stories

After reading a familiar story, the student usually works on stories containing words with sounds that have been presented in class but that have not yet been mastered. These stories may be the ones that the student is working on in class, may be parallel stories that use the same letters and sounds as the one being read in class, or may be stories that the tutor makes up containing similar word sounds. Parallel stories are provided for Reading Roots Shared Stories 4 through 37, and tutors can use KinderRoots stories, which also follow the same sequence and introduce most of the same letters and sight words as Reading Roots. When learning new letter sounds, the student needs repeated practice with words that contain these sounds in the context of a story. The repeated practice and exposure to the sounds in different words help the student learn and recall the letter sounds. Also, presenting words in the context of a story helps the student attach meaning to these words while using letter and sound correspondences. Meaningful material is learned more quickly than isolated material.

Listening to the student's oral reading allows the tutor to understand precisely where he or she needs instruction. Frequently, it is the blending of individual sounds to make a recognizable word rather than the memory of individual sounds that is the most difficult task for the student. When the student is reading a real story out loud, the tutor is able to model repeatedly how to solve the problem of an unknown word through the use of the sound-blending strategy, as well as through the use of rereading, context, and pictures. Knowledge of sounds and sound blending are not ends in themselves but tools to be used to read real texts. The use of oral reading in tutoring helps teach the student how to use his or her knowledge of sounds in reading. In addition, metacognitive comprehension-monitoring strategies learned with familiar stories can be called on to understand new ones. See the sample dialogue in Appendix 3.4 for an example of this.

Skill-Focused Writing

Reading and writing are closely connected. Skill-focused writing helps develop the same skills students need for reading. During the writing activity, students learn to produce and write sounds and letters they are learning during reading.

Skill-focused writing develops phonemic awareness and recall of letter sounds as well as concepts about print, all in the meaningful context of written sentences.

Specific lesson guides are provided at four levels to provide appropriate challenges at different stages. Four primary activities are used. The goals of each are clearly explained to the student to enable the student to be an active participant in the process.

1. Introduction: The specific sound goal of the lesson is explained, along with the activities that will be used to provide practice.
2. Listening to sounds: The Say-It-Fast and Break-It-Down activities are used with the target sound to ensure that the student can hear and work with the sound at the word level.
3. Dictation: The tutor guides students to use the sound in dictated words and later, as skill develops, in sentences.
4. Sentences: The tutor guides the student to create a sentence using a word with the target sound and then has the student write it, providing as much assistance as needed. At first, the student may write only the target sound. Later, the student may be able to write all the letters in the word containing the target sound and later, perhaps the entire sentence. Appendix 3.5 shows the pertinent section from the *Tutoring Manual*.

The Tutoring Process in Reading Wings

Tutoring Goals

Because the emphasis of tutoring is on children in the primary grades who are having difficulties with reading, almost all tutoring involves Reading Roots, the first-grade model. However, sometimes children receive tutoring in Reading Wings. There are several goals in tutoring students in Reading Wings. One is to teach comprehension-monitoring skills. The emphasis in Reading Wings is to teach students how to get meaning from what they have read. This involves getting meaning from individual words as well as connected text. Other goals in Reading Wings are to help students build their vocabulary, develop fluency in reading, and teach students to effectively express ideas in words.

The first step in tutoring in Reading Wings is to determine the student's reading problems. The Assessment Checklist is used to do this. After this diagnostic evaluation is completed, a plan is made to target the areas on which the student needs to work. For example, a student may be having problems figuring out the meaning of specific words, and this may be interfering with his or her comprehension of the text. Another may not understand how to answer the comprehension questions in the Treasure Hunts. A third may be having trouble tracking what he or she is reading. Although all of these problems interfere with understanding what has been read, the ways these problems are dealt with in tutoring are very different.

Activities in Tutoring Reading Wings

The specific activities done in tutoring a student in Reading Wings are as follows.

Vocabulary Review

The Vocabulary Review gives the student the opportunity to practice pronouncing words with which he or she is having difficulty. Repeated practice of words that the student encounters frequently when reading helps reinforce correct pronunciation of these words. In addition, the student has the opportunity to clarify the definitions of words.

Reading Sections of Stories Used in Class

Reading stories helps develop comprehension-monitoring strategies. Poor readers often have difficulty monitoring their comprehension as they read. When reading sections of the basal stories, novels, or other texts being used in class, the student can be taught comprehension-monitoring skills. As the student reads sections of the story, the tutor asks questions that check understanding of the parts that he or she has read. If the student is unable to answer the questions, the tutor provides him or her with helpful strategies. For example, the tutor may guide the student to reread a section of the text where the answer is located or may guide his or her thinking through a response to an inferential question. In both cases, the tutor is modeling comprehension strategies that facilitate comprehension.

Rereading Familiar Stories

Rereading familiar stories helps even older readers read with fluency and expression. Rereading also helps the student gain a sense of mastery over reading. This repeated practice builds confidence in the student's self-perception as a reader.

Reviewing a Treasure Hunt

Reviewing the answers to the Treasure Hunts helps develop comprehension skills. Using the specific Treasure Hunt questions from a story being studied in class provides direct support and reinforcement for class work. If the student does not know an answer, the tutor will work with him or her on the strategies needed to find the answer, such as looking back in the text, thinking beyond the literal meaning of a section, and so on. Tutor and student also work to develop comprehension-monitoring strategies while reading that can be used in subsequent first readings. The student receives immediate feedback on the quality of his or her answers to Treasure Hunt questions in the tutoring situation and can learn to develop more complete answers.

Writing

During tutoring, the students and teacher work on written expression, primarily through developing high-quality answers to the Treasure Hunts. Writing the answers requires the student to express his or her thoughts clearly in short sentences. The tutor provides immediate feedback, modeling, and instruction as the students work.

Tutor and student can also work on story-related writing activities. The one-to-one tutoring situation once again provides an opportunity for feedback, modeling, and guidance that is tailored specifically to the individual student's needs.

CHAPTER 3 APPENDICES

Appendix 3.1.
Assessment Checklist

Tutoring

Assessment Checklist

Student: _____

Tutor: _____

Date: _____

PART I : SKILLS FOR SOUNDING OUT WORDS:
Phonemic Awareness; Letter Sounds and Sound Blending

Phonemic awareness is the ability to recognize different speech sounds. Skills in this area help children learn to sound out words as they learn to associate speech sounds with written letters and blend them to identify words in print.

Phonemic Awareness (PA)
Provide more examples if necessary.

PA 1 Recognizes words that rhyme   Number Correct: _____

Some words sound alike because they have the same ending; they rhyme. For example, "Mad" sounds like "Sad" and "Dad." "Ghost" doesn't sound like "sad, mad, and Dad" though, does it? What about "bad"; does it sound like "sad?" (Pause for response). *I'm going to say two words together. Tell me if they rhyme — if the endings sound alike, O.K?*

Say each word pair and circle those correctly identified by the student as rhyming or not rhyming.

Sam Pam	mop pop
cat did	late hate
dig pig	cot sag
Dad miss	bug rug
sing mud	Tim pan

PA 2 Recognizes words that begin with the same sound   Number Correct: _____

Some words start with the same sound, like "Sad," and "Sam" (say, then say again, stretching the beginning sound of both words). *"Sad" and "sit"* (stretch the words, then say them fast) *start with the same sound, too. All these words begin with /sss/. Do "sad" and "big" start with the same sound?* (Do not stretch the beginning sound. Pause for response.) *"SSSad, bbbig; no they do not start with the same sound. "Bend" and "bat?"* (Pause for response.) *I'm going to say some more words and you tell me if they start with the same sound, O.K?*

Say each word pair without stretching the words and circle those correctly identified by the student as having or not having the same beginning sound.

mad mit	sit Dad
pot tap	cap sat
did Dad	tip Tom
cat cap	sit man
pig sag	hop him

PA 3 Discriminates between one- and two-syllable words   Number Correct: _____

Words have different numbers of sound groups, too. "Sad, Matt, and dog" have one sound group (say each word and simultaneously clap once). *"Happy, wagon, and party" have two sound groups* (say, slightly exaggerate syllables, and clap twice). *I'm going to say some words and I want you to tell me if they have one or two sound groups.*

Say each word clearly, but not exaggerated; circle those the student correctly identifies as having one or two syllables.

Sam	picnic
patted	ant
sitting	fill
hiccup	hop
began	Sid

Assessment Checklist, part 1, cont.

PA 4 Identifies words from the individual sounds

Number Correct: _____

When we say words slowly we can hear all of the sounds. Listen: /m/ /a/ /n/. (Say each sound distinctly, stretching just slightly; also, slightly pausing between sounds.) Now I'll say it fast: Man. Listen to another word: /r/ /u/ /n/ (say as before), run. This time I'll say a word slowly and you say it fast: /r/ /a/ /n/ (say as before and pause for student response). Let's play a game like that—I'll say the sounds in a word slowly. See if you can tell me what the word is by saying the sounds fast.

Say the <u>sounds</u> in each word as directed with the first example above. Circle the word if the student pronounces it correctly.

/m/ /e/ me	/n/ /o/ /t/ not
/s/ /e e/ see	/r/ /a/ /m/ ram
/m/ /u/ /g/ mug	/s/ /u/ /n/ sun
/n/ /a/ /m/ name	/s/ /e a/ /t/ seat
/m/ /ai/ /n main	/f/ /e a/ /r/ fear

PA 5 Breaks words down to separate the individual sounds

Number Correct: _____

Let's try that game another way. I'll say a word and you say the sounds slowly. For example, if I say "fog," you would say, "/f/ /o/ /g/." Let's try another example. What if I said "mats"? What would you say? (Pause for response.) "That's right, there are four sounds in mats: /m/ /a/ /t/ /s/." Be sure to say each sound clearly. For example, if I say "ran," you should say, /rrr/aaa/nnn, not /rrr/annn/. O.K.? Let's start.

Say the words. Circle the sounds the student says clearly.

Sam /s/ /a/ /m	nut /n/ /u/ /t/
mean /m/ /ea/ /n/	rain /r/ /ai/ /n/
seem s/ /e e/ /m/	phone /ph/ /o/ /n/
shut /sh/ /u/ /t/	near /n/ /ea/ /r/
rush /r/ /u/ /sh/	slam /s/ /l/ /a/ /m/

Letter Sounds and Blending (LS) <u>Use the Student Letter Sheet for these activities.</u>
Model responses for the first item if necessary.

LS 1 Letter Name Identification

Number Correct: _____

You've been learning about letters and their sounds in class.
Tell me the names of these letters as I point to them.
Circle those correctly identified. Point L-R, top-to-bottom.

m	a	s	d	t	i	n	p
g	o	c	k	u	b	f	e
l	h	r	j	v	y	w	q	z	x

LS 2 Letter Sound Production

Number Correct: _____

Now I'm going to point to the letter and I want you to
tell me what sound that letter makes. Let's try one.
Circle those correctly identified. Point L-R, top-to-bottom.

m	a	s	d	t	i	n	p
g	o	c	k	u	b	f	e
l	h	r	j	v	y	w	q	z	x

LS 3 Sound Blending

Number Correct: _____

You're doing great! Now I want you to read some words for me.
Think about what you know about letters and sounds, stretch and say
these words, and then say them fast.
Point to words L-R. Circle correct responses.

Sam	mat	nip	pad	gap	kid
cup	cot	sip	top	got	big
fun	fed	him	ran	van	jar
yet	yes				

Assessment Checklist, cont.

Student: _____

Tutor: _____

Date: _____

PART II: READING A FAMILIAR STORY: Concepts about Print, Tracking and Fluency

Before they can read children must know basic concepts about print: how to hold a book, where the title is, and that the message is in the print. As they begin to read they must be able to follow the direction of the print, not lose their place or confuse words. They must also learn to read with a one-to-one correspondence between spoken and written words. This visual tracking evolves into fluent reading as children become more proficient readers.

	Check Yes or No:	Y	N
Concepts about Print (CP) Place a familiar story on the table between you and the child. *This is a story you've read before. Tell me, why would I want to read this story? Why do people read things like stories? Cookbooks? Newspapers?* (accept logical answers)	**CP 1** *Knows a reason for reading*		
Can you show me where the title is? Additional prompts: *Is it here?* (point to place other than title)	**CP 2** *Points to (identifies) the title*		
The title, or name of the story, is (read the title). You have read this story before. Why do you think the writer gave it this name? Additional Prompt: *What does it tell about the story?*	**CP 3** *knows that the title tells something about the story*		
Can you turn to the first page? Observe how the child holds the book. If necessary, prompt further: *Is this how I hold the book* (hold upside down, backwards)?	**CP 4** *Holds the book correctly for reading (right-side up, front forward)*		
Show me with your finger what you would read on this first page.	**CP 5** *Finds the first page*		
If necessary, prompt further: *Do I read here* (point to pictures) *or here* (point to print)?	**CP 6** *Identifies print, rather than pictures, as where one reads*		
Tracking and Fluency (TF) Use the same familiar story presented above and ask the child to read:	**TF 1** *Reads from left-to-right; starts at left of next line*		
You're doing great! Now, I'd like you to read a few pages of this story for me. Observe tracking: following the print, matching spoken and written word (one-to-one correspondence), and not losing the place.	**TF 2** *Reads with one-to-one correspondence*		
If the student does not track print, ask him or her to use a guide; demonstrate if necessary. *Why don't you use your finger or this piece of paper to guide your reading?* Check here if the student must use a guide to track print: _____ .	**TF 3** *Reads without losing place or skipping words*		
	TF 4 *Reads words in units of meaning (phrases)*		
Observe fluency (grouping and stressing words for meaning and reading smoothly)	**TF 5** *Reads fluently*		

Stop *after several pages and discontinue the assessment if the student has significant difficulty reading connected text. Otherwise, continue with the assessment.*

Assessment Checklist, cont.

PART III: READING A CURRENT, NEW, OR ALTERNATE STORY:
Comprehension and Word Strategies, Memory and Recall, and Literal Comprehension

When students read material that is less familiar, they need to use comprehension strategies to help themselves understand the text and fix comprehension problems, word strategies to figure out unknown words, and memory to recall difficult words and what has taken place so far in the story. If they are successful with these skills and strategies, they are likely to understand what they read.

	Check Yes or No:	Y	N
Comprehension Strategies (CS) Use a current story and say: *Here is another story I would like for you to read. The name of it is (read name).* If appropriate, ask: CS 1. beginning at Roots Lesson 9: *What do think this story will be about, looking at the title and pictures?* Answer: the student makes logical predictions or statements about the story using the title and pictures. CS 2. beginning at Roots Lesson 16: *What should you always try to do as you read?* (Answer: accept various answers, but check if the student says: "understand what I'm reading." Prompt to get this, asking, "What else?") Does the student *independently* recognize and try to fix errors? How (check): ☐ Sounds out words? ☐ Rereads? ☐ Uses context? ☐ Asks for help?	**CS 1** *Previews material before reading to predict content*		
	CS 2 *Knows to monitor for meaning*		
	CS 3 *Recognizes and attempts to correct errors*		
Word Strategies (WS) Observe the student's ability to use different word strategies. Elicit the use of different strategies if possible: • *Can you sound out that word?* • *Think about that word; try to reread it.* • *Are there other ways you can find out what that word is, besides sounding it out? asking me?* Provide help if the child continues to ask after attempting other strategies.	**WS 1** *Sounds out words effectively*		
	WS 2 *Rereads effectively*		
	WS 3 *Uses context effectively*		
	WS 4 *Asks for help when other strategies fail*		
Memory and Recall (MR) Observe the student's memory for phonetic (green) words that were difficult. Prompt, if possible. *"Remember we sounded out that word?"* Observe the student's memory of sight words that were corrected. Prompt, if possible. *"Remember we read that word before?"* Check the student's memory for story information. Periodically ask: *What have you read so far?* [Ask this the following day: *Remember the story we read yesterday?* (Show the book or say the title.) *What was it about?*]	**MR 1** *Remembers phonetic words that were difficult*		
	MR 2 *Remembers sight words that were corrected*		
	MR 3 *Remembers the general meaning of the story*		
	MR 4 *Remembers the story the following day*		
Literal Comprehension (LC) When the child has finished reading, ask questions to assess comprehension of the story. *Who was in the story? Was anyone else in the story? How did the story begin? What happened first? What happened next? etc. How did the story end?*	**LC 1** *Identifies main characters*		
	LC 2 *Identifies main events correctly*		
	LC 3 *Correctly sequences important events*		
Comprehension Strategy (CS) CS 4: beginning at Roots Lesson 26, ask: *Can you tell me the main ideas about the story? Use the book to help yourself remember.*	**CS 4** *Reviews to summarize what was read*		

Appendix 3.2.
Reading a Familiar Story

Activities for Reading Roots – Activities for Tutoring   **3.9**

Activity 1 Reading a Familiar Story	Terrell is a first grader in Reading Roots. He is up to lesson #18 and has selected *The Costume Party* (Shared Story #11) to read as his familiar story. Terrell knows most of his sounds and how to blend them, but sometimes forgets. Building independence in this area is a goal.
Introducing the story; prompting memory	Tutor: Do you remember what this story, *The Costume Party*, is about?
Working on comprehension, memory and recall	Student: Yes, it's about dressing up.
	T: What about dressing up?
	S: Well, this boy wants to go to a costume party and doesn't know what he can be.
	T: Yes, why can't he decide what he wants to be?
	S: Because all his friends are the things he wants to be.
	T: What does he want to be?
	S: I'm not sure. I think he wants to be a fireman.
Prompting the student to read fluently	T: Let's read to find out. Since this a familiar story, I won't read the teacher part. You read the story yourself. Use expression and read as smoothly as you can.

3.10   Activities for Tutoring – Activities for Reading Roots

Rereading Familiar Stories, cont.

	S:	*Matt sits on /Niiiccckkk/, Niiicccckk, Nick, Nick's cot. He says, "I am a cot," I mean "cat,"*
Reinforcing self correction; reading for meaning	T:	Good thinking, you corrected yourself. Keep reading.
	S:	*Tim's cap is on Nnnick's cot. Tim's bat is on Nick's cot. He says, "I am a baseball player." Nick looks at Tim and Matt. He says, "I can be a cat. I can," Oh no, "I can not be a cat, I can not be a baseball player." He is says.*
Prompting the student to read for meaning; to monitor comprehension	T:	Hmmm. You read, "He is says." Does that make sense?
	S:	No!
Prompting the student to remember to use sound blending	T:	What will you do now?
	S:	Stretch the Sounds
	T:	Great. Go ahead.
	S:	Saaa, Saaaa,
Reviewing letter-sound recognition	T:	What sound does this letter make? (Points to the /d/.)
	S:	/d-d-d-d/
Prompting the strategy	T	What do you do now?
	S:	Keep going.
	T:	Yes. Go ahead
	S:	Saaaddd, sssaaaddd, sad.
	T:	Great job, the word is sad. Keep reading.
	S:	*He is sad. Tim says, "You can be a dragon! I cccaaann, can, put on the, I mean, I can pin on the tail." Don is a dragon.*
Reinforcing self correction; monitoring for meaning;	T:	I like the way you corrected yourself when you said put instead of pin.
	S:	What is this word?

Activities for Reading Roots – Activities for Tutoring   3.11

Rereading Familiar Stories, cont.

Encouraging the student to read independently; to apply a word strategy (sounding out) to a comprehension problem	T:	How can you figure it out?
	S:	Stretch the sounds
	T:	Go for it.
	S:	NNNiiiiccckkk, Nnniiiccckkk, Nick, Nick. *Nick sits on the cat. Wait that doesn't make sense. Nick sits on the cot. He says, "I can not be a dragon." He is sad. Don says, "You can be a pirate! I can get a pirate cap."*
Reinforcing reading for meaning; monitoring comprehension	T:	I like the way you asked yourself if what you read made sense and then reread when it didn't. Keep reading. You are doing a great job!
Reinforcing the student for reading more fluently and for strategy use	S:	*Ann is a pirate. Nick sits on the cot. He says, "I can not be a pirate." He is sad. Nick says, "Dad is a policeman. I can be a policeman!" Nick gets Dad's jacket. Nick gets Dad's hat.*
	T:	Helmet. (This is a sight word so it is just stated, not stretched.)
	S:	*Nick gets Dad's helmet. Nick gets Dad's badge*
	T:	You did a great job. Your reading gets smoother all the time and you are reading with a lot of expression. It really sounds like a good story when you read that way. And you remembered how to figure out words when you were stuck. Fantastic. Now let's do a quick review.

Appendix 3.3.
Sample Dialogue:
Quick Review of Letter Sounds and Words

Activities for Reading Roots – Activities for Tutoring   3.13

Sample Dialogue: Quick review of letter sounds and words

Activity 2 Quick Review	In this tutoring session, the tutor has the student review words that he had difficulty with from the familiar story, such as *Nick* and *sad*, as well as some sight words that are challenging. The tutor will also have the student review words that begin with the /f/ sound since the story being read in class, *Fang*, presents the /f/ sound. As in the last activity, the tutor focuses on sound blending.
Working on recognition of words the student read with difficulty or missed	T: What does this say? (Shows the word *Nick* on a small card.)
	S: Nnniiiccckkk. Nick.
	T: Good. (Shows *sad*.)
	S: I remember this, *ssaadd. Sad.*
	T: Good stretching. Try this (Dad.)
	S: DDaadd
	T: Great. You've got the /d-d-d/ sound now.
	T: (Shows the word *the*.)
	S: The
	T: Right. *"The" dog runs fast.* is in your story. (Shows the word *on*.)
	S: In
Reinforcing sight word recognition with say/spell/say	T: This is *on*. Let's say/spell/say it.
	S/T: On, "o" "n", on.
	T: Good. The kids got "on" the jungle gym when they were afraid of Fang. (Shows the word *be*.)
	S: Did.
Working on the distinction between be and did. These are two sight words that the student constantly confuses	T: No. This word is *be*. Let's say/spell/say it.
	S/T: Be, "b" "e", be.
	T: We will look for this word in the story before we start to read.

May 1999   **Tutoring Manual**

3.14   Activities for Tutoring – Activities for Reading Roots

Quick review of letter sounds and words, cont.

	T:	Now try this word (shows *Fat*). This is a green word.
	S:	/fffaaattt/, Fat.
Working on the current letter-sound /f/ and sound blending.	T:	Yes, good stretching, the word is *Fat*. Let's change the beginning sound and see what other words we can say (the tutor puts an /s/ in front of /at/). What is this word?
	S:	/sssaaattt/ sat.
	T:	Now try this. (Shows *fitt*.)
	S:	Fffffiiiiitt. *Fit.*
	T:	Very smooth. This is hard. (Shows *fast*.)
	S:	Fffaaaatt. Fat.
	T:	Stretch them all. Try it with me.
Teacher models and supports at first, pointing to the letters and softly saying the sounds along with the student.	S/T:	Ffffaaaassssttttt. Ffaasstt. Fast.
	T:	Now try a new one! (Writes *fist*.)
	T/S:	/Ffffiiiissstttt/
	S:	/fffiiissstttt/. /fffiiissssttttt/. Ffiisstt/. Fist.
	T:	You did it. You stretched a brand new word. Congratulations. Keep using those great stretching skills. Let's read the current story you are working on in class. Let's read <u>Fang</u>.

Success for All™   /   Roots and Wings™

Appendix 3.4.
Reading Current or Alternate Stories

Activities for Reading Roots – Activities for Tutoring   3.17

Sample Dialogue: Reading Current or Alternate Stories

Activity 3: **Reading the story for the current class lesson**	The student, Terrell, is having difficulty using sound blending and with comprehension. The tutor introduces the story that Terrell is working on in class this week: Fang. Reading the same stories being studied in class during tutoring provides the opportunity to reinforce classroom instruction and enable the student to make better use of class time, too. During this reading of the story, the tutor works on a variety of strategies including sounding out words and using comprehension strategies in the context of the current story.
Introducing the story: prompting memory and activating background knowledge.	T: Let's begin by reading this book. You have read this book before with your class. Can you tell me what the name of the book is?
	S: I remember. It's *Fang*.
	T: Right! Do you remember who Fang is?
	S: Yes.
Working on comprehension; probing for recall	T: Tell me who he is.
	S: He's a dog.
	T: Can you tell me anything else about him?
	S: He's big and he's a Beethoven dog.
	T: Yes, he is big and he's a St. Bernard! Good job remembering. Can you tell me who this little girl is? (Points to the girl next to Fang on the cover of the book.)
	S: I think she is his owner, but I can't remember her name.
	T: Yes, she is Fang's owner. Her name is Lana. Do remember who else is in the story?
	S: Well, I think a kid named Tanya. I can't remember other names.
	T: That's right, Tanya, Paco, Scott, and Derrick are in the story. What's the story about?
	S: About Fang.
	T: Yes, what about Fang?
	S: The dog pushed the girl in the mud.

May 1999   **Tutoring Manual**

3.18   Activities for Tutoring – Activities for Reading Roots

Reading Current or Alternate Stories, cont.

	T:	Right, that's a part of what happened. Let's read to remember what the whole story is. (Tutor begins reading the teacher part of the story.) *Scott and Tanya practice kicking her ball during recess. Lana joins them. What will happen to the ball?*
	S:	*/Sssscott/ Scott rolls the ball. /Bbbbaaammm/. Bam. /Tttttaaa/ /Tttttt/.*
Providing assistance with a sight word so the student can continue reading.	T:	Tanya. It is the little girl's name. (Tanya is a sight word)
	S:	*Tanya kicks it. She runs fat.*
Prompting the student to read for meaning—to monitor comprehension	T:	Does what you read make sense?
	S:	No.
Prompting the student to use word strategies: rereading and sounding out the word	T:	Read it again.
	S:	*She runs far.*
	T:	Let's sound it out.
	S/T:	*/Ffffaaaasssstttt/, /ffaasstt/.*
	S:	*/Fffaaassttt/.*
	T:	Now say it faster.
	S:	*/ffaasstt/, fast.*
Giving explicit explanation about why the student is doing certain activities and what he needs to work on. This builds metacognitive skills.	T:	Good. */fffaaassstttt/, fast.* We will work on saying the words faster when we sound them out. Keep reading.
	S:	*She runs fast. Lana says, "The ball is..."* What is this word?
Tutor states the red word to maintain flow of reading.	T:	*Off*
	S:	*Lana, says, "The ball is off the fence!"*
Prompting the student to monitor comprehension and to use a word strategy—to examine the context (pictures) to correct an error (fence)	T:	Does that make sense? The ball is off the fence? Look at the picture. Do you see a fence?
	S:	No. Oh, yeah, field. The ball is off the field!

Activities for Reading Roots – Activities for Tutoring   3.19

Reading Current or Alternate Stories, cont.

	T: (Tutor reads her part.) *Scott and Tanya look for the ball in the bushes while Lana looks on the other side of the playground. Suddenly, Scott sees something. What is it?*
	S: *"Look!" gggaaapppsss, gaps Scott.*
Supporting the student's use of the word strategy—sounding out the word—for accuracy;	T: Look at that word again. Good job sounding it out but there is one more sound. Try it with me.
Checking literal comprehension of the word (gasp)	S/T: *Gggaaassspppsss. Ggaassppss. Gasps.*
Giving direct explanation of the word and how to monitor for meaning: use context or ask for help rather than pass over words you don't understand	T: Good job. Now can you tell me what the word *gasps* means?
	S: No, I'm not sure what it means.
	T: A person gasps when they are surprised. (The tutor demonstrates gasping.) If you read a word and you don't understand its meaning either try to figure it by rereading or ask someone what it means.
Prompting the student to 1) sound out the word and then 2) reread for meaning and fluency (students should always reread sentences after sounding out a word)	S: *"Look Tanya!" gasps Scott. Tanya looks. She sees a big fat dog. It....* (The student looks to the tutor for help with the word.)
	T: Try to sound out the word.
	S: *Bbbuuummmpppsss, bbuummppss, bumps.*
	T: Great! Now read these two sentences again so you understand what you are reading.
Modeling how to read fluently and with expression	S: *The dog runs fast. It bumps into Tanya. She sits in the mud.*
	T: I'll read this part. *Poor Tanya! How do you think she feels about being pushed into the mud?*
Prompting the student to identify a strategy	S: What is this word? (The student points to the word *ick*.)
	T: How could you find out?
Checking for literal comprehension of the word	S Stretch it.
	T Let's do it together.
	S/T: /Iiiicccckkkk/ /Iicckk/. Ick.
	T: Say it fast.
	S: Ick.

3.20   Activities for Tutoring – Activities for Reading Roots

Reading Current or Alternate Stories, cont.

Checking for literal comprehension of the word	T:	Do you know what it means? (The tutor wants to be sure that the student understands the meaning of the word.)
	S:	Yes, when something is icky, it is not good or doesn't taste good.
	T:	Yes, *ick* means that you don't like something. Keep reading.
	S:	*"Ick!" says /TTT/ Tanya. Mud is not fun. Go, dog!*
Checking comprehension with background knowledge	T:	Why do you think the mud is not fun?
	S:	Because the girl, Tanya, got all dirty.
	T:	Yes, the mud can be icky and make you all dirty. Good job. Keep reading.
	S:	*The /bbbiiiggg/ /bbbiiiggg/ the big dog says.* No that's not right the big dog can't talk. *The big dog /sssiiitttsss/ /sssits/ sits. The big dog sits. He pants?* This doesn't make sense either. He pants. He wears pants?
Giving the student direct explanation of word meaning in response to a comprehension question	T:	The word "pants" has two meanings. One is something you wear. The other means breathing heavily. It's what you do if you've been running fast. Fang is a big dog who breathes heavily. He pants.
	S:	Oh. OK. *He pants.*
	T:	Let me read the teacher part. *Paco starts to shake. He turns pale. What has Paco seen that has scared him?*
	S:	*Paco says, "See the dog's...."* What is this word?
Prompting the student to identify and use a strategy.	T:	How can you find out?
	S	Stretch it.
	T:	Go ahead.
	S:	*Fffaaannn, fan?*
	T:	Look at the word again. Make sure you don't forget that last sound. (The tutor wants to encourage the student to independently sound out the word and say it fast, combining all the letters.)

Success for All™ / Roots and Wings™

Activities for Reading Roots – Activities for Tutoring   3.21

Reading Current or Alternate Stories, cont.

	S:	*/Fffaaannngggg/, fang?*
	T:	Try it with me.
	S/T:	*/Fffaaannngggsss/.*
	T:	Good, now put these sounds together.
	S:	*/Fffaaannngggsss/.*
	T:	Good, say it faster.
	S:	*Fangs.*
Modeling how to say the word fast so the student can hear all of the sounds	T:	Yes, *fangs.*
	S:	*"Fangs!!" says Tanya. The big dog says....* What is this word?
	T:	*"Ruff."* (This word is a sight word so the tutor simply states it for the student.)
	S:	*"Ruff!" The kids clim, clim, clim up the jungle gym.*
Telling the student the sight word so he can continue reading	T:	The word is *climb.*
	S:	*"Can we fit?" asks Paco. Lana runs fast. "Fang!" Lana says. She skips (skids) to a stop.*
Giving direct explanation about how to use word strategies—to try sounding out a word before, or in addition to, using context; this student tends to over-rely on context	T:	Good, but let's take a look at this word. When you come to a word that you are not sure of, slow down and try to sound it out first before you guess at it.
	S:	*Skips?*
	S/T:	Stretch it with me.
Helping the student sound out a word.	S/T:	*/Sssskkkkiiiiddddsss/. / Sskkiiddss/. Skids.*
	S:	*/Sss/ kids, Skids. She skids to a stop. "Fang is not bad," sits,* I mean, *says Lana.*
Reinforcing the student for self-correcting (monitoring for meaning)	T:	Good. You went back and corrected yourself. I'll read my part. *Lana explains that Fang is her St. Bernard. He is very gentle, even though he has big teeth. He follows her to school when he gets lonely. What will the other children do now?*

3.22   Activities for Tutoring – Activities for Reading Roots

Reading Current or Alternate Stories, cont.

	S:	*Lana says, "Fang is a fun dog. He likes kids."* Kids is like skids.
Reinforcing the student's observations about word similarities	T:	That's right! It's good that you noticed. Continue to read.
	S:	*The kids get off the jungle gym.*
	T:	*All of a sudden, Derrick has an idea. What do you think?*
	S:	*Derrick says, "Dogs can /sssnnnniiiffff/ sniff. Can Fang sniff the ball?"*
Checking literal comprehension	T:	What do you think? Can Fang sniff the ball?
	S:	Yes, he has a nose, he can sniff.
	T:	Yes, good job, keep reading.
	S:	*Lana nots.* Oh, wait. *Lana nods. "Get the ball, Fang," says Lana.*
Reinforcing self-correction (monitoring for meaning)	T:	Good job correcting yourself! I'll read. *Fang puts his nose to the ground. Do you think he can find the ball?*
	S:	*Fang runs. He sniffs. He digs fast in a* (long pause) *stack.*
	T:	Stack. (The tutor repeats the word to confirm that the student is correct.)
	S:	*Stack of leaves. The kids say, "Fang got the ball back!"*
Prompting the student to read fluently; modeling fluent reading	T:	*Fang is a hero. He found the missing ball.* You did a great job. Now let's read the last page together so we can practice reading with expression.
	T/S:	*Fang runs. He sniffs. He digs fast in a stack of leaves. The kids say, "Fang got the ball back!"*

Success for All™   /   Roots and Wings™

Appendix 3.5.
Skill-Focused Writing

Activities for Reading Roots – Activities for Tutoring   3.23

Skill-Focused Writing: 7 minutes

Purpose

Skill-focused writing works on phonemic awareness, recalling and blending letter sounds to form words, and developing written sentences. It is also used to teach and model concepts about print. These activities begin with quick oral practices with the writing activities following.

Procedures (see example of activity script below):

- Decide what letter sounds, blends, or words the student needs help with; base the decision on your observations from a previous lesson, your assessments (see Assessment section for detail), or input from the reading teacher.

- Select the appropriate Skill-Focused Writing Script (Appendix) for that lesson.

- Collect the materials you will need based on the script (if any).

- Introduce the activity to establish context for the activity (see sample dialogue).

- Implement the activity according to the script; **at each step, assess and support the student with explanation, modeling, prompting, or reinforcement, as needed.** The scripts provide only basic information about what the tutor should say. They do not include information about how the tutor should react to various responses a student might give.

- As you implement the script, make a point to demonstrate, prompt students to use, and reinforce them for using different *concepts about print*. Examples of these include: capital letters as needed, direction and spacing of print (left to right, spaces between words), and punctuation. Help students learn, too, what a complete sentence is, as well as what it is not.

3.24 Activities for Tutoring – Activities for Reading Roots

Example: Reading Roots: Skill-Focused Writing Activity
Script for Lesson 17

Introduction: Explaining the activities and the goal (working on /b/)	Why?
Today we're going to play a listening game with words that have /b/ in them. We'll write words with that sound in them. We'll also write sentences that have at least one word with /b/ in it. Before we start these activities, though, I would like for you to write your name here, at the top of the paper. (Response) Good job. Are you ready?	to explain the goal(s) of the writing activity.

Sounds: Listening to the sound in words (breaking words down)	Why?
First let's listen to some words in Alphie's special language. You remember Alphie talks so slowly sometimes that you can hear all of the different sounds in his words. Listen: /bbbuuuggg/. Now I'll say-it-fast, the way we do when we're talking: Bug. A fly is a bug. You try it. I'll say the word slowly, the way Alphie does, and you say-it-fast. Try these: /bbbaaattt/ (bat) /bbbuuummmppp/ (bump) /bbbeeelllttt/ (belt). (Response after each.) Let's play that game a different way. I'll say a word fast and you say it in Alphie's language, slowly so I can hear all of the sounds. Do you want to listen to me say some more words slowly before we start? Let's go ahead then and you try it. big boat bell (Response after each.) Oh, you're good at this game. I could hear all of the sounds.	to teach students to listen to the sounds in words by stretching them out. (Phonemic Awareness).

Dictation: Writing words and sentences with words that have the sound in them	Why?
We use that same way of saying words slowly to help us write. Let's try that with some words that have /b/ in them. I'll write one first, and then you. I'll show you how I say the word slowly, like we did in the game, so that I hear and write letters for all of the sounds. Watch and listen while I write "bang." /bbbaaannnggg/. Now it's your turn; you write "bump." Remember to say it slowly at first, then say it fast after you've written it. (Response) Good Job! Let's write a sentence with a work that has /b/ in it— let's use the word "big." Can you write, "Sam's dog is big?" Show me. Remember to stretch the green words, say the sounds slowly, as you write them. (Response) Excellent! Can you read it back to me?	To make letter/sound connections; to give direct instruction in, and model, stretching words out to writing words.

Success for All™ / Roots and Wings™

Sentences: Creating sentences that have the sound in at least one of the words	Why?
Now let's make up sentences that have at least one word with /b/ in it. We can pick any word with that sound in it. I'll go first. Let me think; I know, "bug." "That bug is big!" Which word(s) in my sentence has /b/ in it? Now it's your turn. What's your sentence (Response)? That's good. Which word has /b/ in it? (Response) Let's write your sentence. You can write the words you know. Tell me which ones you want help with and I'll write those. Be sure to say the words slowly as you write so you won't miss any of the sounds. (Student and tutor write.) There! Can you read it back to me? O.K., we're finished for today. We've thought a lot about the /b/ sound today and you've worked really hard. You may take the paper with you. Why don't you show it to your parents and tell them what you worked on today?	To reinforce using letter sounds and phonemic awareness in the context of writing sentences.

Note: The scripts are slightly different for students in Roots Lessons 1-4, 5-10, 11-15, 16-37, and 38-48. For example, students are gradually given more responsibility for writing (and teachers demonstrate less) as they progress. Also, phonemic awareness activities (listening to sounds in words) phase out and students begin to work on learning how to write meaningful sentences out at higher levels.

4

Prekindergarten and Kindergarten Programs

Success for All and Roots & Wings emphasize prevention, doing everything possible to ensure that students succeed in school the first time they are taught so that they will never need remediation. Prevention of learning problems takes many forms in Success for All, including providing high-quality curriculum and instruction and involving parents in their children's education. Some of the most important program elements directed at preventing learning problems are those provided before students enter first grade, in prekindergarten and kindergarten.

Because disadvantaged students often enter kindergarten well behind middle-class children in their oral language development, it is critical that they participate in preschool and kindergarten experiences that will help them develop the kind of oral language skills necessary for success in school (Barnett, Tarr, & Frede, 1999). Preschool attendance alone does not lead to higher achievement (Karweit, 1994); the nature of the program substantially determines its effects. Mounting evidence indicates that for preschool to have a lasting impact on achievement, programs must

AUTHORS' NOTE: Bette Chambers and Barbara Wasik contributed to this chapter.

focus on oral language, emergent literacy, and social development (Schweinhart, Barnes, Weikart, Barnett, & Epstein, 1993).

Success for All and Roots & Wings emphasize the importance of children attending quality prekindergarten and kindergarten programs. Research demonstrates that for disadvantaged students, prekindergarten experience reduces the chances of being retained or assigned to special education (Karweit, 1994). There is some evidence of long-term effects of high-quality preschool experiences on high school completion, increased employment rates, and other outcomes (see Schweinhart et al., 1993). Full-day kindergarten has been found to consistently increase end-of-kindergarten achievement more than half-day programs (Karweit, 1994). However, the philosophy of Success for All and Roots & Wings is to build success one year at a time. Our prekindergarten and full-day kindergarten programs stand on their own but are also designed to better prepare students to profit from a high-quality first-grade experience.

Attendance in prekindergarten and kindergarten is not sufficient to ensure that students succeed; these programs must provide an enriched curriculum. Success for All and Roots & Wings provide experiential, child-centered curricula designed to ensure that all students enter first grade with the self-confidence, positive attitudes toward school, and orientation to reading they will need to succeed in the elementary grades. Also, these programs emphasize involving parents in their children's early learning experiences and creating a strong home-school connection.

The prekindergarten and kindergarten programs in Success for All and Roots & Wings (Wasik & Bond, 1999) use thematically based curricula intended to develop oral language, literacy, listening skills, numeracy, and creative expression. The curricula balance child-centered and teacher-directed instruction and focus on the integration of language and communication skills in the context of literacy experiences.

The Preschool Program: Curiosity Corner

The prekindergarten program used in Success for All is called Curiosity Corner. The goals of Curiosity Corner are to foster children's language, cognitive, social, physical, and emotional development and to involve families in their children's education (Bredekamp & Copple, 1997; Chambers et al., 1999). Curiosity Corner's integrated curriculum incorporates language-focused, problem-solving activities designed to achieve these goals (Kostelnik, 1991). The program is one of prescribed flexibility with specific directions, a wide variety of children's literature, and manipulative materials provided to teachers to help them carry out activities that offer children a balance of teacher-directed and self-selected experiences focused around a theme that is relevant to the children's lives.

Curiosity Corner is used with 3-year-olds and 4-year-olds, usually either in Success for All schools or in community-based programs in which children are likely to graduate into Success for All elementary schools. Language-related activities, such as interactive story reading and storytelling, action songs and rhymes, verbal guessing games, and discussions of thematic concepts, promote children's phonemic awareness and oral language development. Children choose among learning labs, such as art, water and sand, science, manipulatives, construction, dramatic play, library, and writing, and they participate in guessing games and reflection activities to promote their creative problem-solving abilities.

A variety of strategies promote parents' involvement in their children's education. These strategies include home visits, storybook kits aimed at promoting literacy that parents borrow and share with their children, videos that promote parenting skills (e.g., reading to children), a family support team, and daily activities that link what children are learning at school to their home life.

District-level Curiosity Corner coaches mentor and support teachers in their implementation of the program. Curiosity Corner trainers, from the Success for All Foundation, also monitor the implementation of the program and provide training for teachers, assistants, and Curiosity Corner coaches.

The following sections describe the main activities used in Curiosity Corner.

Greetings & Readings

Each day during Greetings & Readings, the teachers welcome the children and whomever brings them to school with a smile and a personal greeting. They use this opportunity to make a positive connection between the child's home and school. Children's language and social abilities are enhanced through informal conversation with the educators. Teachers use attendance taking to promote learning as well. The children find their name tags and hang them on a picture of a schoolhouse near their cubbies.

During Greetings & Readings, children ease into the day by snuggling up with an adult looking at a book, playing with some puzzles or play dough, making productive use of every minute while everyone gets ready to begin another fun-filled, learning-rich day.

At the end of Greetings & Readings, the class gathers for a short whole-group activity in which children share information and ideas through the Daily Message. On Monday, the teacher quickly assigns weekly jobs to all of the children.

Clues & Questions

The Clues & Questions component introduces the children to the concepts highlighted that day. The teacher brings out the class mascot, Curiosity Cat, and stimulates the children's curiosity about an aspect of the theme, for example, by giving oral clues and having children guess what object Curiosity has in her bag. The teacher acknowledges their efforts at guessing, prompts the children to explain their predictions, and encourages them to ask questions and say what other things they would like to discover about the theme.

Phonemic Awareness: Rhyme Time

Children love the sounds and rhythms of the music and rhymes that they chant during Rhyme Time. The goal of Rhyme Time is not to have children memorize poems but to build their phonemic awareness, to have them learn that words are made up of sounds, and to recognize similar sounds in words (Adams, Foorman, Lundberg, & Beeler, 1998). Phonemic awareness is an essential skill that children must learn on their way to learning how to read. They do this by learning and repeating nursery rhymes, songs, fingerplays, and poems. The children move, dance, sing, and act their way to phonemic awareness. These strategies are used to highlight similar beginning and ending sounds of words and are used at any time of the day, particularly during transitions.

Learning Labs

Learning Labs are engaging discovery or problem-solving learning centers at which children explore and experiment with concrete objects related to the theme under study (Kostelnik, 1991). Most of the activities at these labs are tasks that the children can do independently, requiring minimal teacher supervision. Examples of Learning Labs include Dramatic Play Lab, Science Lab, Construction Lab, Art Lab and Paint Easel, Library and Listening Lab, Letter and Writing Lab, Sand and Water Lab, Manipulatives Lab, and Cooking Lab.

Language and literacy are promoted in each of the labs. Writing implements and written materials are regularly provided in the labs. For example, in the Blocks Lab, road signs are incorporated into the road building. Cookbooks and shopping lists are an integral part of the Dramatic Play Lab. In the Science Lab, children record their observations.

In each lab, elaborated language is modeled and enhanced. For example, teachers thoroughly describe what they are seeing and doing when interacting with the children in the labs. The children are encouraged to speak in complete, elaborated sentences as well.

Story Tree

Research demonstrates that storybook reading is clearly related to children's language and literacy development (Adams, 1990). Story Tree is an interactive, literature-focused segment of the schedule. In this engaging story experience, the teacher enthusiastically introduces the story, author, and illustrator and has the children make predictions about what will happen in the story. One of the most important goals is to build children's expressive and receptive language skills.

The teacher reads the story, involving the children by asking open-ended, predictive questions. After finishing reading the story, the teacher has the children recall events from the story and ask and answer questions (covering a range of levels) about the story. Teachers often reread stories on successive days and again in subsequent units. Story Tree activities include regular and big-book story reading; storytelling with puppets, felt characters, and other props; and extension activities.

Print and Alphabet Awareness

Curiosity Corner classrooms are covered with printed material. The goal is not to teach 3-year-olds or 4-year-olds letters or words but to create an environment in which children will see the functions that print serves. Everywhere you look, there are signs and labels, letters, posters, poems, songs, instructions, recipes, and words related to the theme. The 4-year-old program includes a systematic introduction to letters, conducted in the meaningful context of the theme, literature, and children's experiences (Wasik, in press).

Outside, Large Motor Play

Children need to spend time each day running, jumping, throwing balls, and climbing to enhance their large motor development. To improve their skill and fitness and to feel successful and develop positive attitudes toward an active lifestyle, Curiosity Corner offers ample opportunities for children to engage in locomotor, balance, and manipulative activities.

Children not only develop their physical abilities through this large motor play, they also develop their interpersonal skills through the sharing, turn taking, and negotiating that is involved in these activities. Children's cognitive abilities are fostered through learning about thematic concepts that many of the activities reinforce. Outside play is also a good time for promoting children's language development, particularly their understanding of positional terms, such as under, beside, on, and down.

Snack Time

Snack time offers opportunities to foster children's social development by modeling and reinforcing the use of polite social conventions (Warach & Lazorchak, 1999). Children are also encouraged to pour their own water, milk, or juice and to serve themselves as much as possible.

Question and Reflection

At the end of the class period, the children gather to review what they have learned that day or week. Through active engagement with not only thematic concepts but other knowledge and skills, children deeply process their newfound knowledge (Hohmann & Weikart, 1995).

For example, in a unit on bread, children experience bread of many kinds from many cultures. They recall types of bread that they have eaten and where they came from, analyze the ingredients of bread, and evaluate which ones they liked the best.

The class creates a graph of their favorite types of bread. The children take turns placing bread pictures in the column representing the bread that they prefer. Together, they count the number of pictures in each column to determine the most popular. This activity reinforces learning about the different types of bread and also exposes the children to rudimentary graphing.

Home Links

The importance of family involvement in young children's education cannot be overstated. Curiosity Corner engages parents and other family members in many ways, beginning with home visits. Making a positive initial contact with families can help everyone feel like they are a team with the common goal of fostering the child's learning. Other ways that families are involved in their children's education include instructional videos and opportunities for volunteering.

On the last day of each unit, the children take home a Home Link Page to inform their families about what they will be learning in the next unit. The newsletters typically include titles of some books they might like to read to their children, a poem to recite together, and a request for someone to come to school to help out during a particular activity or contribute a special material.

Each day, the teacher suggests to the children something that they can do at home that day that connects with what they have learned in school. The next day, the teacher leads a discussion with the children about the home activity.

Children and their family members are encouraged to borrow Book Bags from the lending library, the goal of which is to help families promote their children's literacy. Book Bags contain a book and a sheet of ideas on how to interact with their children around the book, questions to ask, fingerplays, activities, and sometimes, a manipulative related to the story.

The following tables show sample schedules for half-day and whole-day prekindergarten programs, and Appendix 4.1 shows a day from a typical Curiosity Corner theme guide.

Sample Half-Day Schedule

Component	Allotted Time
Greetings and Readings	15 to 20 minutes
Clues and Questions	10 to 15 minutes
Rhyme Time	5 to 10 minutes
Learning Labs	45 to 60 minutes
Story Tree	10 to 20 minutes
Outside, Large Motor Play	20 to 25 minutes
Snack	10 to 15 minutes
Question and Reflection	5 to 15 minutes
Departure	5 to 10 minutes

Sample Whole-Day Schedule

Component	Allotted time
Greetings and Readings	20 to 30 minutes
Curiosity Corner	10 to 15 minutes
Rhyme Time	5 to 10 minutes
Learning Labs	45 to 60 minutes
Story Tree	10 to 20 minutes
Snack	10 to 15 minutes
Outside, Large Motor Play	25 to 40 minutes
Lunch	40 to 50 minutes
Rest	30 to 60 minutes
Learning Labs	40 to 60 minutes
Story Time	10 to 20 minutes
Question and Reflection	10 to 15 minutes
Outside Play	40 to 50 minutes
Departure	5 to 10 minutes

The Kindergarten Program: Early Learning

Children come to kindergarten with a range of developmental levels, cultural backgrounds, and experiences. The purpose of Early Learning is to accept children where they are and to facilitate their continued development (Wasik & Bond, 1999). The goals of the curriculum are to develop oral language, literacy skills, listening skills, numeracy skills, creative expression, and positive self-esteem.

The Early Learning curriculum emphasizes the acquisition of such language skills as the use of elaborated, descriptive language, recognition and production of the alphabet, understanding the conventions of print, and understanding the communicative function of language, as well as such specific skills as letter knowledge. The components of the kindergarten curriculum include STaR, with integrated oral language and writing experiences; a phonemic awareness program; emergent writing; Eager to Read and KinderRoots (initial reading experiences); and learning centers, all taught in the context of integrated, thematic units.

Thematic Units

The Early Learning thematic units primarily integrate instruction around science and social studies topics to help children make sense of the world. The program expands children's horizons by starting from the familiar and gradually exposing them to novel experiences (Kostelnik, 1991). Thus, the thematic units begin with topics such as Special Me, extend to the larger community with such topics as Community Helpers, and finish with exposing them to novel concepts, such as Space.

Each thematic units consists of several components:

- An introduction that includes Learning Essentials (the main concepts to be introduced), a letter to parents, and a dictionary of terms related to the units
- Theme-learning lessons about the related concepts
- STaR, an interactive story-reading component with related oral language and writing activities
- Shared Book experiences that use big books to teach concepts of print
- Emergent writing activities
- Learning center activities
- Math, science, music and movement, cooking and home learning activities
- A unit assessment

The thematic units are comprehensive resource guides that teachers use to plan and implement an integrated curriculum. Teachers are not expected to complete every activity in each unit; rather, they pick specific learning essentials and activities that fit the needs and developmental levels of their children and determine the time line they will follow. Therefore, if the class is to spend 2 weeks on the Plants in Our Lives unit, the teacher determines which Learning Essentials best fit the needs and developmental levels of the students, selects the activities in each component that focus on those essentials, and maps out a plan for the intended time line.

The thematic units currently available for kindergarten include Special Me, Community Helpers, Transportation, Japan, Dinosaurs, Kenya, Plants in Our Lives, The Environment, Healthy Me, and Space.

Learning Center Activities

Learning centers are an important aspect of the kindergarten program in Success for All and Roots & Wings. Center areas recommended in the thematic units include Art, Construction, Dramatic Play, Water and Sand, Manipulative, Science, Writing, and Listening-Media (Library). The activities in each center are related to and reinforce the theme that is being explored in class. The purpose of center activities is to allow young children to have the opportunity to play independently and learn, in a hands-on exploration of concrete objects, concepts that are presented in the thematic unit.

Concept development and skill practice are emphasized in the kindergarten center activities. Center time is carefully planned to support the specific concepts that relate to the theme. For example, if the class is working on the Community Helpers unit, an art center activity presented in the unit suggests that the children make a fire fighter ladder. Such concepts as counting the number of rungs on the ladder, spacing the rungs of the ladder, and comparing and contrasting are also highlighted when doing this activity. Teachers incorporate higher-order concepts into the center activities and guide children to think about many concepts that can be learned from the tasks as they circulate from center to center.

Story Telling and Retelling (STaR)

STaR (Karweit, Coleman, Waclawiw, & Petza, 1990) is a beginning literacy program that employs children's literature as an important avenue for expanding children's experience and knowledge. The goal of STaR is to enhance oral language, understanding of story structure, and comprehension skills. STaR structures storytelling activities to increase student involvement with and attention to children's literature.

Stories expose children to the communicative function of language and to how print works. In discussing and retelling stories, children learn that narratives have predictable elements (characters, settings, problems, and solutions), which helps with reading comprehension later on. Stories also expose children to other worlds and other usages of language that provide models and metaphors for the child's developing communication abilities.

Evaluations of STaR indicate positive effects on the important prereading skills of receptive vocabulary, production of language, and story comprehension. STaR is used in kindergarten and first grade. The STaR procedure organizes storytelling and retelling and includes ways to introduce a story and maintain student interest during the story and techniques for reviewing and retelling the story. A story kit consists of guide sheets (which include questions for introducing and reviewing the story) and story retelling aids (in some cases, story sequence cards or illustrations to cut out and make into flannel board figures or stick puppets). A list of the storybook titles used in the STaR program is included at the end of this chapter.

STaR is designed for a whole-class format with a teacher and an assistant. The activities take between 20 and 30 minutes a day. The teacher sets up a special area of the classroom where the children can sit together, see the book clearly, and interact about the story.

Story Introduction

The teacher selects a STaR book to read to the class that is appropriate to their developmental level and is related to the thematic unit being implemented. The story guide sheets include some suggested ways to set the stage and pique the children's curiosity for the story they are about to hear. The teacher discovers the children's prior knowledge to help them make connections to the story. The teacher also establishes the setting for the story. It is important to give the children some idea of when and where the story takes place to prepare them for what they are about to hear.

In every STaR story, three new vocabulary words are introduced. STaR focuses on comprehension. Children make predictions after hearing the title and vocabulary and looking at the cover. They share and justify their predictions.

Interactive Story Reading

During Interactive Story Reading, the teacher thinks aloud to model for students what good readers do when reading. While reading the story, the teacher asks predictive, summary, and other high-level questions. Asking predictive and summary questions during the storytelling keeps students involved and thinking about the story and helps the children recall the events in the story.

Story Structure Review

After reading the story, a review of story structure elements helps give the lesson closure while children recall the title, author and illustrator, characters, setting, main events and problem, and story resolution and ending.

Group Story Retelling and Individual Story Conferences

The purpose of story retelling is to give students an opportunity to make the story their own, understand the nature of stories, enhance vocabulary, and improve oral language skills. The story kits include questions for story retell as well as sequence cards that can be used as aids for story retelling. There are two forms of story retelling—the group retell and the individual story conference.

In the group retell, the whole class participates in recounting the story in some manner. Sometimes, this is done by dramatizing the story, with children playing the roles of different characters. Sometimes, students recall events from the story by taking turns elaborating on each others' ideas in a Story Circle. Another method of retelling is for the children to organize story events with a Story Map.

While the teacher is conducting a group retell with the rest of the class, the assistant usually calls individual students to conduct the individual story conferences. The individual retell allows a student to practice telling a story from beginning to end. It is not expected that every child will retell every story. The assistant's job is to schedule the students for conferences and record the story retell. The assistant uses the individual retell questions provided for each story.

Story Critique

Children are also given an opportunity to critique the story. This critique activity gives children an opportunity to share their opinions about the story in a risk-free setting. It is important to provide ways in which children can voice their opinions. Story Critique allows the children to play the role of critic and learn a variety of techniques, such as story rating and story frames, to express their opinions about the stories.

Story Extension Activities

STaR Story Extensions provide children with a variety of ways to further respond to literature in a meaningful way. Each STaR guide sheet provides suggestions for extension activities, such as story rereading; story dramatization; art and cooking activities; story exchange, where children tell their related experiences to the other children; story group, where children tell the STaR stories to their peers; and story journal. Appendix 4.2 is an example of a STaR Story Guide Sheet.

Emergent Writing

Oral language, reading, and writing are inherently connected. In Success for All and Roots & Wings, young children begin exploring writing as soon as they begin school. As soon as children begin to make marks with writing instruments, they are beginning to learn about language and how it works. The Emergent Writing component of the curriculum begins with where the child is at the time and encourages the developmental progression of writing. Children are taught that print conveys meaning and that they are able to manipulate print to provide meaning to the reader and show the purpose of their writing through multiple forms of text.

Teachers are taught the developmental progression of writing, from scribbles, to linear repetition, to random letter formation, and eventually letter name writing. Teachers provide numerous opportunities for the children to write and to be exposed to print. The thematic units and the STaR materials include suggestions for writing activities. Teachers are given strategies for making their classroom a print-rich environment and teaching the editing process to young children.

By modeling the different ways kindergartners write, teachers provide their students with a platform to begin experimenting with writing while making them feel safe and encouraged. This technique provides an effective framework in which teachers can discuss and demonstrate the many ways that young children can write. Using this technique reinforces children's writing attempts and motivates them to write.

Oral Language Development

Through the Success for All and Roots & Wings oral language component, children expand their vocabulary and learn elaborated speech patterns. The active, engaging oral language activities are related to the theme and either the STaR or Shared Books that are currently being studied. Some of the skills that are enhanced through the oral language activities include classifying, describing, matching, labeling, discussing, sequencing, and reasoning. Lessons include concepts such as shapes, colors, classification, neighborhoods, foods, and clothing and such language concepts as over-under and before-after. The daily lessons typically take about 15 minutes and are meaningfully integrated into the children's learning experiences (Galda, Cullinan, & Strickland, 1993).

In Grade 1, the oral language and writing activities are related to the Shared Stories or STaR stories, following the same 3-day schedule that those components follow. These components flow together to form an integrated Reading Roots program.

Phonemic Awareness

Phonemic awareness, the ability to recognize and manipulate sounds in words, is one of the most important building blocks of literacy. In a playful way, children learn how letter sounds are related to words. Phonemic awareness is not direct instruction of phonics. Instead, young children learn about sounds in words through the exposure to phonemic awareness games, based on a program designed by Adams et al. (1998).

The phonemic awareness program exposes young children to the variety of sounds letters make in words and provide them the opportunities to manipulate these sounds. Children learn about sounds and how they are combined. The children engage in game-like activities that focus on listening, words and sentences, awareness of syllables, initial and final sounds, and phonemes. The phonemic-awareness activities are done every day in full-day kindergartens.

Shared Book Experience

The Shared Book Experience focuses children's attention on the conventions of print. It uses big books that contain short, predictable stories with illustrations and other forms of enlarged text. Teachers read the books to children, pointing out where they start to read (front of the book, left side of the page), how the pictures illustrate the story, how each spoken word corresponds to a written one, and so on. Through several rereadings of predictable text, students began to isolate phrases on pages, words in phrases, and so on. The purpose of the Shared Book Experience is to reinforce not only that print carries meaning but also how books and print are related to reading for meaning.

The big books, which are chosen to feature rhythm, rhyme, and repetition, are used with the related themes and focus children's attention on the mechanics of print. In the 3-day cycle, on the first day, the teacher simply reads the story through, pointing out words and pictures. On the second day, the teacher reads again and encourages the children to chime in. The third day focuses on the details, such as cutting up sentence strips to convey the relations of words to phrases.

Alphabet Activities

Children need to learn letters of the alphabet and their sounds to become independent, fluent, and strategic readers and writers (Wasik, in press). Letter learning is one of the best predictors of future reading success. Our goal is to immerse children in letter-learning activities that highlight the various contexts in which letters exist and promote letter and letter sound recognition.

Alphabet instruction is built into Success for All and Roots & Wings using a wide variety of activities. Letter Investigations provides a framework of activities that allow children to explore the physical nature of letters as well as the role letters play in our everyday lives. Environmental print, names, and books are just a few of the contexts through which children explore and learn about letters.

Letters are introduced in various parts of the daily routine and are connected with the thematic unit or STaR story (or both) that is being studied. Typically, the letter that is being worked on is presented during morning routine as a part of a morning message or a calendar activity. The letter activities are then woven throughout the daily theme. Children are given opportunities during writing or journal time to see the letter in print. During the STaR activity, the letter that is being worked on is presented again to the children. Often, an alphabet book is used to reinforce the letters that have already been presented and to expose the children to new ones.

Eager to Read

The goal of Eager to Read is to prepare children to learn to read. It is an early literacy program that encourages reading behavior and exposes children to the conventions of print. It consists of a series of little books for each child with simple, regular text and pictures that represent the text. There is an accompanying big-book version of each story for the teacher. Each week, children participate in repeated readings of two stories, allowing them to memorize or approximate the text. This modeling of reading behavior helps children see themselves as readers.

The Eager to Read stories are related to the thematic units. Students become familiar with six characters, Kinderfriends, that are in most of the books. Children read the stories as a whole group, in partners, and independently. Children record the stories they have read in their Reading Log. In the second half of the school year, Eager to Read is replaced by KinderRoots.

KinderRoots

KinderRoots provides kindergarten students with an introduction to reading. The goal of the program is to expose students to the use of sound blending and general strategies for word recognition and text comprehension so they will become independent, thinking readers who enjoy reading (Madden, Rice, Livermon, Wasik, & Slavin, 1999).

About halfway through the school year, after much exposure to books, concepts of print, phonemic awareness, and names and sounds of letters, kindergarten classes begin KinderRoots. It is structured along the same lines as the Reading Roots program, described in detail in Chapter 2. KinderRoots uses its own Shared Stories and lessons that introduce letters and their sounds and use them in phonetically regular text. These stories use the same general format and letter sequence as the Reading Roots Shared Stories.

KinderRoots's structured, fast-paced lessons are implemented for 30 minutes each day and follow a 5-day schedule. Lessons include instruction in metacognitive strategies; presentation of the story; sound, letter, and word development activities; story activities; reading aloud; and review.

By the end of the school year, students will have experienced between 10 and 20 KinderRoots lessons. Some will have gained mastery of the strategies during this time and will begin Reading Roots at an advanced level, whereas others will need another opportunity to experience similar lessons at the beginning of Reading Roots in first grade.

Although the different components are described separately here, they are in fact presented in a seamless fashion as an integrated curriculum. Sample full-day and half-day kindergarten schedules follow.

Sample Full-Day Kindergarten Schedule

Component	Allotted Time
Arrival (journal writing)	5 to 10 minutes
Beginning Routines (message, calendar)	10 to 15 minutes
STaR	20 to 30 minutes
Specials	30 minutes
Theme Learning, Oral Language	20 to 25 minutes
Learning Centers	40 to 45 minutes
Letter Investigations	10 minutes
Eager to Read	10 to 15 minutes
Lunch	30 minutes
Rest (independent reading)	20 to 30 minutes
Phonemic Awareness	15 to 20 minutes
Shared Book	10 to 15 minutes
Recess and Snack	15 minutes
Math	20 to 30 minutes
Writing	10 to 15 minutes
Sharing	10 minutes
Departure	5 minutes

Sample Half-Day Kindergarten Schedule

Component	Allotted Time
Arrival (journal writing)	5 to 10 minutes
Beginning Routines (message, calendar)	5 to 10 minutes
Theme Learning, Oral Language	15 to 20 minutes
Specials	30 minutes
STaR	15 to 20 minutes
Learning Centers	30 to 40 minutes
Letter Investigations	5 to 10 minutes
Phonemic Awareness	15 minutes
Shared Book, Eager to Read	10 to 15 minutes
Recess and Snack	15 minutes
Math	15 to 20 minutes
Writing	10 minutes
Sharing	5 to 10 minutes
Departure	5 minutes

At the time of writing, we are working on the creation of a revised kindergarten program that will flow in logical sequence from Curiosity Corner, the 3-year-old and 4-year-old program, and clearly articulate with the Success for All and Roots & Wings elementary programs.

CHAPTER 4 APPENDICES

Appendix 4.1. Ready, Set . . .
Appendix 4.2. Mr. Gumpy's Outing

Appendix 4.1.
Ready, Set . . .

Ready, set...

Focus

Night and day
are opposites.

How will children grow today?

- Name some
  characteristics
  of day and night

- Match pictures
  representing
  common opposites

- Dramatize day
  and night activities

- Carry out a
  simple experiment
  with a flashlight

Thinking ☆ about you...

"Childhood shows
the man as the morning
does the day."
(John Milton, in Lincoln,
1986, p.16)

Materials for Day 1

Learning Activities	Materials
Greetings & Readings	• Theme-related books and favorites from previous units • Lakeshore bedtime story puzzle • Opposites Basic Skills Puzzles • Theme-related puzzles • Pre-written daily message: "Today is _____. Today we will learn about day and night."
Clues & Questions	• Curiosity Cat • Chart divided into two headings, "Day" and "Night" • Marker • Bag with pajamas, a backpack, "day" and "night" opposites puzzle pieces • *Sun*
Rhyme Time	• "Wake Up"
Art	• Easel, easel paper, large brushes, day (white, yellow, green, pink, and other pastels) and night (dark blue, black, white) colors of paint on opposite sides of the easel • *Listen, Learn, and Grow* (Mozart's "Eine kleine Nachtmusik–Night Music") tape
Blocks	• Unit blocks; paper with the following words written on them - "tall," "short," "big," "small" (two of each)
Dramatic Play	• Props for day (e.g., empty cereal boxes, empty milk cartons, clothes, paper, crayon, Legos, books) and night (e.g., alarm clock, pajamas, slippers, robes) activities

Ready, set... CONTINUED

Materials for Day 1

Learning Activities	Materials
Letter	• Beaded letters • Magnetic letters • Variety of paper • Crayons, markers, pencils
Library/ Listening	• *A Child's Book of Art; Good Morning, Good Night; Hot, Cold, Shy, Bold; How Many Stars in the Sky?; Sun; Sun Song* • Other theme-related books and favorites from previous units • *Listen, Learn, and Grow* tape
Manipulatives	• Day and night sorting pictures made from magazine pictures mounted on cardboard • Two pieces of paper with the "day" written on one and "night" written on the other • Opposites Basic Skills Puzzles • Theme-related puzzles (including Lakeshore bedtime story puzzle)
Science	• Flashlight(s) • Small pieces of black construction paper • Scissors, circles of black construction paper pre-cut to fit the lens of the flashlight • Paper punch, paper clip, sharpened pencil, tape • Large piece of black construction paper • Large piece of light blue construction paper
Water	• Water table • Variety of items from your classroom materials to experiment with sink and float (e.g., small/large, heavy/light, soft/hard, long/short) • Chart with two columns and the headings "Sink" and "Float"

Good Morning, Good Night 4s   Day 1

Ready, set... CONTINUED

Materials for Day 1

Learning Activities	Materials
Story Tree	• *Good Morning, Good Night* • Leaf with title
Outside Play	• Large and small balls
Snack Time	• Biscuits, butter, milk
Question/ Reflection	• *Sun* • Chart from Clues & Questions, marker • Opposites Basic Skills Puzzles puzzle pieces for day/night, full/empty, tall/short, far/ near, in/out • Magazine or any other pictures of day and night opposites discussed throughout the day

Day 1

Greetings & Readings

ABOUT 15 MINUTES

▷ As the children and adults arrive, greet each one by name and make comments relating to day and night, such as **Jason, you seem full of energy. You must have had a good sleep last night,** or **Nakia, what did you do during the day yesterday?**

▷ Notice all of the opposites that you could talk about during a discussion of the bedtime story puzzle (i.e., night/day, black/white, boy/girl, young/old, tall/short, or soft/hard). Note also that the little girl has a hearing aid.

▷ Ask the children if they notice anything different about the girl. If they mention the hearing aid (if they don't, you mention it) say, **Remember when we talked about how we use our ears for hearing? Sometimes people cannot hear very well and so they use something called a hearing aid. It makes words and sounds louder for them so they can hear better.**

▷ If the children in your class are familiar with microphones, you could add, **A hearing aid works like a microphone to make sounds louder.**

♪ "The More We Get Together"

Gathering Circle

▷ Discuss Friday's Home Link activity. Sing a favorite song or say a favorite rhyme from a previous unit.

While interacting with the children using the materials, point out how they are related to the theme and each other and provide guidance in their proper use, if necessary. You may want to suggest that a child who has had experience with certain materials work with one who is first exploring the materials.

Are children signing in on a daily basis?

It may be a good idea to provide just some of the opposites puzzles for the first day or two. Twenty would probably be too many for children to experience success with at first. Start with five, observe children's performance and when they have mastered those, add five more. Add more before they get bored. Start with the ones that are most common and related to the concepts in the theme. Be sure to acknowledge alternate answers (e.g., in/out can be inside/outside, enter/exit could be in/out).

Daily Message

▷ Welcome the children to school and then use the previously written message Today is _____ as you write, say and spell the day. Then read the prewritten message for the day. **Today we will learn about day and night.**

▷ Point to each word as you read. Assign jobs for the week.

Clues  & Questions   10–15 MINUTES

▷ Have the "Day and Night" chart and a marker ready. Bring out Curiosity and the bag of day and night objects. Have Curiosity greet the children and say, **Today we are going to learn about day and night. Day and night are called opposites because they are not the same. Opposites are things that are very different from each other.**

▷ Show the first three and the last three pages of Sun as you read the text. **When the sun rises, it is day. When the sun sets, it is night.** Move your hand up and down to represent rises and sets. Repeat the sentences and have the children join you in the hand motions.

▷ Have Curiosity say, **I have some things in this bag. We will hear a clue for each item and you try to guess what it is. Then we will write the name of it here on this chart under day or night.**

▷ Point to the chart and the day and night columns when Curiosity mentions them.

▷ Then give the first clue. **This is something that you wear when you go to bed. Some of them you put on like a shirt and pants. They are usually very soft.**

▷   Give as few clues as possible and listen to all replies. When someone guesses correctly ask, **Do you usually wear these in the day or the night?** *[replies]*

▷   **Yes, you usually wear pajamas at night. I will write the word pajamas right here under the word "Night."**

▷   Take the pajamas out of the bag and invite a child to come hold the object while you write. Point to the night column and spell the word as you write it. Ask the child to put the object on the floor under the column in which it belongs. Thank the helper who can then rejoin the group.

▷   Follow the same procedure for the next items giving the following clues:

This is something that some children carry to school with them. It is sometimes used to carry books, notes, food, or clothes. It can be carried on your back using the arm straps. *[backpack]*

This is what shines in the sky during the daytime. It is round. It usually looks yellow. It is hot. *[sun]*

This is what shines in the sky at nighttime. It is sometimes round. It usually looks white. *[moon]*

    "Penny, Nickel, Dime"

Good Morning, Good Night 4s Day 1

Rhyme Time 🔔   5–10 MINUTES

▷   Read the rhyme through twice. Then have the children repeat each line after you several times (My Turn, Your Turn).

▷   Have them Jump Right In on the second of each pair of rhyming words. Then say the rhyme several times together.

Wake Up

In the morning when I wake
Sun is warm and pancakes bake.

Many things I want to do,
Learn new rhymes and play
   with you.

Soon the dark will come around
When the moon shines
   on the ground.

Learning Labs   45–50 MINUTES

▷   As you tour Learning Labs ask the children to name the labs
and tell what new materials they see.

Lab	Activity and Notes for Facilitating
Art Cooperative Painting	**When you tour:** Show the children the different colored easel paints that are available. Ask which colors they think are for "day" pictures and which colors they think are for "night" pictures. **Directions:** Let the children know that they can use "day" colors or "night" colors to paint a picture of their choice. Suggest that two people can paint a picture together if they would like to. Play "Night Music" as background music while the children paint. **Notes:** Young children can increase their skills in cooperation if given opportunities to do so. You may find that some children will enjoy creating a picture together, while others prefer to work independently. Some will enjoy both at different times. If children gain satisfaction from a cooperative activity, they will be able to generalize this skill to other activities in the future.
Blocks Opposites Structures	**When you tour:** Point out the paper on which you have written the words "tall," "short," "big," and "small." **Directions:** Let the children know that they can use the blocks to build tall, short, big, and small structures. Tell them that an adult will come around to talk with them about their creations and help select the correct piece of paper to label their work. **Notes:** While working with the children in this lab, discuss the concept of opposites represented by each label and structure (i.e., tall/short, big/small). Say, **Things that are not the same and are very different from each other are sometimes called opposites like big and small, short and tall, day and night, high and low.** Throughout the rest of the week, as children are in the Blocks Lab, use opposite words as you talk with them about the structures they are making.
Dramatic Play Day and Night Play	**When you tour:** Point out the new materials in the lab. Ask the children how they could use them. **Directions:** Remind the children that day and night are very different from each other and that people usually do different things during the day than they do during the night. The children might need to have an activity suggested to them to get started in dramatic play. You could say, **I woke up this morning at 6:00 when my alarm rang. Then I crawled out of bed and got ready for school. What did you do? Can you pretend that you are just waking up this morning? What did you do next?** **Notes:** The children may not stick to the theme or act out the day chronologically. That's okay. Now they are manipulating individual materials, using them to suggest what they will do, and practicing "grown-up" roles. They may fix breakfast first, then play with the alarm clock, then go to school, and then take their pajamas off. As their concepts of time and sequence develop, they will be able to act out the whole day chronologically.

Good Morning, Good Night 4s   Day 1

Learning Labs

CONTINUED

Lab	Activity and Notes for Facilitating

Science
Day/Night Flashlight

When you tour: Have the large black and light blue pieces of construction paper taped to the wall or shelf in the lab. Display the flashlight, scissors, black paper, paper circles, hole punch, paper clip, pencil, and tape. Tell the children they will be able to use the flashlight and other materials to make suns and stars shine on the paper.

Directions: Let each child who chooses to do this activity select the tool they want to use to punch holes in the small circles. Provide supervision and assistance as needed as they punch holes in the circles. They can cut out their own circles or use the pre-cut circles. They then use tiny pieces of tape to attach the circle to the lens of the flashlight before they shine it onto the black paper to represent stars in the night sky. Change the distance from which the flashlight is held to get the best effect of stars on the paper. It may have to be held as close as five or six inches from the paper. They can also shine the flashlight, without the star disk, onto the light blue paper to represent the sun in the day sky. Count the holes in the paper. Count the stars that shine on the paper. Are they the same or different?

Notes: If children do not choose all three hole-punching tools, make sure that you punch holes using the one(s) not used. This way the children can see the effect of the different sized holes. Experiment with the paper with holes in it held at different distances from the flashlight with the flashlight shining through the paper.

Water
Sink or Float

When you tour: Show the children the new objects added for the water table. Ask if they know what they could do with the objects. Let them know they will be experimenting with these objects to see which sink and which float, as they did with apples and pumpkins.

Directions: As the children are using the objects in the water, talk with them about why they think a particular item sinks or floats. **Why does this float/sink? Does it float/sink because it is big/small, heavy/light, soft/hard, wood/plastic?**

You can record what sinks and what floats on a chart or piece of paper with the two columns labeled "Sink" and "Float."

Remember to rotate through the labs to give the children five minute and two minute warnings before the Zero Noise Signal.

Sing "This is the Way We Tidy Our Labs" as you clean up and as the transition into Story Tree. While you wait for everyone to arrive for Story Tree, talk with the children about what they did in and liked about their Learning Labs today.

Good Morning, Good Night 4s Day 1

Story Tree

10–15 minutes

Good Morning, Good Night
Author/Illustrator: Michael Grejniec
This softly and brightly illustrated book
will help children learn common opposites.
The simple text describes familiar events
in a girl's and a boy's day, from morning
to night.

Before Reading

▷   Practice reading the book while doing the hand gestures several
times to yourself before reading to the children.

▷   **The name of our book today is Good Morning, Good Night.
The author and illustrator of the book is Michael Grejniec.
Look at the picture he made for the cover of the book.
What do you think this book is about?** *[replies]*

▷   **Let's read and see if any of your ideas are in the book.**

While Reading

▷   **I am going to read the book all the way through without
stopping. Then I'll go back to read it again so we can all act
out the story. Listen carefully.** Read through the book
(it will take about two minutes) using the changes in your voice
and hand motions below to illustrate the concepts. Be sure
that each child gets a chance to see the pictures that illustrate
the concepts.

   It is dark. Lay your head on your hand.

   It is light. Lift your head up and open your eyes wide.

   Good morning. Wave.

▷ **The book was about opposites or things that are very different from each other. We will be learning a lot about day and night and other opposites this week.**

▷ Put the leaf on the tree.

↳ Have children move to the next activity by responding to you when you say:

"If you take a bath or shower in the morning you may go to the next activity. If you take a bath or shower at night you may go to the next activity."

Outside/ Large Motor Play   15–25 MINUTES

▷ In addition to unstructured play which most children will need throughout the week, there are two activities that can be done in which opposite concepts can be learned and reinforced. Introduce them on Day 1 or one on Day 1 and the other on Day 2. Continue using them throughout the week if interest continues. They can even be done indoors.

▷ Large and small balls can be used for rolling, kicking, and throwing. Be sure to mention the sizes of the balls. You could say things like, **Jason, get the large ball and roll it to Alison. Alison, get the ball that is the opposite of the one you have now. Yes, the opposite of large is small. Roll it to Jason.**

▷ You can play a Simon Says type game using opposites. Pick a Simon and a Simone. Have them alternate taking turns telling the others what to do. You may have to whisper the opposite words to Simon and Simone. Have them say, **Jump high. Jump low. Take a short step. Take a long step. Walk fast. Walk slowly.**

▷ For this activity it is not important to play the game in the traditional way in which the children can only move if Simon says, "Simon says," before the instruction. The focus here is on opposites and following simple directions.

 Return to the class in pairs of opposites (e.g., one boy and one girl, one tall and one short, one with black shoes and one with white shoes).

Snack Time

5–15 MINUTES

▷ Discuss who eats biscuits at breakfast and who eats them at dinner. **Sometimes we eat the same foods at breakfast that we eat at dinner. Some foods we only eat at breakfast and some foods we only eat at dinner.**

▷· Discuss favorite breakfast and dinner foods including your own. Talk about whose cup is empty and whose is full.

 "Wake Up"

Good Morning, Good Night 4s Day 1

Question/ Reflection **?**

5–15 MINUTES

▷ Display the chart from Clues & Questions. Have the following Opposites Basic Skills Puzzles puzzle pieces you have discussed today available (i.e., day/night, in/out, far/near from Story Tree, tall/short from Blocks, and full/empty from Snack). Say, **Let's talk about some of the things we learned today about day and night. We talked about some day and night things earlier today. Who can remember what we wrote here in the "Day" column?** [replies]

▷ **Yes, we wrote the word "backpack" because that is something that is usually used in the daytime.**

▷ Repeat the same procedure for the pajamas, the day (sun) puzzle piece, the night (moon) puzzle piece and any other words you wrote on the list. Have the children act out some of the words, for instance putting on the backpack or pajamas and sleeping and waking up.

▷ Then say, **Can anyone think of any more words of day and night things that we can add to our list?** [replies]

▷ Try to keep the focus on things that were discussed in class today, such as sun/moon, or the opposites represented by the puzzle pieces you have with you. If necessary, in order to stimulate a discussion, you may need to use the puzzle pieces or other pictures or give a few clues such as, **What is in the sky during the day? What is in the sky during the night?** Keep this activity short, adding just one or two words to each column. Ask the children to pick the correct column and as you write the word, have a child come and hold up the corresponding picture or puzzle piece.

Looking Back   GOOD MORNING, GOOD NIGHT 4s

	What went well?	What would I do differently?
GREETINGS & READINGS ✋ Gathering Circle Daily Message		
CLUES & QUESTIONS 🐈		
RHYME TIME 🔔		
LEARNING LABS — Art		
Blocks		
Dramatic Play		
Letter		
Library/Listening		
Manipulatives		
Sand/Water		
Science		
Small Group		
(Other)		
STORY TREE 🌳		
OUTSIDE/LARGE MOTOR PLAY		
SNACK TIME 🍎		
QUESTION/ REFLECTION ?		
HOME LINK 🏠		
Additional Notes		

Home Link 🏠♡

▷ **When you go home today, tell your family that you learned about day and night and other opposites today. Talk with them about the different things that they do in the day and in the night.**

Departure

▷ Be sure to say good-bye to each child and family individually. Remind them of the Home Link activity and sing "I'll Miss You."

What Else  Can We Get Into?

- Take a trip to the library to find more books related to the unit. Use the Resource Corner list as your guide.

- Make clouds on paper or directly on the art table using shaving cream. The texture and temperature of the shaving cream will help children expand their tactile experiences and add to the development of their sense of touch.

- Take a dark piece of construction paper with several small items (e.g., a leaf, a moon cut from paper, a key) outside. Put the paper with items spaced out on top of the paper in the sun. Leave them in the sun for as long as possible, at least several hours, depending on the sun's intensity that day. You may have to continue this experiment over more than one day. Note what happens to the paper in the areas covered by the items. If you have a very bright, sunny window you could put these objects on the windowsill.

Good Morning, Good Night 4s Day 1

Slavin, R.E., & Madden, N.A., *One Million Children: Success for All.* © Corwin Press Inc.

Appendix 4.2.
Mr. Gumpy's Outing

by John Burningham

STORY SUMMARY

One fine day, Mr. Gumpy decided to take some of his friends on a ride in his boat. Before boarding the boat, each friend was given an instruction they would need to follow in order to ride on Mr. Gumpy's boat. However, after a while, no one followed Mr. Gumpy's instructions and the boat tipped over and everyone fell into the river. Luckily, everyone knew how to swim and were able to reach the river bank safely and in time for tea!

MATERIALS

- Star Sheet
- Individual Conference Form
- Book

VOCABULARY

outing   river   squabble

DAY 1

STORY INTRODUCTION

Our story is about a man named Mr. Gumpy and an adventure he and his friends had one afternoon. Look at the book's cover. What do you think Mr. Gumpy and his friends did? What do think will happen to them? Can you name some of Mr. Gumpy's friends? Let's read our story and find out how the day will turn out for *Mr. Gumpy's Outing.*

INTERACTIVE STORY READING

Begin reading the story, stopping when appropriate to ask predictive, summative, and inferential questions that will motivate children to interact with the story. Depending on the length and complexity of the story, select approximately five interactive story reading questions.

Page 2: Where did Mr. Gumpy live?

  (He lived near a river.)

Page 3: What do you think Mr. Gumpy will do today? Why?

Page 4: What did Mr. Gumpy ask the children not to do? Why?

   (He asked them not to squabble on the boat.)

Page 6: What did Mr. Gumpy tell the rabbit? Why?

   (Mr. Gumpy told the rabbit not to hop on the boat.)

Page 8: What do you think Mr. Gumpy will tell the cat? Why?

Page 10: Why do you think Mr. Gumpy doesn't want the dog teasing the cat?

Page 12: What did Mr. Gumpy tell the pig? Why?

   (Mr. Gumpy told the pig not to muck about on the boat.)

Page 14: What do you think Mr. Gumpy will tell the sheep? Why?

Page 16: What did Mr. Gumpy tell the chickens? Why?

   (Mr. Gumpy told the chickens not to flap around on the boat.)

Page 18: What did Mr. Gumpy tell the calf? Why?

   (Mr. Gumpy told the calf not to trample about on the boat.)

Page 20: What did Mr. Gumpy tell the goat? Why?

   (Mr. Gumpy told the goat not to kick the boat.)

Page 23: What do you think will happen now? Why?

Page 26: How did they get back home?

   (They swam to the bank and walked home across the fields.)

Page 29: How did they end their day?

   (They had a tea party.)

STORY STRUCTURE REVIEW

Encourage children to recall the story title, characters, setting, story problem, and ending.

DAY 2

STORY REVIEW AND INTERACTIVE RETELLING

Briefly review the elements of the story, *Mr. Gumpy's Outing.* Encourage children to recall the story title, characters, setting, problem, and ending. A story map could be used to record this information.

Provide a framework for children to interactively retell the story. The following is a list of activities that will foster communication about story details between teacher and children:

▪ *Interactive Story Circle:* Students take turns elaborating on the details and ideas expressed by the last participant without repeating the sequence but instead try to add to the sequence of events to complete the story.

SC1—Mr. Gumpy lived near the river. One day, he went for an outing on his boat.

SC2—The children asked if they could come along. Mr. Gumpy said yes, but no squabbling.

SC3—The rabbit wanted to come along, too, so Mr. Gumpy said yes, but no hopping on the boat.

SC4—The cat wanted to come along, too, so Mr. Gumpy said yes, but do not chase the rabbit.

SC5—The dog wanted to come, also, so Mr. Gumpy said yes, but do not tease the cat.

SC6—The pig wanted to come, too, so Mr. Gumpy said yes, but no mucking about.

SC7—The sheep wanted to come, too, so Mr. Gumpy said yes, but no bleating.

SC8—The chickens wanted to come, too, so Mr. Gumpy said yes, but no flapping.

SC9—The calf wanted to come, too, so Mr. Gumpy said yes, but no trampling.

SC10—The goat wanted to come, too, so Mr. Gumpy said yes, but no kicking.

SC11—No one listened to Mr. Gumpy. They each did what they were asked not to do, and the boat tipped over.

SC12—Everyone swam back to shore and enjoyed a nice tea party.

- *Sequence Cards:* There may be occasions when story sequencing material can be used to foster the group retelling of the story.
- *Story Dramatization:* Students share the sequence of the story through dramatization. Many stories lend themselves to dramatization.
- *Sharing:* Teacher and children share their favorite story events with one another.
- *Story Maps:* Children organize the story structures to convey the sequence (or path) of the story and pattern of the story.
- *Discussion Prompts:* The answering of higher-order questions lends itself to the understanding and retelling of story elements.

Looking at the size of Mr. Gumpy's boat, how many people or animals do you think should be allowed to ride in the boat at one time?

Who wanted to go on a boat ride with Mr. Gumpy?

Why did Mr. Gumpy tell each of his friends not to do certain things while they were on the boat?

Why did the boat tip over?

What would you have done to prevent Mr. Gumpy's boat from tipping over?

How did the story end?

What important lesson do you think the children and animals learned? Why?

Why is it important to practice boating safety?

Explain how the animals and children could have prevented the boat from tipping over.

What was your favorite part of the story? Why?

STORY CRITIQUE ACTIVITIES

Provide children with an opportunity to share their opinions about the story. Any of the following activities can be used to foster the story critique experience.

- *Thumbs Up or Thumbs Down?* Invite children to respond to a story by either giving it a thumbs up for "Yes, I liked that story," or a thumbs down for "No, I didn't care for that story." Record children's responses on chart paper.

- *Story Rating:* Assist children in developing a story-rating system. As a class, evaluate the story according to the rating criteria.

  For example: 1 star—engaging title   1 star—enjoyable characters
  1 star—eye-catching   1 star—interesting story
  illustrations

- *Story Critique Frames:* Encourage children to tell what they either liked or disliked about the story.

  I liked the story _____ because _____.

  I disliked the story _____ because _____.

- *Story Recommendations:* Encourage children to think of reasons why they would or would not recommend a given story. As a class, write a story recommendation.

STORY EXTENSION ACTIVITIES

- Design a boat that would be large enough to carry Mr. Gumpy and all of his friends.
- Brainstorm a list of rules that Mr. Gumpy should post on his boat.
- Explain why is it important that everyone knows how to swim.
- Design a poster that highlights boating safety procedures.
- Pretend you are one of Mr. Gumpy's friends from the story. Write a letter of apology to Mr. Gumpy.
- Brainstorm a list of water vehicles.
- Read a factual book about boats and record newly learned information on the chart.

INDIVIDUAL STORY CONFERENCE FORM

Name _____ Date _____

Teacher _____ School _____

QUESTIONS FOR INDIVIDUAL STORY RETELLING

1. Recall the name of the story. *(Mr. Gumpy's Outing)*

   _____

2. Recall the characters. *(Mr. Gumpy, children, rabbit, cat, dog, pig, sheep, chickens, calf, and goat were the characters.)*

   _____

   _____

3. Where did Mr. Gumpy and his friends go? *(They went for a boat ride.)*

   _____

   _____

4. What happened on the boat? *(It tipped over and everyone fell into the river.)*

   _____

   _____

5. Why did the boat tip over? *(Everyone was doing what Mr. Gumpy had asked them not to do.)*

   _____

   _____

6. How did the story end? *(Everyone enjoyed a nice tea party.)*

   _____

   _____

7. What was your favorite part of the story?

   _____

   _____

   _____

Slavin, R.E., & Madden, N.A., *One Million Children: Success for All.* © Corwin Press Inc.

5

Roots & Wings

Adding Social Studies, Science,
and Mathematics to Success for All

In the auditorium of a school in a small town in Southern Maryland, 10-year-old Jamal rises to speak. "The chair recognizes the delegate from Crest School," says the chairwoman, a student from the local high school.

He begins, "I'd like to speak in favor of House Bill R130. This bill would tell farmers they couldn't use fertilizer on land that is within 200 feet of the Bay. Fertilizer goes into the Bay and causes pollution and kills fish. Farmers can still grow a lot of crops even if they don't plant close to water, and we will all have a better life if we can stop pollution in the Bay. I yield to questions."

A hand goes up. The chairwoman recognizes a delegate from Washington Elementary.

"How does fertilizer harm the Bay?" she asks. Jamal explains how the fertilizer provides nutrition to algae in the Bay, and when too much algae grows, it deprives the other creatures of oxygen and sunlight. When he finishes, a delegate from Oak Street School is recognized.

"I'm a farmer," says 11-year-old Maria. "I can hardly pay all my bills as it is, and I've got three kids to feed. I'll go broke if I can't fertilize my whole field!"

AUTHOR'S NOTE: Cecelia Daniels and Kathleen Simons contributed to this chapter.

The debate on the bill goes on for more than an hour. Student delegates who are playing the role of water men speak about how their way of life is disappearing because of declining catches due to pollution. Business owners talk about how pollution ruins the local economy.

Finally, the committee amends the bill to prohibit farmers from planting near waterways unless they are poor. The bill passes and later on is voted on by the whole House of Delegates.[1]

It is essential to ensure that every child can read, but this is not enough to fully restructure elementary schools. Students must also know mathematics, social studies, and science. They need to be able to creatively and flexibly solve problems, understand their own learning processes, and connect knowledge from many disciplines.

The opening vignette illustrates one aspect of a program that builds on the base of success established by Success for All. This program, called Roots & Wings, was initially developed, piloted, and disseminated under funding from New American Schools, a private foundation established to create school designs for the 21st century.

Roots & Wings schools use the prekindergarten, kindergarten, reading, tutoring, writing and language arts, and family support integrated services programs of Success for All but adds two major elements. One is an integrated social studies and science program called WorldLab. The other is a new cooperative learning approach to mathematics instruction called Math Wings. These are described in the following sections.

WorldLab

The debate in the "House of Delegates" illustrates WorldLab, one of the most distinctive and innovative elements of Roots & Wings. In WorldLab, students take on roles as people in history, in other countries, or in various occupations. The students in the vignette's "House of Delegates" were participating in a 12-week unit called BayLab. They studied a local waterway, focusing on sources of pollution, watersheds, tides, the water cycle, and the ecology of aquatic organisms. They also learned about government, economics, geography, and politics. Their work on these topics was done in preparation for a model state legislature, in which students write, propose, and debate many bills relating to cleaning up and protecting the waterway. In other WorldLab units, students take on roles as inventors, delegates to the Constitutional Convention, engineers designing efficient vehicles, explorers in the 15th century, and physicians seeking a cure for smallpox. In these simulations, students work in small, cooperative groups to investigate topics of science and social studies. They read books and articles about their topics, write newspapers, broadsides, letters, and proposals, use mathematics skills to solve problems relating to their topics, and use fine arts, music, and computer, video, and other technology to prepare multimedia reports. Students ultimately learn all the usual content of elementary science and social studies (plus much more), but they do so as active participants in the scientific discoveries, historical events, and other political and economic systems they are studying.

The idea behind WorldLab is to make the contents of the entire elementary curriculum useful and relevant to children's daily lives by immersing them in simulations in which knowledge and skills are necessary. One key problem of traditional elementary schooling is that the content students are learning is not immediately useful to them. It is entirely possible to be a happy and successful 10-year-old with no knowledge whatsoever about the American Revolution, the water cycle, how to add fractions, or how to write a persuasive letter. Students may work to please their teachers or parents or to get a good grade, or they may be interested in some parts of the content they are studying, but motivation, curiosity, and insight are certain to be much greater when students need information or skills to solve problems that have meaning to them.

Simulations provide ideal opportunities to make information immediately useful. In a well-designed simulation, students fully identify with the roles they take on. Maria, in the House of Delegates example, is a farmer with serious responsibilities: three children, a mortgage, bills, and taxes. She is also an elected representative to the Maryland House of Delegates. As a real-life kid and as a simulated farmer and delegate, Maria cares about the ecology of the Chesapeake Bay. However, she cares about it from a particular perspective. She pays great attention to information about the effects of fertilizer runoff because this has direct relevance to her role. To participate intelligently in the debates, she has to have a deep understanding of watersheds, erosion, eutrophication, photosynthesis, and the needs of sea life for oxygen, tides, economics, and the economic impact of pollution on the Bay, government, laws, and many other topics. She has used math to solve real economic problems, written impassioned letters to support her views, and read books relating to the Bay to build her understanding of the issues she confronts in her simulated roles. The BayLab unit is not only an interdisciplinary thematic unit. Because of its use of simulations, it is an opportunity to make knowledge and skills not only integrated but also useful.

Simulations can give students an emotional investment in the material they are studying. In a unit called Rebellion to Union, fifth graders received a distressing note from their principals. The note announced taxes (against the classes' simulated economies) on certain activities, such as using the pencil sharpeners, to help support the costs of WorldLab. The students in each class assembled their class governments, wrote back notes of protest, and decided to boycott the pencil sharpeners. After a while, additional notes taxed the use of desks. Some classes moved their desks into the hall and sat on the floor. Exasperated, the principals dissolved the class governments. At this, classes decided to "secede," and wrote a declaration of independence to explain and justify their actions.

Even though they knew it was a simulation, the students were deeply emotionally involved. They wrote letters, picketed the principals' offices, and took great pleasure in defying their authority. When they then read the various drafts of the real Declaration of Independence, they could identify not only with the framers' words and logic but with their emotions. They were really there, not acting out a script but wrestling with similar questions, fears, and uncertainties. Later, the students became delegates to the Constitutional Convention and debated positions appropriate to the interests of their states and occupations. These children will never forget the American Revolution or Constitutional Convention. They were there, in their hearts and minds. They participated in the debates, stood up for their points of view, heard, saw, and felt what it was like. Everything they had learned in a 4-week unit was relevant and important to them.

The world outside the school is a crucial part of the WorldLab program, accessed by means of field studies, telecommunication, computer technology, and the involvement of community resource people. WorldLab units are designed to enhance student motivation and higher-order thinking processes by engaging students in the dynamic interdependence of economic, political, social, physical, and biological systems. This "systems approach" to curriculum development represents a significant departure from traditional curricula because it requires integration rather than compartmentalization of information. In WorldLab, students are continually encouraged to ask questions, collect data, investigate, and predict how elements of one system will affect another system and their own personal outcomes in the ongoing simulation. Yet, students in WorldLab do more than merely study real-world problems; they take an active part in planning and implementing projects that contribute to the community, such as conducting a stream quality survey or participating in efforts to promote the health of a waterway.

The WorldLab process is structured to provide frequent use of scaffolds for scientific experiments and other information-gathering investigations so that students' skills in thinking through the investigation process are continuously honed during their years in WorldLab. The questions that students formulate as they experience a unit become the basis for informational or scientific investigations.

As students conduct a scientific experiment, they learn how to develop a testable hypothesis, describe the procedure for experimentation, identify materials needed, record their data, and communicate their conclusions. Laboratory report formats used in all units assist them in understanding the experimentation process as a tool. Laboratory reporting requirements are simpler in the early grades and become more elaborate as students' skills grow. Figure 5.1 shows an example of a laboratory report filled out by a fourth grader using the Inventors unit.

An information-gathering investigation has a similar scaffold that is used in every WorldLab unit. Students first determine whether the question they are interested in can be investigated. When questions have been narrowed and focused, students learn how to use a variety of resources to find information related to their question. They use classroom books and texts, library books, encyclopedias, CD-ROM information bases, and community members, reached by phone, Internet, or in classroom visits, to piece together the needed information.

Students work as members of a team in all WorldLab activities. Whereas each student is individually accountable for a product related to the topic being explored, the team works together to plan, assist, and provide feedback to each of its members as the work goes on. Team members are responsible for ensuring that each member of the team understands the concepts being presented and is prepared with his or her

Figure 5.1. Sample Student Lab Report

1. Problem: Do different surfaces affect how far a battery will travel?

2. Hypothesis: I think that the battery will go the farthest on the cardboard.

3. Procedure: We made a track. Then put a book under the board. Then we put the cardboard at the end, then the cloth, then the towel.

4. Results: Our table found out the battery went the farthest on the cardboard.

Surface	1	2	3	Average
Cardboard	185 cm	164 cm	159 cm	169.3 cm
Cloth	158 cm	150 cm	134 cm	147 cm
Towel	119 cm	11 cm	118 cm	116 cm

5. Conclusions: Our hypothesis has been supported by the data we had on our experiment. It has been supported because the battery went the farthest on the cardboard.

—Clifford

portion of the work for the team's task. Weekly team scores provide feedback and goals that help the team work together. Scores on a weekly assessment, which use improvement points to allow every student to contribute equally to the team, are one component of the feedback.

Like the other components of Success for All and Roots & Wings, WorldLab units are structured. Units are organized into 5-day cycles of instruction as well as a daily lesson sequence. This provides structure to support both teachers and students as they take on the many extraordinary opportunities that WorldLab provides. The daily cycle is made up of five parts:

Setting the stage: The agenda for the day is laid out, along with several key concept questions. Each student answers the key questions at the end of the day, so students know what they must focus on. Daily goals for cooperation are also established at this time.

Active instruction: Basic information about the science or social studies content being studied is provided using a variety of presentation modes, including interactive discussion, videos, discovery opportunities, or presentations. Relevant process skills and strategies are modeled and practiced. For example, students learn skills needed to glean information from expository text, and they learn how to summarize it for their partners. Last, instructions for subsequent teamwork activities are provided.

Teamwork: Students work in their teams to carry out investigations, gather information, or conduct scientific experiments. Simulation activities are also carried out at this time. Each team member has an individual task that he or she is working on that contributes to the team product.

Time for reflection: At the end of each day, students integrate the information they have gained with the goals for the day. Students review major concepts, discussing them with their teammates; they answer the concept questions and write in their journals to express their understandings of the work done.

Assessment: Assessment is done on a daily basis in daily conferences called "one-to-ones." These provide informal opportunities for the assessment of each student's product and allow for individual goal setting. In addition, a more formal assessment comes at the end of each 5-day cycle and takes a variety of forms. A letter taking a position supported by information gathered during the week, a completed lab report, a summary of information gathered, or a demonstration of mastery of content may be the basis for the end-of-cycle assessment. A sample WorldLab lesson is provided in Appendix 5.1 at the end of the chapter.

WorldLab is a laboratory in which students can use and enhance the skills they are learning in other components of the Roots & Wings program, including reading, writing, and mathematics. Some of the materials included in WorldLab units are designed to be used during reading and language arts periods, and there is a close integration of reading and writing activities with WorldLab themes. Likewise, mathematics skills required in WorldLab investigations and simulations often become the subject of lessons in a mathematics class. Physical education, music, and the visual arts are integral components of WorldLab, used to enhance student investigations and participation in simulations.

The BayLab unit for Grades 4 and 5 is illustrative of the key components of the WorldLab model:

- A design that promotes an understanding of the interdependence of economic, political, biological, and physical systems
- Use of simulation, group investigation, experimentation, and cooperative learning
- Involvement of community resource people
- Encouragement of problem solving and other higher-order thinking processes
- Projects, completed by students, that help solve community problems

In the simulation component of the BayLab unit, students become citizens of a fictional place called Baytown, where they have a simulated family and occupation (such as farmer, builder, water man, etc.). Students receive incomes in their occupations but must pay taxes and bills for food, clothing, utilities, and shelter. In addition, students experience various "life events," which are pleasant and not-so-pleasant occurrences, such as inheriting a sum of money or needing a washing machine repaired. Other events occur that affect the income they earn in their occupations, such as a decrease or increase in the fish harvest or additional people moving into Baytown. Community resource people, such as water men and farmers, are asked to share their knowledge about their occupations' impact on the bay with students. Students are engaged in activities that encourage them to think about different viewpoints on environmental issues. They quickly begin to realize that people in different occupations and family situations may have quite dissimilar perspectives about problems facing the bay.

BayLab also engages students in a series of lessons designed to lead to investigations of important problems and topics that affect the bay and how these may affect their simulated lives in BayLab. Students try to identify "mystery objects" from the bay, investigate plant and animal life in the waterways near the school, experience food webs and food chains, and learn about watersheds and the impact of oil spills on aquatic environments. They also carry out experiments to determine the effects of water salinity and dissolved oxygen levels on ecosystem relationships, using lab report forms designed to guide them in learning the steps in the scientific process. As BayLab lessons progress, student-generated questions about the bay are continuously posted in the classroom. Using these questions, cooperative teams begin to investigate topics about the bay, such as "What causes the yearly algae bloom in the bay?" or "Why have sea grasses in the bay been disappearing?" Students give presentations describing the outcomes of their research on specific BayLab topics. Students are continuously asked to estimate and predict outcomes as well as analyze and interpret data about the bay. Students also begin a project to enhance local waterways, such as participating in a Save Our Streams survey of stream quality in their area or painting storm drains to warn people that pollutants should not be poured into storm drains.

Students are informed that they will next have an opportunity to run for election in a simulated State Legislature so that they can sponsor bills to help the bay. In writing campaign speeches, students are asked to use the information they have learned about the bay to propose bills they promise to introduce if elected. Students learn how to register to vote in the upcoming BayLab election and conduct extensive campaigns. Issues that arise in campaigns may require students to do additional research about particular bay topics. Once the election has been held and the results announced, the class helps the elected delegates and state senators write bills to help enhance bay life. Again, students use the information learned about the bay in writing and revising these bills. Bills that are recommended by the classroom delegates and state senators are introduced at the culminating activity of the BayLab unit: a meeting of the BayLab Model State Legislature. Students from different classes (sometimes different schools) and their elected representatives come together to deliberate about bills to preserve and enhance the bay. In committee meetings and on the floor of the House of Delegates and State Senate, students have opportunities to bring to bear the knowledge they have learned in debating and revising submitted bills. A local notable may act as governor and will sign or veto the bills passed by the model legislature. Once the legislature session is completed, taxes are assessed for any programs that require new revenues (with accompanying groans from the tax-payers).

WorldLab units include the following:

Trees (First Grade)

In the primary wing, young botanists are busy classifying leaves that they collected at home and on the school grounds. These students are going beyond the usual first-grade activity of sorting autumn leaves by colors. They are interested in how much green is left in their leaves. They are learning about chlorophyll and its role in producing food for the tree. Each team of scientists has adopted a tree and is keeping a journal to record any changes they observe throughout the school year. They need to know not only that leaves change color in the fall but also how this affects their tree. These first graders will measure their tree, plant bulbs around it, and conduct experiments to help them answer questions that they have about plant life. Students build thinking, reading, and writing skills as they complete lab reports, investigate different kinds of trees, and perform a play for their parents about the importance of trees. Last, students decide where more trees should be planted in their community and plan for their care.

Harvests (First Grade)

As students prepare for Thanksgiving, they first investigate modern farming practices and simple economic principles that affect both farmers and consumers. They grow their own plants, comparing seed and vegetative propagation. To find out why we celebrate the third Thursday in November, first graders travel back in time and investigate the origins of our modern Thanksgiving celebration. They explore the relationship between the Pilgrims and the Northeast Woodland Indians and participate in the customs and traditions of both. Last, students recreate the colorful sights, sounds, and aromas of the First Thanksgiving or Harvest Home. The students host parents and other visitors as they celebrate their harvest of new ideas.

Birds (First Grade)

Young scientists huddle around the incubator anxiously awaiting the arrival of the new chicks. First graders gasp and watch in awe as the young chicks break through their shells and enter the world. These primary students have become bird experts by carefully observing the hatching eggs, candling eggs, and observing birds outside their window. As students try to learn more about birds, they discover that few field guides are written for first graders. They decide to solve this problem by creating a field guide of the birds native to their state and sending copies of the guide to WorldLab classrooms across the country. Information about local birds in every

WorldLab site creates an extensive and easy-to-use field guide for all WorldLab schools to place in their media centers.

Changes (Second Grade)

"Oh, you've gotten so big!" How often do second graders hear that exclamation? Changes is a one-cycle introduction to WorldLab and a companion unit to Life Cycles. By studying changes in the seasons, trees, birds, and themselves, children learn that there are many predictable patterns, trends, and cycles in nature. In Changes, students gather and record data about themselves in the beginning of second grade and compare it to the same data collected at the end of second grade during the Life Cycles unit. Students learn about their growth and development as they marvel at the changes taking place in themselves in just one school year.

Life Cycles (Second Grade)

"Can we keep them?" This is a question that students will ask when they receive a special delivery package from Nanny Nurture. The package contains butterfly and praying mantis eggs. Their investigation takes them on a journey through the animal kingdom to learn about different animal groups, their life cycles, and their needs. The classroom becomes a living laboratory as caterpillars turn into butterflies and praying mantises hatch from egg cases, molt, and grow. Students develop skills in recording data and conducting experiments. At the end of the unit, students debate the question, "Can we keep them?" and defend their position on this issue. Students plan and plant a butterfly garden.

Adventures (Third Grade)

Adventurers-in-training embark on a quest to meet the challenges initiated by the Map Maniac, a mysterious world traveler on a mission to do good deeds around the world. Adventures, Africa, and Japan are units designed to be taught consecutively. They focus on geography, economics, and physical and earth sciences. As part of their preparation for worldwide explorations, students learn map and research skills as they design a visitors' center and map of their school community. Along the way, they identify elements common to all communities. The students' last challenge is to conduct experiments about buoyancy and navigation as they prepare to simulate a ship's crew on a voyage of discovery. They apply their findings while they make critical design decisions and build a clay ship that carries "passengers" and cargo. They learn about the economic concepts of scarcity, supply and demand, and opportunity costs as they choose what to bring on their expeditions. Last, they set sail for Africa on their first trip as official adventurers!

Africa (Third Grade)

"Land ho!" voyagers shout as the shore of Africa emerges along the horizon. The ship approaches land and anticipation builds as the travelers set foot on the

African continent. Rehema, a young girl who lives in a Tanzanian village, needs help. Being the daughter of a game reserve tour guide, Rehema is torn between her desire to see the wildlife continue to thrive and the needs of the people surrounding the national parks for additional land for farming. The Map Maniac challenges students to learn more about the land, people, animals, and their common ecosystem. The ultimate goal is to devise a plan to use the natural resources in an economical fashion that still meets the needs of both animal and human communities. Students use a village council as a forum to negotiate and reach a win-win resolution to Rehema's conflict.

Japan (Third Grade)

Third graders fly on to their next challenge, which is to help citizens of Kobe, Japan, rebuild their community following the devastating earthquake of January 1995. Students learn about the causes of earthquakes and use this information to help them design buildings to withstand earthquakes. They investigate the theory of plate tectonics, conduct experiments to understand the movements that occur during an earthquake, and study instruments used to measure earthquakes. Using spaghetti and minimarshmallows as their materials, students construct building models to withstand earthquakes. As students learn about the strengths of different shapes and the effects of various foundations, they continue to revise their design to make it as earthquake resistant as possible. The unit concludes with an investigation of elements of a Japanese community. Students customize the exterior of their buildings to meet the needs of the Japanese community. They establish a concrete understanding of the interdependence of social and environmental systems in a community.

Encounters (Fourth Grade)

Students learn how the interactions among three major cultural groups—African, European, and Native American—shaped the development of our nation. Instead of merely memorizing a litany of facts about the origins of our nation, students become historians and scientists-in-training. They explore the methods historians use by studying a local historic site. They become scientists as they investigate how scientific discoveries affected early U.S. societies. Students recreate Ben Franklin's Traveling Electrical Show, using Franklin's original experiments in static electricity. The unit includes both authentic experiments to replicate and primary historical documents to investigate. Later in the unit, teams experiment with methods for growing typical colonial crops. They collect data to help them decide how to produce the most bountiful harvest for their families. Ultimately, teams harvest and enjoy their crops. Students develop their roles as Africans, Europeans, or Native Americans during specific historical periods by composing "Day in the Life" stories about a typical day in the life of the characters they are role-playing. Writing historical fiction personalizes learning and helps students appreciate what people thought and felt as historically significant events unfolded. Students may use computers to research and publish their "Day in the Life" stories and then assemble them into class books. At the conclusion of the unit, students plan and present an Encounters Fair to share their learning and insights with the local community.

Inventors (Fourth Grade)

Four design engineers are huddled around their newest prototype. "Looking at our data so far, I think the rear spoiler has really made drag go down." "I think so too, but we have to make sure the extra weight doesn't make it tip over. It might change the center of gravity. I think we need to run some more trials." It's time for lunch, and the engineers carefully place the model inside a case to keep its design secret. Is this a glimpse inside General Motors or Chrysler? No! It's a WorldLab classroom where fourth and fifth graders are designing vehicles as part of a unit called Inventors.

This class of fourth graders is working cooperatively, simulating engineering design teams. Their goal is to design the most efficient vehicle they can. With the help of a volunteer engineer, they complete experiments about forces, Newton's laws of motion, aerodynamic shapes, friction, and balance. They *learn* the scientific method because they must use it every day.

Designing the vehicle is only one part of this integrated unit. The students also read biographies of famous inventors and investigate the effect great inventions have had on their lives. They understand the inventive process that these famous inventors used because they are writing plans for an invention of their own.

Archaeology (Fifth Grade)

Fifth graders dig in to discover the past. Archaeology is a companion unit for Encounters, as it is designed to enhance the students' historical research. Students discover how the scientific process is an essential tool in uncovering information from the past. They analyze artifacts, experiment with decomposition, and create their own fossils. Young archaeologists create their own archaeological site in a shoe box. Students incorporate their writing skills as they write stories to match the contents of their archaeological sites. Teams excavate each other's sites and make inferences to piece together the story that discoveries unmask. They investigate the best ways to preserve clues so that historians in the future can discover their past.

BayLab (Fifth Grade)

This unit is designed to help students understand the problems of water pollution that confront many communities in today's world. Students become science detectives as they investigate who or what is responsible for the pollution problems of the Nashua River in New Hampshire. Students learn about the town of Nashua and its citizens through newspapers, letters, books, and video testimonies. They are then introduced to the basic concepts of physical science. They study and experiment with matter and its properties. Students receive a sludge sample of the Nashua River. They analyze the sludge and discover some substances that belong in a river and others that do not. The primary objective of this unit is accomplished as students find out what is causing the pollution and make specific suggestions to the people of Nashua for cleaning up the river.

Rebellion (Fifth Grade)

Chairs are stacked in piles against the classroom walls and students sit with their books on the floor. Are these students being punished? No, they are boycotting the use of their chairs to protest the unfair taxes being levied upon them by their principal. The tax on the use of their chairs is just one of the numerous taxes their principal is imposing. Is she levying taxes because she miscalculated this year's school budget? No, the simulation teaches students about the feelings of the American colonists prior to the Revolutionary War. Students pretend to be American colonists. Each team is a colony, and their challenge is to determine the fate of America and whether or not to claim independence from Great Britain. Students learn about the events of the period through newspaper accounts by Loyalists and Patriots. As tensions rise, students conduct debates and cast their final votes for or against independence from Britain. They compare their experiences with that of the delegates at the Second Continental Congress and examine the language of the Declaration of Independence. Students finish this unit with a knowledge of the events that led to the Revolutionary War and an understanding of the lives and motivations of early Americans.

MathWings

MathWings, the Roots & Wings mathematics program for Grades 1 through 6, is based on the standards of the National Council of Teachers of Mathematics (NCTM) (1989) and correlates well with the Principles and Standards for School Mathematic 2000. A program to prepare students for mathematics in the 21st century needs to actively involve students in the conceptual development and practical application of their mathematics skills. The MathWings program reflects a balance of solid mathematical conceptual development, problem solving in real-world applications, and maintenance of necessary mathematics skills.

Students enter school with a great deal of mathematical knowledge. They know about combining and separating, halves and wholes, and so on. What they need is a bridge between their preexisting knowledge and the formal representation of this knowledge in mathematical symbols. This requires the use of manipulatives, demonstrations, and discovery to help students build mathematical understanding. MathWings uses cooperative learning at all age levels while incorporating problem solving in real situations, skill practice and reinforcement for efficiency in application, calculator use, alternative assessments, writing, connections to literature and other disciplines, and application to the students' world and personal experiences. Although students help each other learn, they are always individually accountable for their own learning and are frequently assessed on their progress in understanding and using math (see Slavin, 1995).

Critical Components of MathWings

The MathWings program objectives are a close fit with the Principles and Standards for School Mathmatics (NCTM, 2000) objectives. The Standards advocate emphasizing problem solving rather than rote calculation with algorithms. MathWings lessons involve the students in problem solving in "real" situations to give validity and purpose to their mathematics explorations and in daily problem solving as part of the routine of math class. MathWings lessons also make connections to literature, science, art, and other subjects, as well as students' experiences to provide this real-world problem-solving context.

Two other strands of the Standards are mathematical reasoning and representaton. Students develop their ability to think through and solve mathematical problems when they use manipulatives to develop concepts and then represent what is actually happening with symbols. MathWings units are constructed to develop concepts from the concrete to the abstract so that each step of the reasoning is clarified and represented. The Standards also promote the use of calculators for developing concepts and exploring advanced problem-solving situations rather than checking answers or replacing skills and mental math. MathWings students use calculators in this way to increase both their mathematical reasoning skills and the scope and complexity of the problems they can solve and to focus their energy on mathematical reasoning rather than mere mechanical calculation.

The NCTM Standards emphasize communication, both oral and written, to clarify, extend, and refine the students' knowledge. MathWings students constantly explain and defend their solutions orally and regularly write in their logbooks. This emphasis on communication extends to the assessments as well. The Standards suggest the use of alternative assessments, which incorporate communication as well as calculation. MathWings units involve the students in many different types of ongoing formal and informal assessment. Intermediate students complete Concept Checks in which they explain their thinking as they solve problems after every few lessons. They work on performance tasks at the end of each unit to use the skills they have learned to solve practical real-world situations and explain and communicate about their thinking. Primary students complete a written assessment at the end of each unit. Teacher observations of both primary and intermediate students at work with manipulatives, collecting data, and so on, and students' written and oral communications are also used to assess understanding.

The use of cooperative learning in MathWings is based on years of research regarding effective strategies for classroom instruction. This research has shown that the cognitive-rehearsal opportunities presented by cooperative learning, as well as the opportunities for clarification and reteaching for students who do not catch a concept immediately, have positive effects on academic achievement. Research has also shown that using cooperative learning in the classroom can have positive effects on interethnic relationships, acceptance of mainstreamed academically handicapped students, student self-esteem, liking of others, and attitudes toward school and teachers (Slavin, 1995). In cooperative learning, students work together to learn; the team's work is not done until all team members have learned the material being studied. This positive interdependence is an essential feature of cooperative learning.

Research has identified three key components that make cooperative-learning strategies effective: team recognition, individual accountability, and equal opportunities for success. In MathWings, as in other Student Team Learning strategies (Slavin, 1995), students work in four-member, mixed-ability teams. Starting in second grade, teams may earn certificates and additional means of recognition if they achieve at or above a designated standard. All teams can succeed because they are working to reach a common standard rather than competing against one another. The team's success depends on the individual learning of all team members; students must make sure that everyone on the team has learned, because each team member must demonstrate his or her knowledge on an individual assessment. Students have an equal opportunity for success in MathWings because they contribute points to their teams by improving over their own individual performance, bringing in their homework, and meeting particular behavior goals set by the teacher, accomplishments that are within the capabilities of every student but that are also demanding for every student. Students who are typically seen as lower achievers can contribute as many points to the team as high achievers.

The MathWings program is designed to use the calculator as a tool, not a crutch. Calculators enable the students to explore and demonstrate concepts in an appealing way. Students discover that they need to check their calculator answers for accuracy because the calculator is only as accurate as the information and process that is keyed into it. Thus, students develop their skills in estimating and predicting outcomes. Students also spend more time actually thinking about math and the processes that will most efficiently solve a given problem rather than focusing completely on tedious and lengthy calculations. Because of the speed of calculation with calculators, students are more willing to try several approaches to solving a problem situation or to reevaluate their answers and try a different method of solution. Last, calculators build students' confidence in mathematics as they receive much positive reinforcement from correct solutions. This leads, in turn, to a greater willingness to tackle more challenging mathematical situations in the belief that they have the ability and the tools to solve them.

Manipulative use is a basic building block of the MathWings program at all levels. Students construct understanding and develop original methods for solving problems using manipulatives. As they work with manipulatives and discuss and defend their thinking, they gradually make the concepts their own. Once a problem can be solved with manipulatives, students draw a picture and then write a number sentence to represent what was happening with the manipulatives as they solved the problem. This gradual progression from concrete to pictorial to abstract provides a solid foundation of understanding on which the students can build. Every method or algorithm can be understood, and even reinvented, with manipulatives, thus replacing rote learning of algorithms with understanding of concepts and ways to efficiently apply them. Once the concepts have been firmly established and students understand how the algorithms work, they move away from using concrete manipulatives. However, manipulatives can be revisited at any time to remediate or extend a concept as needed.

Most MathWings Action Math units have a literature connection, which is an integral part of the concept development. Literature provides a wonderful vehicle for exploring mathematical concepts in meaningful contexts, demonstrating that mathematics is an integral part of human experience. The use of literature incorporates the affective elements and demonstrates the aesthetic aspect of mathematics. Last, the use of literature encourages students to pose problems from real and imaginary situations and to use language to communicate about mathematics.

MathWings involves the students in daily routines that frame each lesson and are efficient ways to provide for team management, problem solving, and skill practice and reinforcement to facilitate efficiency in calculation and application. Once the students have mastered the facts and basic algorithms, they become tools for the students to use as they develop concepts and problem solving. These routines include facts practice at both levels. In Intermediate MathWings, there are weekly timed facts tests to encourage mastery of the basic facts and then practice problems at varying difficulty levels to provide for fluency in the use of the essential algorithms. There are also daily real-world applications in Primary MathWings and daily problem solving in Intermediate.

MathWings has two major forms. Primary MathWings is used in Grades 1 and 2, Intermediate MathWings in Grades 3 through 5. The MathWings program is quite similar at the two levels, with one key exception. In Primary MathWings, the main element of daily lessons, called Action Math, is taught every day to the entire class and an additional interactive bulletin board activity called 15-Minute Math is included daily. Intermediate MathWings also uses Action Math but intersperses Action Math Units with Power Math, which provides individualized work to help students gain facility and confidence in algorithms, remediate gaps in prior skills and concepts, master grade-level material, or accelerate their mathematics skill development. Otherwise, Primary and Intermediate MathWings use similar routines, procedures, and teaching methods, as appropriate to children's age levels.

Primary MathWings

In Primary MathWings, students spend 75 minutes in math daily. There are two start-up routines: 15-Minute Math and Check-In. 15-Minute Math can be done at the beginning of the lesson or at any other time during the school day. It uses an interactive bulletin board that contains activities based on everyday mathematical experiences. Students use a calendar, look at patterns, create a weather graph, keep a tally to show the number of days they have been in school, and do many other "thinking tasks." The activities are revisited repeatedly to provide opportunities for developing fluency with basic math skills. During 15-Minute Math, students also practice their basic facts during a daily 3-minute facts practice session. With a facts partner, students work on a weekly facts game or activity. There is a menu of different games and activities for facts practice.

The lesson begins with Check-In, which lasts approximately 5 minutes. The teacher quickly collects the Home Connection from the night before and assigns partners for the day. A Review to Remember activity gives students a chance to practice their basic facts and other skills that were introduced earlier in the year. Skills and concepts are reviewed and spiraled throughout the school year. Flashback follows the Review to Remember activity and is a time for students to recall mathematics concepts and activities from the previous lesson to build on in the new lesson.

The Primary MathWings lesson is made up of Active Instruction, Teamwork, and Direct Instruction. Active Instruction provides a springboard for new ideas, concepts, terminology, and so forth. It is the part of the lesson that invites students to draw from their background knowledge while discussing new ideas and concepts. This part of the lesson might contain a new literature piece or poem, the teacher might introduce a new problem situation, or the students might brainstorm ideas, create a web, make a list, make observations about something, predict outcomes, or estimate.

Teamwork is intended to provide students with an opportunity to test their ideas, practice what they have discussed in Active Instruction, generate and organize data, and communicate about mathematics. Students in first grade most often work in pairs, especially in the earlier parts of the year. Students in second grade work in pairs or teams, with a greater emphasis on teamwork during the second half of the year. Teachers begin the Teamwork phase of the lesson by clearly explaining and modeling the team or paired activity. In most lessons, students work with manipulatives. Prior to using these manipulatives, students are given approximately 2 minutes to explore. Students then work with a partner or with their team to complete the mathematics activity while the teacher circulates to assist and informally assess them. During Teamwork, students may complete handouts, collect and record data, draw illustrations, or write about the activity.

Direct Instruction is the part of the lesson where the whole class shares the results of Teamwork, analyzes data, and discusses what they have learned. This is also a time for the teacher to clarify confusions, review any terms that have been introduced, and ask specific questions to ensure that the mathematics concepts involved in the lesson activities become clear to students. Sometimes, students write in their Mathematics Log during this part of the lesson.

The closure routines are included in Reflection. During Reflection, students discuss what they have just done. They share what they liked about the lesson, what they have learned, and where they are confused. Then the teacher summarizes the key concepts, reviews vocabulary, and explains the Home Connection assignment. Reflection ends with Team Wrap-Up to have the students get ready for the next class.

Intermediate MathWings

In Intermediate MathWings, students spend at least 60 minutes daily in their mathematics class, although 75 minutes is recommended. Daily lessons consist of three components: Check-In, Action Math or Power Math, and Reflection.

The first 15-minute segment is Check-In, an efficient class start-up routine in which the teams regularly complete one challenging real-world problem and then discuss their various strategies together. They also complete a facts or fluency study process twice a week and briefly check homework every day.

The next 40 to 55 minutes in either Action Math or Power Math is the heart of the lesson. When the class is doing an Action Math unit, the lesson involves the students in active instruction, teamwork, and assessment. During active instruction, the teacher and students interact to explore a concept and its practical applications and skills. The teacher may present a challenging problem for students to explore with manipulatives to construct a solution, challenge the teams to use prior knowledge to discover a solution, and ask the teams to find a pattern to develop a rule.

During teamwork, the students come to consensus about their solutions to problems, their understanding of concepts, and their thinking. A team member is chosen randomly to share his or her ideas with the class. Then, students individually practice similar problems with teammates available for support. The team members check answers with each other and rehearse to be sure that every team member can explain them.

At the end of the teamwork, there is a brief feedback opportunity. The teacher randomly chooses a team member to share the ideas or solutions of the team and to explain their thinking. This enables the teacher to assess the understanding of the group as a whole and ensures that teammates are invested in making sure that all members of the team are mastering the concepts.

The final portion of an Action Math lesson is assessment. One or more brief problems are used as a quick individual assessment of mastery of the concept or skill explored in the lesson.

Intermediate classes intersperse 1-week to 2-week Power Math units among Action Math units. During these units, the 40- to 55-minute heart of the lesson involves each student in remediating, refining, or accelerating his or her skills. This component is an adaptation of Team Accelerated Instruction, an individualized math program found to be effective in several studies (Slavin, Leavey, & Madden, 1984). Power Math covers a range of skills from basic addition to statistics and algebra. Students work at their own pace on the skill that they need to practice, completing check-outs and mastery tests successfully to move to another skill they need to practice. Teammates check each other's work and provide help as needed. Students who have mastered the basic skills explore accelerated units at their own pace. The teacher teaches mini-lessons to small groups of students (working on the same skills) gathered from various teams while the other students continue to work individually.

The last 5-minute segment of class is Reflection. This is an efficient routine to bring closure to the class time. During Action Math units, reflection involves a quick summary of the key concepts by the teacher. During both Action Math units and

Power Math units, homework sheets are passed out, and a short entry is written in the MathWings Logbook in response to a writing prompt about the lesson.

All students should not only be given the opportunity to establish a solid foundation in mathematics but also the opportunity to extend and stretch their knowledge and experience in mathematics. Thus, a program of mathematics should include a structure to accommodate a diversity of abilities and prior mathematical knowledge, while ensuring that all students experience the depth, breadth, and beauty of mathematics. The Math Wings curriculum incorporates this philosophy in its development.

Samples of Primary and Intermediate MathWings lessons are included in Appendix 5.2 at the end of this chapter.

Future of Roots & Wings

Roots & Wings is the future of Success for All. It is enormously important to ensure that every child succeeds in reading, but this is not enough. Every child must also become a thoughtful, strategic, and enthusiastic scientist, mathematician, historian, economist, and geographer. Children must know how to find and integrate information, solve problems, use their minds well. This is the goal of Roots & Wings.

There will always be schools that are only interested in the components that constitute Success for All, just as there will be schools that are only interested in MathWings or WorldLab. Each of these can stand on its own and make a contribution to student success. As of Fall 1999, only 130 of the 1500 Success for All schools were also implementing MathWings, WorldLab, or both, but this number is growing rapidly. We hope and expect that many schools will seek a broader, coherent vision of what elementary schools could achieve with all students, a comprehensive approach encompassing curriculum, instruction, professional development, prevention, early intervention, and school organization, touching on all subjects and grade levels. These are the schools for which Roots & Wings was designed.

Research on Roots & Wings, summarized in Chapter 8, shows that the full program can add to the effects of Success for All. In particular, studies of 10 early adopters of MathWings found substantial gains in student achievement on state accountability measures; in every case, gains for schools with MathWings were greater than those for their respective states (Madden, Slavin, & Simons, 1999). Research on WorldLab is at a much earlier stage, but schools implementing WorldLab have shown significant gains on measures of social studies, science, and writing, as well as reading (Slavin & Madden, 2000).

Note

1. This vignette was adapted from Slavin, Madden, Dolan, and Wasik (1994). All names are pseudonyms.

CHAPTER 5 APPENDIX

Appendix 5.1. Solutions, Solutions

Appendix 5.2. Examples of Primary and Intermediate MathWings Lessons

Appendix 5.1.
Solutions, Solutions

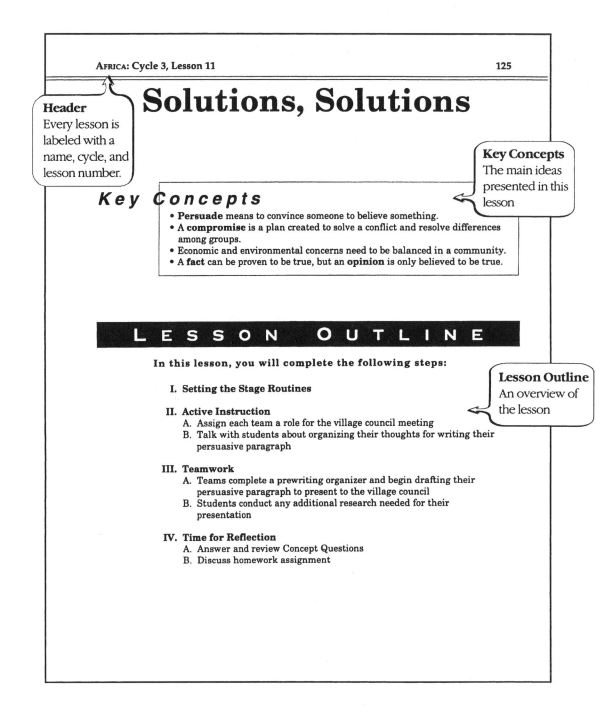

Solutions, Solutions

Header
Every lesson is labeled with a name, cycle, and lesson number.

Key Concepts

Key Concepts
The main ideas presented in this lesson

- **Persuade** means to convince someone to believe something.
- A **compromise** is a plan created to solve a conflict and resolve differences among groups.
- Economic and environmental concerns need to be balanced in a community.
- A **fact** can be proven to be true, but an **opinion** is only believed to be true.

LESSON OUTLINE

In this lesson, you will complete the following steps:

I. **Setting the Stage Routines**

II. **Active Instruction**
   A. Assign each team a role for the village council meeting
   B. Talk with students about organizing their thoughts for writing their persuasive paragraph

III. **Teamwork**
   A. Teams complete a prewriting organizer and begin drafting their persuasive paragraph to present to the village council
   B. Students conduct any additional research needed for their presentation

IV. **Time for Reflection**
   A. Answer and review Concept Questions
   B. Discuss homework assignment

Lesson Outline
An overview of the lesson

126 LESSON 11: SOLUTIONS, SOLUTIONS

Advance Preparation

Advance Preparation
Things that need to be prepared before the lesson is taught

Cut up the names of roles on the "Role Assignment Sheet." Figure out the best way to assign roles for the village council meeting. One idea is to put the names in a basket or hat and have teams pick one. Half the teams will take on the role of their team's animal, and the other teams will take on the role of village farmers, Ashraf, or a Maasai tribe. Fold up "Role Cards" and give to appropriate teams to display on their tables during the simulation.

Students will write a persuasive paragraph stating whether or not they feel that the farmers should be able to use some of the land of the Serengeti. The purpose of this lesson is for students to take on the perspective of another person and to apply the facts that they have learned in this unit.

Materials

Materials
List of items needed during the lesson

Per teacher:
"Role Assignment Sheet" to assign roles for village council meeting

Per team:
Assigned "Role Card" to display on their table during the simulation

Objectives
What students should be able to do by the end of the lesson

OBJECTIVES
Students will:
- Express their opinion in a proposal to resolve a conflict
- Use persuasive language to convince others that their opinion is correct
- Identify ways to balance economic and environmental issues in a community

PRODUCTS OR ASSESSMENTS

- Completed prewriting organizer for their persuasive paragraph

Products or Assessments
List of written products to be completed by the student and checked by the teacher during One-to-Ones

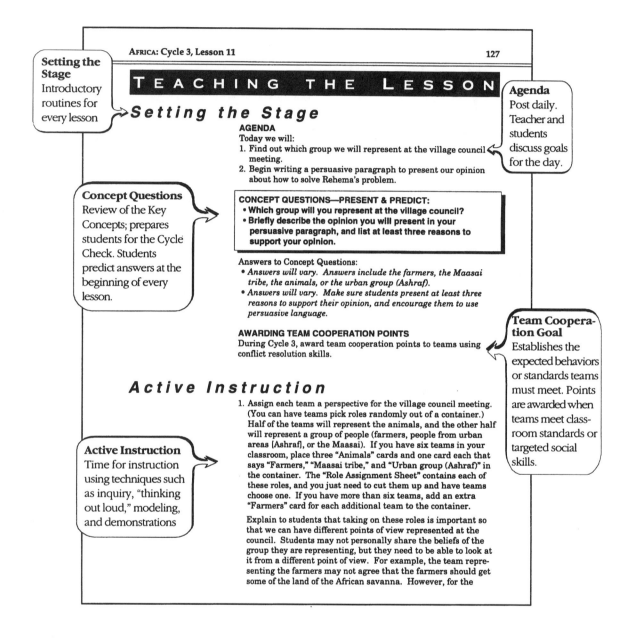

Setting the Stage
Introductory routines for every lesson

TEACHING THE LESSON

Setting the Stage

AGENDA
Today we will:
1. Find out which group we will represent at the village council meeting.
2. Begin writing a persuasive paragraph to present our opinion about how to solve Rehema's problem.

Agenda
Post daily. Teacher and students discuss goals for the day.

Concept Questions
Review of the Key Concepts; prepares students for the Cycle Check. Students predict answers at the beginning of every lesson.

CONCEPT QUESTIONS—PRESENT & PREDICT:
• **Which group will you represent at the village council?**
• **Briefly describe the opinion you will present in your persuasive paragraph, and list at least three reasons to support your opinion.**

Answers to Concept Questions:
• *Answers will vary. Answers include the farmers, the Maasai tribe, the animals, or the urban group (Ashraf).*
• *Answers will vary. Make sure students present at least three reasons to support their opinion, and encourage them to use persuasive language.*

AWARDING TEAM COOPERATION POINTS
During Cycle 3, award team cooperation points to teams using conflict resolution skills.

Team Cooperation Goal
Establishes the expected behaviors or standards teams must meet. Points are awarded when teams meet classroom standards or targeted social skills.

Active Instruction

Active Instruction
Time for instruction using techniques such as inquiry, "thinking out loud," modeling, and demonstrations

1. Assign each team a perspective for the village council meeting. (You can have teams pick roles randomly out of a container.) Half of the teams will represent the animals, and the other half will represent a group of people (farmers, people from urban areas [Ashraf], or the Maasai). If you have six teams in your classroom, place three "Animals" cards and one card each that says "Farmers," "Maasai tribe," and "Urban group (Ashraf)" in the container. The "Role Assignment Sheet" contains each of these roles, and you just need to cut them up and have teams choose one. If you have more than six teams, add an extra "Farmers" card for each additional team to the container.

Explain to students that taking on these roles is important so that we can have different points of view represented at the council. Students may not personally share the beliefs of the group they are representing, but they need to be able to look at it from a different point of view. For example, the team representing the farmers may not agree that the farmers should get some of the land of the African savanna. However, for the council meeting, the students have to present the opinion of the village farmers.

2. Give each team the appropriate "Role Card" for their assigned role. These cards are included with this lesson, and you may want to laminate them. You will need to fold them so that they can be displayed on teams' tables. Fold each card twice to display the names on the front and back of the card and the concerns listed on the inside. The concerns are listed to sum up for each team how their group feels about the issue. Make sure students set their role cards out on their tables so that they can see which group each team will be representing at the council.

3. Talk with students about how they will prepare for the council meeting. Each team is to write a proposal for what they think should be done with the land of the African savanna. Remind students that they are taking on the role of a particular group and that they need to think about how their group feels about this issue.

Ask:
Do you know what a proposal is?
(A proposal is a plan.)

Students will write their proposal or plan in the form of a paragraph. Since we are trying to convince others that our plan will work, we will write a **persuasive** paragraph. Talk with students about using persuasive language in their paragraph.

Ask:
What does *persuade* mean?
(Persuade means to convince someone to believe something.)

How do you persuade someone?
(You persuade someone by using convincing language and by presenting facts to support your position.)

Discuss examples of persuasive language with students.

Ask:
When is a time that you have used persuasion before?
(Answers may vary. Students will probably give examples involving convincing their parents to let them do something or go somewhere, convincing their teacher not to give them homework, convincing their friend to do something, etc.)

How did you persuade this person? What types of things did you say to convince them?
(Answers may vary. Accept any logical responses. Focus on the type of language they used to sound convincing to the other person.)

Good examples of persuasive language can be found in advertising campaigns. Discuss commercials and other advertisements and how advertisers try to persuade consumers to buy their products.

4. Students will use the writing process to write their persuasive paragraphs. Review the steps of the writing process with students.

Ask:
What is the first step of the writing process?
(The first step of the writing process is prewriting.)

Part of prewriting is to identify the **topic, audience, purpose,** and **form** (TAPF) for our paragraph. Post the following on the board and elicit responses from students. See the sample answers below:

> **Topic:** A plan for how to use the land of the African savanna
> **Audience:** Village council
> **Purpose:** To convince others that my plan is the best solution
> **Form:** Persuasive paragraph

The next step in prewriting is to complete a graphic organizer. This will enable students to organize their thoughts before they start writing. Students can use an organizer similar to the one below. Students can be as creative as they wish with their graphic organizer.

My Opinion

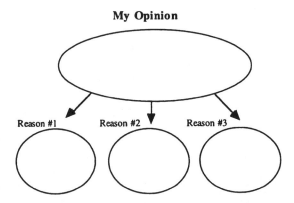

Depending on how much experience your students have with persuasive writing, you may want to do some minilessons on different aspects of writing. If you have a separate Language Arts block, you could use this time to teach writing techniques and skills. Possible minilessons include:
- Writing a clear position or opinion statement (topic sentence)
- Using supporting details
- Using transitions in writing
- Writing a conclusion statement

Slavin, R.E., & Madden, N.A., *One Million Children: Success for All.* © Corwin Press Inc.

Today students will focus on expressing their opinion and reasons to support it. Remind students that this information will be written in a prewriting organizer. You may want to model a sample prewriting web for your students, including a sample opinion with at least three supporting reasons. An example (from a team representing the animals) is included below:

My Opinion

The land of the African savanna should continue to be preserved for the wild animals.

Reason #1
Animals are an important part of the food chain.

Reason #2
Animals need the land to survive.

Reason #3
Animals in the park attract tourists to Tanzania.

Briefly review with students the difference between fact and opinion.

Ask:
What is a fact?
(A fact is something that is true or can be proven to be true.)

What is an opinion?
(An opinion is what someone thinks or believes to be true.)

Students are sharing their opinion in their persuasive paragraph. Explain to students that using facts to support their opinion will help to convince their audience. If they simply state their opinion without any supporting evidence or facts, then they will most likely not succeed in being persuasive.

Remind students that we are trying to develop solutions to Rehema's problem that will be win-win solutions. Tell students to try to suggest ideas in their proposal that will meet the needs of both sides involved in the conflict.

Teamwork
Teams complete investigations, experiments or simulations. The teacher acts as a facilitator, conducting One-to-One confer-

Teamwork

1. Teams discuss the opinions that they will present in their persuasive paragraphs and then organize their thoughts using a prewriting web. Students can make their prewriting web on a piece of loose-leaf paper, and they can select any organizer they think is appropriate. Each team member is responsible for writing her or his own persuasive paragraph. Tell students you

will be using Numbered Heads to call on students to present to the council. Each student needs to be prepared to speak for his or her team.

2. If students finish their prewriting web, have them begin drafting their persuasive paragraph.

3. Allow students to do any additional research needed for their presentation. Encourage them to look up any facts that they can use as evidence to support their opinion. Suggest that students try to incorporate visual aids into their presentation. They can make a poster, do a slide show, show a video clip, etc. We want to try to encourage students to design multimedia presentations.

4. Conduct **One-to-One.** Check to see that students are completing their prewriting webs. Encourage students to ask their partners the following questions:
   - Is my opinion clearly stated?
   - Do I have at least three convincing reasons to support my opinion?

Time for Reflection
After each student answers the Concept Questions on his or her own, the team uses Discuss and Defend to reach consensus and ensure that all team members understand the concepts involved. Whole class discussions or sharing of information may also take place here.

Time for Reflection

Have students write their answers to the Concept Questions on a sheet of paper. Have them trade with a partner and discuss their answers. If there is disagreement, have them check with the rest of their team.

Extend & Connect
Application of concepts to other situations

EXTEND & CONNECT
Compare the process students are going through to that of writing a bill. Explain to students that when people want a law to be passed, they first have to propose a bill. The bill is presented to the local or federal government, and then the government discusses it and decides if it should be a law. (The process is more complicated than this, but for these purposes this type of explanation is sufficient.) People support their bill with facts and evidence to try to persuade the government to pass it into law. Talk with students about how this is similar to the process they are going through with their village council.

HOMEWORK
Have students finish drafting their paragraph. Remind students to use their prewriting web as a guide, and encourage them to be creative and to use persuasive language.

Slavin, R.E., & Madden, N.A., *One Million Children: Success for All.* © Corwin Press Inc.

Appendix 5.2.
Primary MathWings Lessons

LESSON 3

GOAL: Students will find the values of sets of coins that include pennies, nickels, dimes, quarters, and half-dollars.

Vocabulary:	no word wall cards used

OUTLINE OF LESSON

I.	**15 MINUTE MATH**
II.	**CHECK-IN**
III.	**ACTIVE INSTRUCTION**
	Model counting the value of a set of coins out loud and allow students a chance to practice. Model using a **Hundreds Chart** to count the value of a set of coins.
IV.	**TEAMWORK**
	Have team members play the **Memory Match** game with coin value cards and coin cards.
V.	**DIRECT INSTRUCTION**
	Have team members work together to solve logic problems about coin combinations.
VI.	**ASSESSMENT**
VII.	**REFLECTION**

Introduction for the Teacher:

In today's lesson, your students will count the values of sets of coins that include pennies, nickels, dimes, and quarters. Throughout the lesson, continue to point out how it is easiest to start counting with the coin that has the greatest value. In sets of coins with pennies, nickels, dimes, and quarters, your students should count the value of any quarters first, then any dimes, then any nickels, and finally any pennies. There will be a couple of sets with half-dollars, but since this is a coin that is not as commonly used as the others, the emphasis on it will be minimal.

Help your students practice counting the value of a set of coins out loud. For example, in a set with 1 quarter, 2 dimes, 1 nickel, and 3 pennies, they would say 25¢ for the quarter, 35¢, 45¢ for the dimes, 50¢ for the nickel, and 51¢, 52¢, 53¢ for the pennies. You will also introduce your students to using the Hundreds Chart to count the value of a set of coins. They will start by placing the coin with the greatest value on the square that matches its value on the Hundreds Chart and continue by adding on the values of the other coins. They will be able to practice counting the values out loud or using the Hundreds Chart as they play a matching game in **TEAMWORK**.

Key Concept:	When we count the value of a set of coins, it is easiest to count the coins in the order of their values, starting with the coin of the greatest value.

Dollars, Cents, and Change B   1999   Lesson 3

PREPARE:
Transparencies:
  Hundreds Chart (from Lesson 2)
  Logic Problems
Copies:
  Matching Coin Bookbag cards (5 pages, 1 set per team plus 1 for teacher, cut apart)
  Matching Money Cards (1 per team plus 1 for teacher, cut apart)
Teacher Materials:
  bag of assorted overhead coins
  Matching Coin Bookbag cards (cut apart)
  Matching Money Cards (cut apart)
Student Materials:
  Team:
    Hundreds Chart (not necessary if each student has a Student Reference Sheet)
    Matching Coin Bookbag Cards (cut apart)
    Matching Money Cards (cut apart)
  Pair:
    pair set of assorted coins

START UP ROUTINES

15 MINUTE MATH

CHECK-IN: Collect the Home Connection assignment.
            Partners/Teams
            Review to Remember
            Flashback

MATHEMATICS LESSON

ACTIVE INSTRUCTION (15 minutes)
    on the floor

  Place 4 pennies, 3 nickels, 6 dimes, and 1 quarter on the overhead projector.

  Say, **Use THINK-PAIR-SHARE and tell your partner something about the coins I put on the overhead.** ♀ Select a few students to share with the class. Here are some possible responses:

I see 14 coins on the overhead.
There are more dimes than nickels.
There is an even number of pennies and dimes.
I see 60¢ in dimes.
If you add the pennies to the nickels, there will be 19¢.

Dollars, Cents, and Change B   1999   Lesson 3

As the students are responding, be sure to ask them how they arrived at their answer. This may involve students coming up to the overhead and pointing to the coins or explaining how they counted the value of the coins.

Explain to the students that today they are going to count the values of sets of coins that have pennies, nickels, dimes, quarters, and sometimes even half-dollars. Place 1 quarter, 1 dime, 1 nickel, and 2 pennies on the overhead.

Ask, **If you were going to explain to someone how to count the value of this set of coins, which coin would you tell him or her to count the value of first?** 💡 (the quarter) **Why?** Here are some possible responses:

The quarter has the greatest value. You should start with the greatest value first.
If I start with the biggest value, it's easy to add smaller numbers to it.
If you start with the pennies, it's hard to add 25¢ at the end.

Agree and say, **We know the value of a quarter is 25¢, so we will count it as 25. The value of a dime is 10¢, so we will count it as 10. The value of a nickel is 5¢ so we will count it as 5, and the value of a penny is 1¢, so we will count it as 1. Let's count the value of this set of coins together.** Point to the quarter and say, **25¢.** Point to the dime and say, **35¢.** Point to the nickel and say, **40¢.** Point to the pennies and say, **41¢, 42¢.**

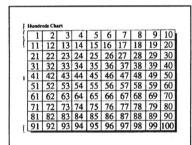

Say, **Let's think about counting the value of this set a different way.** Show the **Hundreds Chart** transparency as you say, **We can use our Hundreds Chart to count the value of the set of coins.** Put the quarter on 25 and ask, **Why do you think I put the quarter on 25?** (Its value is 25¢.) Continue, **How many boxes should I add on to count the value of the dime?** (10, because a dime is worth 10¢.) Agree and say, **We know that on a Hundreds Chart, each number below is 10 more, so I am going to put the dime on 35.** (Put the dime on 35.)

Show the nickel and ask, **How many more boxes should I add on to count the value of the nickel?** (5, because a nickel is worth 5¢.) Say, **I can easily count over 5 from 35 and land on 40.** Model counting on 5 and placing the nickel on the 40. Finally say, **How many more should I add on to count the value of the 2 pennies?** (2, because 2 pennies are worth 2¢.) Ask, **How much is this set of coins worth?** (The value of the coins is 42¢.) Summarize, **This is the same value we got by counting the other way. You can count the value of a set of coins either way. Which coin did we start with when we counted the value each way?** (the quarter)

Agree and summarize:

> 🔑 **When we count the value of a set of coins, it is easiest to count the coins in the order of their values, starting with the coin of the greatest value.**

Dollars, Cents, and Change B   1999   Lesson 3

TEAMWORK (20 minutes)
    in their seats

Say, **You and your teammates are going to practice counting the values of sets of coins. You can count their values out loud to each other or you can use the Hundreds Chart.** Have 3 students come to the front to help you model the team activity.

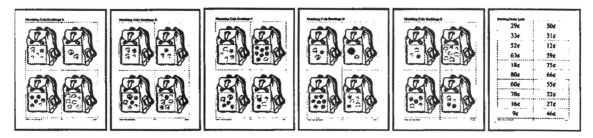

Show one **Matching Coin Bookbag** card and one of the **Matching Money Cards.** Say, **You and your teammates will be matching the amounts of money to the set of coins by playing a Memory Match game.** Explain that for each card with a set of coins on it, there is a matching card that has the correct amount of money written on it. Say, **Our team is going to put all of the cards face down on our desks/tables. Then we are going to take turns flipping over 1 money card and 1 coin card. The coin cards are larger than the money cards, so each time we should turn over 1 large and 1 small card.**

Have the first student volunteer turn over a money card and a coin card. Have her count the value of the coins on the coin card out loud and announce whether she made a match. Continue, **The person who flipped over the card should count the value of the coins out loud to the rest of the team so the team agrees on the value of the set of coins.** For example, if the student turned over the 2 quarters and 2 pennies coin card, she would count, **25¢, 50¢, 51¢, 52¢.**

Continue, **If the 2 cards you turned over do not match, say that these cards are not a match and flip the cards back over in exactly the same spot as they were before.** Have her turn them back over in exactly the same spot they were before. Say, **If the coins and the value match, the person who flipped them over gets to keep the cards. A person who makes a match gets another turn.** Continue modeling until one of you finds a match and say, **Since I (or _____) found a match, I (or _____) get(s) to take another turn.**

Say, **Let's practice the activity once together before we begin.** Give the teams time to put all of their cards face down in several rows on their desks/tables. Designate which team member will go first. Have those students turn over 1 money card and 1 coin card, count the value of the set on the coin card, and announce whether they have a match. If a student has a match, she will keep the cards and go again. If she does not have a match, she will flip the cards back over and the next team member will flip over 2 cards. Continue practicing until all team members have had 1 turn.

Say, **The object of the game is for your team to find all of the matches. You can continue playing the game until there are no matches left. If you finish before time is up, you can shuffle the cards, put them all face down, and play again.**

✔ While your students are working, circulate to assist them and informally assess several students with some of the following questions:

Which value card would match the coin card you just flipped over?
Why did you start counting with the quarter/dime/nickel/penny?
What do you count by when you count the value of a quarter?

DIRECT INSTRUCTION (15 minutes)
in their seats

Tell the students they will be listening to clues and working with their teams to figure out a set of mystery coins. Say, **When we use clues to figure something out, we are solving a logic problem.**

Make sure each team has a bag of assorted coins and a workmat in the middle of the table/group of desks. Tell the students that they are going to hear clues about the coins in a mystery set and are going to try to predict what the coins are from the clue. Say, **As more clues are read, your team can change its prediction. There are no half-dollars in the mystery sets.**

With the overhead off, place 1 dime and 3 pennies at the bottom of the overhead and place a small cup or small sheet of paper over them so students can't see. Explain to the students that you have the first mystery set covered on the overhead.

Show the first clue in Problem 1 on the **Logic Problems** transparency. Cover all of the clues except for the first one with a piece of paper.

Say, **The first clue says, "My set has 4 coins."** Tell them that to place coins on their mats to match the first clue. Give the teams 1 minute to work together to put coins on their workmats that match the clues. Have several teams share the coins they put on their workmats. Here are some possible responses:

We put four pennies/nickels/dimes/quarters on our mat.
We have two nickels and two dimes on our mat.
We put one quarter and three dimes.
We have three quarters and one penny.

Be sure to spend a few minutes talking about the sets teams have placed on their mats. Ask, **Why do you think there are so many different sets of coins on our mats?** Let them think about this and talk about the reasons. Say, **The first clue only tells us how many coins there are and nothing else, so there are many possibilities.**

Reveal and read the next clue, **My set only has pennies and dimes.** Explain that teams may change their sets if they would like. Ask, **What did you do if you had quarters or nickels in your set from before?** (Put dimes or pennies where there were quarters or nickels.) Have teams share what coins are in their sets now. Make sure that all of them still only have 4 coins and these are only pennies and dimes.

Dollars, Cents, and Change B   1999   Lesson 3

Reveal and read the next clue, **My set has an odd number of dimes.** Explain that teams may change their sets if they would like. Have teams share what coins are in their sets now. Make sure that all of them still only have 4 coins and that they have either 1 dime and 3 pennies or 3 dimes and 1 penny.

Reveal and read the last clue, **My set has 13¢.** Explain that teams should now know what the mystery set is. Have teams share what coins are in their sets now. Your students should have 1 dime and 3 pennies because that set is equal to 13¢. 3 dimes and 1 penny are equal to 31¢. Count the value of these sets out loud if you feel they need more practice counting the values of sets of coins.

When you have finished reading all of the clues, check to see that the coins in the set fit all of the clues. Then reveal the mystery set you placed at the bottom of the overhead. Work through as many sets of clues as time permits, following the same process.

Answer to Problem 2: 1 dime, 5 nickels
Answer to Problem 3: 4 dimes, 1 nickel, 2 pennies
Answer to Problem 4: 1 quarter, 2 nickels, 1 penny

ASSESSMENT

ASSESSMENT OPPORTUNITIES	
ACTIVE INSTRUCTION	• none
TEAMWORK	• matches sets of coins to values of sets
	• answers questions about counting the value of sets of coins
DIRECT INSTRUCTION	• none

REFLECTION
Students discuss today's lesson.

⸙ Key Concept Summary:
When we count the value of a set of coins, it is easiest to count the coins in the order of their values, starting with the coin of the greatest value.

No word wall cards are used in this lesson. Read the directions and explain the Home Connection assignment.

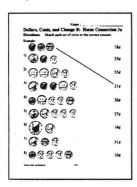 

Team Wrap-Up

Dollars, Cents, and Change B   1999   Lesson 3

Review to Remember

Name: _____   **Unit 9: Lesson 3**

Fill in the missing numbers on the number lines below.

1)
28   30 31   34 35 36 37

2)
62   64 65   68 69   71

3)
77   79 80   83   85 86

- -

Name: _____   **Unit 9: Lesson 3**

Write the numbers in each box in order from least to greatest.

1)
| 71   56   67 |

_____, _____, _____

2)
| 19   17   26 |

_____, _____, _____

3)
| 19   76   39 |

_____, _____, _____

Dollars, Cents, and Change B   1999

Name: _____

Dollars, Cents, and Change B: Home Connection 3a

Directions: Match each set of coins to the correct amount.

Example:

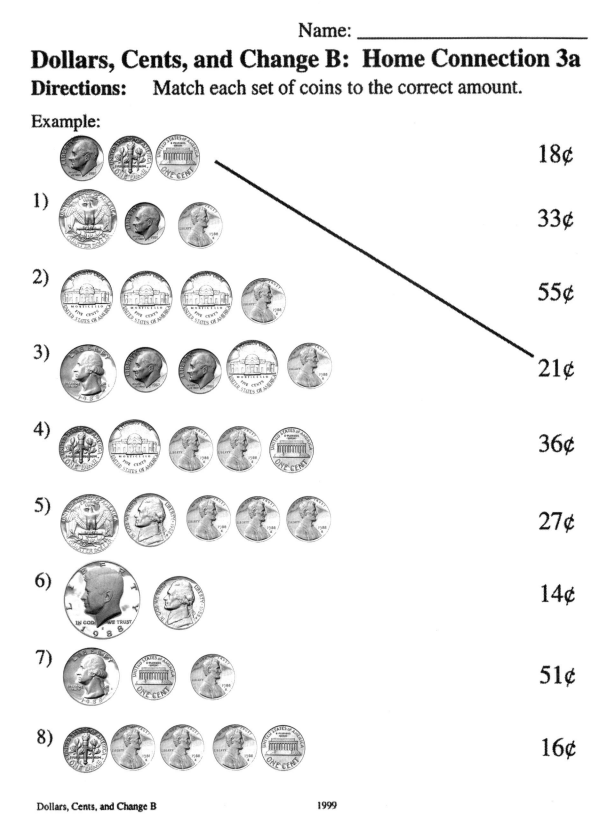

18¢

1)

33¢

2)

55¢

3)

21¢

4)

36¢

5)

27¢

6)

14¢

7)

51¢

8)

16¢

Name: _____

Dollars, Cents, and Change B: Home Connection 3b

Directions: Write how much money each child has.

Example: **Keleigh**		45¢
1) **André**		_____
2) **Tom**		_____
3) **Patti**		_____
4) **Peter**		_____
5) **Alicia**		_____
6) **Abdul**		_____

Dollars, Cents, and Change B   1999

Parent Peek:

In this lesson, your child learned how to count the value of a set of coins that includes pennies, nickels, dimes, quarters, and half-dollars. **She learned that to find the value of a set of coins, it is easiest to count the coins in the order of their values, starting with the coin of the greatest value.** So, in a set of coins with pennies, nickels, dimes, and quarters, she would count the value of the quarters first, then the dimes, then the nickels, and finally the pennies.

25¢   35¢   40¢   45¢   46¢   47¢

Your child also used clues to guess what coins were in a set of mystery coins. There were only pennies, nickels, dimes, and quarters in the mystery sets. After each clue, she would show the coins she thought were in the set. She would change her prediction, if needed, when a new clue was read until the final clue was reached and she knew what the set had to be. You might like to do a similar activity at home.

Make a list of clues or use the clues below. Have all different coins for your child to use. Read each clue and stop to let your child show you what the set could be. Make sure she explains why she chose the coins she did. For example, if the first clue was, "My set has 5 coins," she could show any 5 coins. After each clue you read, allow her time to change her set if needed. Once you have read the final clue, go back and make sure that the set your child is showing fits all of the clues.

Mystery Set #1	Mystery Set #2
1. My set has 4 coins.	1. My set has 5 coins.
2. My set has nickels, dimes, and pennies.	2. My set has no nickels.
3. My set has 1 penny.	3. My set has the same number of quarters as pennies.
4. My set has more dimes than nickels.	4. My set has more than 60¢.
Answer: 2 dimes, 1 nickel, 1 penny	Answer: 2 quarters, 1 dime, 2 pennies

Dollars, Cents, and Change B   1999

Intermediate MathWings Lessons

MEASUREMENT with STATISTICS E

LESSON 1 ★

GOAL: Students will measure to the nearest inch, half inch, and quarter inch, measure height to arm span ratio, and make a category sketch graph of the data.

OUTLINE
I. CHECK-IN
II. ACTIVE INSTRUCTION
   Quickly review attributes and tools of measurement and customary units of measurement for length as a warm-up.
   Model measuring to the nearest inch and have your students extend their skill to measure to the nearest half and quarter inch.
   Challenge: Have your students use calculators to explore mile equivalencies.
   Discuss body ratios and explain the height to arm span ratio and the three categories people fall into with this ratio.
III. TEAM WORK
   Team Consensus
   Have team members work together to measure their height to arm span ratios, cut out a square, tall thin rectangle, or short wide rectangle to represent their ratio type, and post it on the Body Ratio Bulletin Board.
   Model making and interpreting a category sketch graph. Have teams work together to make a class category sketch graph of their body ratios and be able to explain their thinking.
   Team Mastery
   Have each team member write in her Logbook a brief paragraph describing and explaining length to width body ratios and supporting her explanation with data from the category sketch graph.
IV. ASSESSMENT
   Collect Logbook entries for assessment.
V. REFLECTION

Introduction for Teacher:
   <u>Note:</u> Since your students have a wealth of measurement experiences behind them at this point, the focus of this unit is to apply and consolidate their measurement skills in situations involving statistics and probability. If your students need to learn any basic measurement skills, select lessons from earlier grades as needed.

   Quickly review measurable attributes and appropriate tools for measuring. Your students will use **customary units of measurement** for length, **inches (in. or "), feet (ft or '), and yards (yd)** and will measure to the **nearest** $\frac{1}{4}$ **in.** They will use their calculators to explore the length of a mile. A **mile = 5,280 ft** or 63,360 in. It takes 880 men who are 6 ft tall lying end to end to make a mile.

   A **ratio** shows the relationship of two numbers. The relationship of the length of one part of the body to the length of another is a **body ratio.** Have your students explore their height to arm span (length to width) body ratios. This ratio is more variable, and thus more interesting, than other body ratios. People fall into one of three categories: they are squares with arm spans equal to their heights, or tall thin rectangles with arm spans shorter than their heights, or short wide rectangles with arm spans longer than their heights. The students can measure and classify themselves using these ratios. They will then make a **category sketch graph** of their class data.

Measurement with Statistics E   1999   Lesson 1 Page 1

Key Concepts:
- **Standard customary units of measure for length are inches (in. or "), feet (ft or '), yards (yd), and miles (mi).**
- **1 yard = 3 feet or 36 inches, 1 foot = 12 inches, and 1 mile = 5,280 feet.**
- **We measure to the nearest $1/2$"** by measuring up if it is $1/4$" or more and down if it is less than $1/4$" past the last half inch mark. **We measure to the nearest $1/4$"** by measuring up if it is $1/8$" or more and down if it is less than $1/8$" past the last quarter inch mark.
- A **ratio** shows the relationship of two numbers. **Your body ratios** are the relationships of the lengths of various parts of your body.

PREPARE:
Transparencies:
- several blank transparencies
- TABLE OF MEASURES, save for Lesson 2

Copies:
- LESSON 1 HOMEWORK (Pages 10 - 13), one per student

Teaching Materials:
- measuring tape or string and customary ruler and yardstick
- Begin to make a large poster of the TABLE OF MEASURES with the customary units of length. (Save to be added to and used in future lessons as different units of measure are explored.)
- Have a Body Ratio Bulletin Board set up and ready to fill with the students' measurements.
- three construction paper shapes with stick figures drawn on them (see models in lesson) demonstrating the three length:width body ratios (square, tall thin rectangle, short wide rectangle)

Team Materials:
- **Team**
  measuring tape or string and customary rulers
- **Student**
  ruler and string
  calculator
  scissors
  construction paper
  markers
  LESSON 1 HOMEWORK

CHECK-IN: Team Set-up
                  Problem Solving / Facts or Fluency
                  Homework Check

ACTIVE INSTRUCTION:
Quick Warm-up Review:
Have the class discuss some things they have measured in their daily lives. (Might include height, weight, ingredients for cooking, material for sewing or building, temperature, etc.)

Ask them to discuss how they measured these things. (Might include rulers, scales, thermometers, estimates with body parts such as feet, hand span, etc.)

Agree that people have always needed to measure things in their daily lives and they used parts of their bodies, such as hand spans and feet, to measure at first because these were so convenient.

Note that, although we use standard units of measure when we want exact measurement, we still use body parts to help us estimate measurements after we get some idea of how our body measurements compare to the standard units of measure.

For example, someone might have a hand span of about 6 inches or half a foot, and someone else might have a span from elbow to tip of index finger of about 12 inches or 1 foot. They could use these convenient nonstandard units when estimating distances.

Measurement with Statistics E   1999   Lesson 1 Page 2

Remind them:

Standard customary units of measure for length are inches (in. or "), feet (ft or '), yards (yd), and miles (mi).

Remind the class that **inch** is abbreviated as **in. or "**, a **foot = 12 in.** and is abbreviated **ft or '**, and a **yard** is **36 in.** or **3 ft** and can be abbreviated **yd**.

Show the TABLE OF MEASURES transparency, showing the customary units of measure for length.

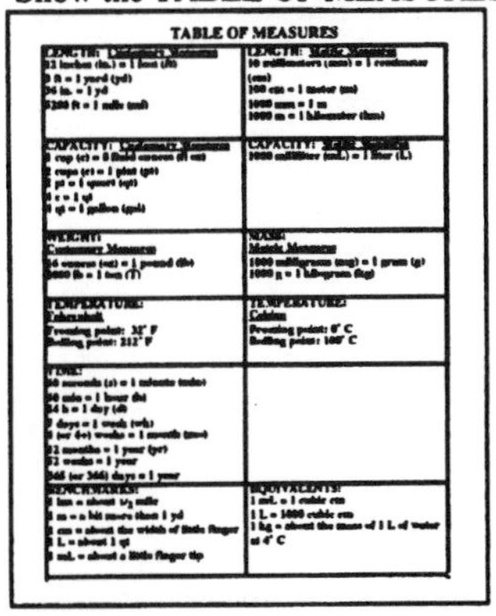
TABLE OF MEASURES

Review:

1 yard = 3 feet or 36 inches, 1 foot = 12 inches, and 1 mile = 5,280 feet.

Customary Units of Length:
Model measuring to the nearest 1 inch with several lines drawn on a blank transparency, reminding the students that measuring to the nearest inch is like rounding; $^1/_2$" or more goes up to the next higher number of inches and less than $^1/_2$" goes down to the smaller number of inches.

T Have team members work together to draw and measure several lines to the nearest inch.

✔ Circulate to observe their understanding of measuring to the nearest inch.

Challenge teams to use what they know about rounding to decide how to measure some lines they draw to the nearest $^1/_2$" and nearest $^1/_4$". Have them be sure every team member can explain her idea.

✔ Randomly choose a team member to share her team's method of measurement to the nearest $^1/_2$" and $^1/_4$". (Measure to the nearest $^1/_2$" by measuring up if it is $^1/_4$" or more and down if it is less than $^1/_4$" past the last half inch mark. Measure to the nearest $^1/_4$" by measuring up if it is $^1/_8$" or more and down if it is less than $^1/_8$" past the last quarter inch mark.)

Agree and summarize:

We measure to the nearest $^1/_2$" by measuring up if it is $^1/_4$" or more and down if it is less than $^1/_4$" past the last half inch mark. We measure to the nearest $^1/_4$" by measuring up if it is $^1/_8$" or more and down if it is less than $^1/_8$" past the last quarter inch mark.

Optional Challenge: Remind the class that 1 mile = 5,280 ft and ask them to use their calculators to find out how many inches are in a mile (63,360 in.) and to find out how many 6 ft men lying end to end it would take to make a mile (880 men).

Length to Width Body Ratio:
Tell the class that artists have discovered certain proportions in the human body and that when they understand them, they can draw people well.

As an example, point out that the eyes are usually about halfway down the face. Although most people think they are higher, if they draw them higher, the face looks funny.

Tell the class that they are going to use customary units of length to measure the lengths of various parts of their bodies to discover their proportions, or their **body ratios**. Explain:

> A ratio shows the relationship of two numbers. Your body ratios are the relationships of the lengths of various parts of your body.

Explain that the most interesting ratio is the height:arm span ratio or length:width ratio because it varies so much. Tell them that their height is their length and their arm span is their width.

Place three construction paper shapes at the top of BODY RATIO BULLETIN BOARD (shown below).

Point out that people fall into three different categories: squares - length and width are about equal (height and arm span are about equal), tall rectangles - length is greater than width (height is greater than arm span), and wide rectangles - length is less than width (height is less than arm span).

TEAM WORK:
Team Consensus:
T Tell team members that each of them is going to measure his partner's length and width to the nearest inch, compare the lengths of each, and determine whether his partner is a square, a tall rectangle, or a wide rectangle. Have partner pairs check each other's measurements.

Ask each team member to cut out a construction paper square or rectangle to describe his length to width ratio, write his name on his shape, and put his shape in the appropriate column of the bulletin board. Have them be sure that every team member rehearses finding and explaining his body ratio and his type.

✔ Circulate as partners work together to check for understanding of the body ratios.

Ask the class to observe the data on the bulletin board and decide what kind of graph would represent it well. (category sketch graph)

Agree that a **category sketch graph** would make an excellent representation of their class length to width ratios. **Quickly** draw a simple category sketch graph on a blank transparency as shown below.

FAVORITE SPORTS

```
                X
                X                    X
    X           X                    X
    X           X        X           X
    X           X        X           X
 Basketball   Soccer  Swimming    Baseball
```

What could they tell about their coins based on the category sketch graph?

Measurement with Statistics E   1999   Lesson 1 Page 4

Quickly review category sketch graph construction and interpretation, which your students have done repeatedly in earlier grades. Point out that we only need a line with the horizontal axis labeled and X's to represent the items in each category. Explain that a category sketch graph is so simple that we do not need a vertical axis.

Work with the class to make a category sketch graph on a blank transparency, with each team contributing a part of the graph in order to review the parts of a category sketch graph that make it communicate information clearly.

As each team fills in the transparency in turn and the class comes to consensus about it, have the team copy the part of the category sketch graph that they contributed onto a piece of chart paper so that there is a complete category sketch graph to be put on the bulletin board by the time the transparency category sketch graph is finished.

Ask one team to draw the line for the horizontal axis and label it with the three types of ratios (square, tall rectangle, wide rectangle) on the blank transparency and the chart paper.

Ask another team to count and record the square data of the category sketch graph on the transparency and the chart paper.

Have a different team count and record the tall thin rectangle data of the category sketch graph on the transparency and the chart paper.

Ask still another team to count and record the short wide rectangle data of the category sketch graph on the transparency and the chart paper.

Have another team make a key explaining that the shapes denote body ratios of height and arm span (length and width) on the transparency and the chart paper.

Ask the final team to make a title for the category sketch graph so that readers know what it represents on the transparency and the chart paper. An example of a possible category sketch graph with 9 square ratios, 11 tall thin rectangle ratios, and 7 short wide rectangle ratios is shown below.

LENGTH TO WIDTH BODY RATIOS

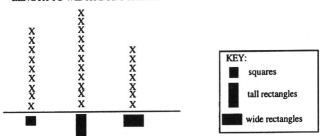

Team Mastery:
Quickly review the data represented by the category sketch graph as you place it on the bulletin board as a summary of the categories of length to width body ratios and point out how much data we can see at a glance when it is displayed in a category sketch graph.

Ask every team member to record her height (length) in her Logbook for use in Lessons 2 and 3. Have each team member write a brief paragraph describing and explaining length to width body ratios and supporting her explanation with data from the category sketch graph.

T Then have her check in with her team members to come to consensus on their explanations. If a team member has an unclear or unreasonable explanation, have other team members explain the process, and then have her write a second explanation. If a team member has a clear and reasonable explanation, have her help other team members who need more practice.

<u>Have them be sure that each team member rehearses how to explain her length to width body ratio.</u>

✔ Circulate to observe their understanding of body ratios and category sketch graphs. When teams have demonstrated understanding, move on to Numbered Heads Together.

✔ **Numbered Heads Together:**
Use Numbered Heads Together, or another strategy, to randomly choose a team member to share her explanation.

✔ **ASSESSMENT:**
Collect the Logbooks for assessment as you review the Key Concepts below. Note whether team members had to rewrite their explanations or had a good understanding right away.

REFLECTION:
Key Concepts Summary:
• **Standard customary units of measure for length are inches (in. or "), feet (ft or '), yards (yd), and miles (mi).**
• **1 yard = 3 feet or 36 inches, 1 foot = 12 inches, and 1 mile = 5,280 feet.**
• **We measure to the nearest $1/2$"** by measuring up if it is $1/4$" or more and down if it is less than $1/4$" past the last half inch mark. **We measure to the nearest $1/4$"** by measuring up if it is $1/8$" or more and down if it is less than $1/8$" past the last quarter inch mark.
• A **ratio** shows the relationship of two numbers. **Your body ratios** are the relationships of the lengths of various parts of your body.

✔ **Logbook:**
Student explanation of the length to width body ratio supported by the category sketch graph data is in the Logbook from this lesson.

Homework:
Lesson 1 Homework

Team Wrap-up

MEASUREMENT with STATISTICS E - LESSON 1 HOMEWORK ANSWERS
<u>Show your work</u>.

SKILL PROBLEMS

1. 72 in. = **6 ft**

2. 5 ft = **60** in.

3. 3 yd = **108** in.

4. $7^1/_4$ in. to the nearest half inch is $7^1/_2$ **in.**

5. $4^3/_4$ in. to the nearest half inch is **5 in.**

MIXED PRACTICE

1.
```
  893
+ 258
-----
1,151
```

2. 739 ÷ 9 = **82 R1**

3.
```
   83
 x 48
-----
3,984
```

4. How many nickels are in 17 dimes?
34 nickels

5. Is 930 even or odd? **even**

REAL WORLD PROBLEMS
1. John has 3 yards of felt to make banners. How many 2 ft pieces can he cut out of his material?
3 yds x 3 = 9 ft; 9 ÷ 2 = 4 R1, so he can cut 4 pieces and have 1 ft left over.
2. Marsha bought $1^1/_2$ yd of lace. How many inches of lace did she buy?
1 yd = 36 in.; $^1/_2$ x 36 in. = 18 in.; 36 + 18 = 54 in. of lace.
3. Darnel's shoe was 12 in. long. The classroom was 7 yards long. How many of his shoe lengths would it take to go from one end of the room to the other?
7 yds x 3 = 21 ft; 12 in. = 1 ft; the room is 21 of his shoe lengths.

PROBLEM SOLVING
A teacher did a survey of his students' favorite colors. Explain what the category sketch graph below tells you about the favorite colors of his students.

CLASS FAVORITE COLORS

```
      X
      X
      X           X
X     X     X     X
X     X     X     X
X     X     X     X
X     X     X     X
X     X     X     X
X     X     X     X
red  blue  green purple
```

There were 28 students in his class. Blue was the favorite color in his class. The same number of students liked red and green the most. More people liked purple than liked red or blue, etc.

Have you studied your FACTS today?

PARENT PEEK

Your child is beginning a unit about measurement. She has gained a wealth of measurement experiences from earlier years. The focus of this unit is to apply and consolidate her measurement skills in situations involving statistics and probability.

In this lesson, she quickly reviewed the **standard customary units of measure for length** which are inches (in. or "), feet (ft or '), yards (yd), and miles (mi).

She knows that **1 yard = 3 feet or 36 inches, 1 foot = 12 inches, and 1 mile = 5280 feet.** She also knows how to measure to the nearest inch, half inch, and quarter inch. **We measure to the nearest** $1/2$" by measuring up if it is $1/4$" or more and down if it is less than $1/4$" past the last half inch mark. **We measure to the nearest** $1/4$" by measuring up if it is $1/8$" or more and down if it is less than $1/8$" past the last quarter inch mark.

A **ratio** shows the relationship of two numbers. The relationship of the length of one part of the body to the length of another is a **body ratio**. Your child explored her height to arm span (length to width) body ratio. This ratio is more variable, and thus more interesting, than other body ratios. People fall into one of three categories. They are squares with arm spans equal to their heights, or tall thin rectangles with arm spans shorter than their heights, or short wide rectangles with arm spans longer than their heights. Your child classified herself using these ratios. You might like to ask her what category she was in and explain how she knows that.

Then the class made a **category sketch graph** of all their data. See a sample category sketch graph below. Your child will need to understand category sketch graphs for this Homework.

                    FAVORITE SPORTS
                        X
                        X   X
        X   X   X
        X   X   X   X
        X   X   X   X
      ───
      Basketball   Soccer   Swimming   Baseball

What are some observations of this category sketch graph?
    Soccer was the favorite sport in this survey. The same number of students liked basketball as liked baseball. Swimming was the least favorite sport.

NAME:_____   DATE:_____

MEASUREMENT with STATISTICS E - LESSON 1 HOMEWORK
Show your work.

SKILL PROBLEMS	MIXED PRACTICE
1. 72 in. = _____ ft	1. $\begin{array}{r} 893 \\ +\,258 \\ \hline \end{array}$
2. 5 ft = _____ in.	2. 739 ÷ 9 =
3. 3 yd = _____ in.	3. $\begin{array}{r} 83 \\ \times\,48 \\ \hline \end{array}$
4. $7\frac{1}{4}$ in. to the nearest half inch is _____.	4. How many nickels are in 17 dimes?
5. $4\frac{3}{4}$ in. to the nearest half inch is _____.	5. Is 930 even or odd?

REAL WORLD PROBLEMS
1. John has 3 yards of felt to make banners. How many 2 ft pieces can he cut out of his material?
2. Marsha bought $1\frac{1}{2}$ yd of lace. How many inches of lace did she buy?
3. Darnel's shoe was 12 in. long. The classroom was 7 yards long. How many of his shoe lengths would it take to go from one end of the room to the other?

PLEASE TURN THE PAGE AND DO THE PROBLEM ON THE BACK.

Measurement with Statistics E   1999   Lesson 1 Page 9

Slavin, R.E., & Madden, N.A., *One Million Children: Success for All.* © Corwin Press Inc.

PROBLEM SOLVING

A teacher did a survey of his students' favorite colors. Explain what the category sketch graph below tells you about the favorite colors of his students.

CLASS FAVORITE COLORS

```
            x
            x
            x              x
   x        x      x       x
   x        x      x       x
   x        x      x       x
   x        x      x       x
   x        x      x       x
   x        x      x       x
  red     blue   green   purple
```

Have you studied your FACTS today?

PARENT PEEK

Your child is beginning a unit about measurement. She has gained a wealth of measurement experiences from earlier years. The focus of this unit is to apply and consolidate her measurement skills in situations involving statistics and probability.

In this lesson, she quickly reviewed the **standard customary units of measure for length** which are inches (in. or "), feet (ft or '), yards (yd), and miles (mi).

She knows that **1 yard = 3 feet or 36 inches, 1 foot = 12 inches, and 1 mile = 5,280 feet.** She also knows how to measure to the nearest inch, half inch, and quarter inch. **We measure to the nearest** $1/2$" by measuring up if it is $1/4$" or more and down if it is less than $1/4$" past the last half inch mark. **We measure to the nearest** $1/4$" by measuring up if it is $1/8$" or more and down if it is less than $1/8$" past the last quarter inch mark.

A **ratio** shows the relationship of two numbers. The relationship of the length of one part of the body to the length of another is a **body ratio.** Your child explored her height to arm span (length to width) body ratio. This ratio is more variable, and thus more interesting, than other body ratios. People fall into one of three categories. They are squares with arm spans equal to their heights, or tall thin rectangles with arm spans shorter than their heights, or short wide rectangles with arm spans longer than their heights. Your child classified herself using these ratios. You might like to ask her what category she was in and explain how she knows that.

Then the class made a **category sketch graph** of all their data. See a sample category sketch graph below. Your child will need to understand category sketch graphs for this homework.

FAVORITE SPORTS

```
                 X
                 X                    X
     X           X          X         X
     X           X          X         X
     X           X          X         X
  Basketball   Soccer    Swimming   Baseball
```

What are some observations of this category sketch graph?
   Soccer was the favorite sport in this survey. The same number of students liked basketball as liked baseball. Swimming was the least favorite sport.

PLEASE TURN THE PAGE AND SEE THE TABLE OF MEASURES.
THESE MEASURES WILL BE USED THROUGHOUT THIS UNIT.

TABLE OF MEASURES

LENGTH: _Customary Measures_ **12 inches (in.) = 1 foot (ft)** **3 ft = 1 yard (yd)** **36 in. = 1 yd** **5,280 ft = 1 mile (mi)**	**LENGTH: _Metric Measures_** **10 millimeters (mm) = 1 centimeter (cm)** **100 cm = 1 meter (m)** **1,000 mm = 1 m** **1,000 m = 1 kilometer (km)**
CAPACITY: _Customary Measures_ **1 cup (c) = 8 fluid ounces (fl oz)** **2 cups (c) = 1 pint (pt)** **2 pt = 1 quart (qt)** **4 c = 1 qt** **4 qt = 1 gallon (gal)**	**CAPACITY: _Metric Measures_** **1,000 milliliter (mL) = 1 liter (L)**
WEIGHT: **_Customary Measures_** **16 ounces (oz) = 1 pound (lb)** **2,000 lb = 1 ton (T)**	**MASS:** **_Metric Measures_** **1,000 milligrams (mg) = 1 gram (g)** **1,000 g = 1 kilogram (kg)**
TEMPERATURE: **_Fahrenheit_** **Freezing point: 32° F** **Boiling point: 212° F**	**TEMPERATURE:** **_Celsius_** **Freezing point: 0° C** **Boiling point: 100° C**
TIME: **60 seconds (s) = 1 minute (min)** **60 min = 1 hour (h)** **24 h = 1 day (d)** **7 days = 1 week (wk)** **4 (or 4+) weeks = 1 month (mo)** **12 months = 1 year (yr)** **52 weeks = 1 year** **365 (or 366) days = 1 year**	
BENCHMARKS: **1 km = about ½ mile** **1 m = a bit more than 1 yd** **1 cm = about the width of little finger** **1 L = about 1 qt** **1 ml = about a little finger tip**	**EQUIVALENTS:** **1 ml = 1 cubic cm** **1 L = 1,000 cubic cm** **1 kg = about the mass of 1 L of water at 4° C**

6

Family and Student Support

Timothy Jones lives in a Baltimore housing project and attends a Success for All school in which virtually all children are in poverty. He had completed kindergarten the year before Success for All began at his school. According to his teachers' reports, Timothy was already headed for serious trouble. He was angry and aggressive, dealing with both teachers and other students as if they were out to get him. Timothy had to be removed from class frequently because of his disruptive behavior. He had little energy to put into learning when he was in school, and he was not in school very consistently. Even when he did come to school, he often arrived late, closer to 10:30 than 8:30.

Timothy was born when his mother was a young teenager. His mother felt helpless. She loved her son and wanted him to succeed in school but had few resources to help him, being hardly more than a child herself. Her son's response to school was just like his mother's. The only way she knew how to react to Timothy's problems in school was to become angry and aggressive. In the first weeks of first grade, when the school contacted her about problems that Timothy was having, her response was to stomp into school cursing, threatening to take him out of the school because it couldn't deal with him.

Coordinated efforts by teachers, the facilitator, family support team members, and Timothy's mother worked to turn things around for Timothy. After the social worker made the mother feel respected and welcome, she was able to

AUTHORS' NOTE: This chapter was written primarily by Barbara Haxby.

encourage her to participate in parenting classes held at the school. She became more confident in her ability to handle her son. With assistance from the attendance monitor, Timothy's attendance started to improve. At first, the school called his mother early every morning to get her started early enough to get her son to school. For a while, the attendance monitor met the mother halfway to school. Everyone made a concerted effort to make Timothy's mother feel welcome at the school, showing her respect and treating her as a partner. Timothy's teacher sent good news notes home with Timothy when he met the behavioral goals he and his teacher set together. Timothy practiced solving conflicts peacefully at the weekly Class Council meeting. When Timothy experienced a problem with another student, he was able to go to the Roundtable at the back of the classroom and use a method to think through better solutions to conflict. Time for reflection and practice in win-win solutions to conflict reduced Timothy's problems with other students.

Even as his behavior improved, Timothy still had very serious academic problems; on all tests given at the beginning of first grade, he showed no evidence of having any prereading skills. Timothy was given an instructional program in which he could be successful and was given one-to-one tutoring, which not only provided the academic support that he needed but also gave him emotional support. His tutor was a special person with whom he could share his struggles and successes. The tutor and Timothy's classroom teacher met frequently with the family support team to coordinate plans and activities around his needs and strengths.

As Timothy's mother began to work cooperatively with the school, Timothy's attitude toward school improved. He still has a strong temper, but he is learning how to deal with angry feelings in a constructive way. Timothy is in school on time every day. Learning still does not come easily for him, but he knows that if he works hard, he can learn, and he is proud of the steady progress he is making. He loves to bring his Reading Roots books home to read to his mother, who is delighted with his reading success. His mother has developed a good deal of self-confidence as well and is now employed in a store in the neighborhood.[1]

Timothy's experience, which is like that of many students in Success for All, shows the importance of a relentless, coordinated approach to meeting all students' individual needs. Ensuring high-quality instruction, tutoring, and other academic supports is not enough for a child like Timothy who may be failing for reasons that have little or nothing to do with academics. Some children fail because of erratic attendance or poor behavior. Some have serious health problems or need eyeglasses or hearing aids. Some lack adequate nutrition or heat at home. Some are homeless or are threatened with losing their homes. If a school is serious about ensuring success for every child, then it must have the capacity to recognize and solve all of these nonacademic problems that are barriers to a child's success in school.

Composition of the
Family Support Team

The Success for All program places a strong emphasis on increasing the school's capacity to relate to parents and to involve parents as well as health and social service agencies in solutions to any nonacademic problems students may have. Each Success for All school establishes a Family Support Team for this purpose. The composition of the Family Support Team varies from school to school depending on the personnel available and the school's needs. The school's Title I parent liaison, counselor, social worker, nurse, and other resource staff usually make up the Family Support Team, along with building administrators (principals or vice principals) and the facilitator. In schools with serious attendance problems, an attendance aide may be added.

Family Support Teams are led by a Family Support Coordinator. Although some schools hire a full-time Family Support Coordinator, most schools use the school guidance counselor, social worker, principal, or vice principal. Although additional personnel are not usually required, existing school personnel must have their duties redefined so they have the time to oversee a quality implementation of the Family Support components. For the Family Support Team to function well, it is vital that each member has the time to meet and implement decisions. This may involve changing people's schedules or responsibilities. For example, if a school cannot hire a clinical social worker, other school personnel will need to implement the classroom and family-based behavior modification programs. Other personnel may also need to make occasional home visits to families who are hard to reach. These interventions are time-consuming but necessary; Success for All is predicated on the belief that *every* student can succeed, and there are always some children who would fail without the services Family Support Teams provide.

The focus of the Family Support Team is on identifying and building on the strengths of parents, communities, and individual children. All parents want their children to succeed in school, but some have such difficult lives that they need help to create home environments conducive to school success. Family Support Teams begin with a fundamental respect for parents. They see parents as partners in achieving success for their children, a goal shared by parents and school staffs alike. They enlist parents in a cooperative quest to do whatever it takes at home and at school and to engage whatever community resources may be available to ensure that each child succeeds in school.

Family Support Teams usually meet weekly. The team is responsible for two areas. One is planning for schoolwide programs that will help enhance the academic achievement of children. This might include activities to increase parent involvement, improve the school's ability to monitor and respond to truancy, and so on. For example, the team may plan a program for parents on helping children with homework or plan a session with teachers on dealing with behavior problems. The second area discussed by the Family Support Team involves solving problems with individual children. Teachers and other staff refer a child to Family Support because they believe the child is having problems in school that have not been resolved by normal classroom intervention. Examples of such problems might include truancy, behavior problems, health problems, and psychological problems. In addition, students who are not making adequate academic progress despite classroom and tutorial assistance are referred to the Family Support Team even if there are no obvious family problems. The team's goal is to investigate to find out if family interventions may help get the child on track.

The Family Support Team implements a standard set of Success for All activities. In addition to these, each team also uses school data to determine any additional support activities that might increase achievement for their own particular school community. The activities of the Family Support Teams vary depending on available staff, student and family needs, and community investment in the school. All teams must make sure that the needs of children who are having difficulty are being met, school attendance programs are working, and parents are encouraged to participate in school. Other activities will depend on the time and resource constraints of the team.

The multifaceted role of the Family Support Team is crucial for addressing the needs of students who are at the highest risk of school failure. An effective team not only attempts to meet the needs of at-risk students but also creates a schoolwide climate that fosters respect for parents, high family involvement, and a proactive approach to the complex problems faced by many students and families in Success for All schools.

The main activities of the Family Support Team are summarized in Figure 6.1 and described in the following sections (see Haxby, Lasaga-Flister, Madden, Slavin, & Dolan, 1999, for more details).

Parent Involvement

Parent involvement is a key component for student success in Success for All. Research indicates that parental involvement is correlated with increases in attendance, increases in achievement, and decreases in behavior problems (see Epstein, 1995). Success for All stresses the need for a strong parent involvement program that is linked to improvements in curriculum and instruction.

Traditionally, schools and families have seen themselves as separate institutions that interact with the child. However, this separation can be detrimental for many children. In particular, it is clear to schools working with children from disadvantaged families that problems from the community and the family impinge every day on the academic life of students. Students who arrive at school hungry, homeless, angry, or depressed about family problems are unable to concentrate on educational tasks. Schools have become increasingly aware that they cannot address the needs of

Figure 6.1. Family Support

FAMILY SUPPORT

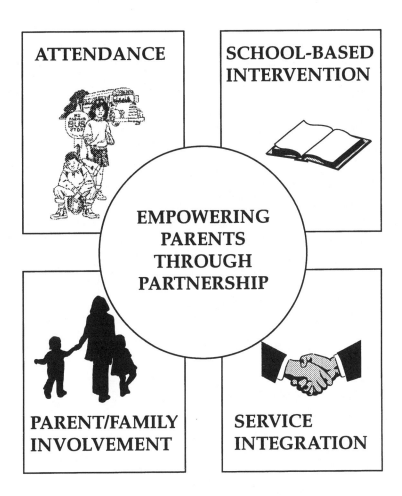

these children alone. The needs of disadvantaged children demand involvement by the family and community for schools to be most effective. It is the job of a school to recognize the family as an integral part of the school system and to work with families in devising ways to increase parent participation and encourage community support of schools.

Parent involvement is recognized as a valuable component of a school system, but there is no one type of parent participation that is "right." Because the goal of any parent involvement strategy is to involve as many parents as possible, a range of activities is necessary to suit the needs and preferences of a variety of parents, from participation in the governance of the school to helping a child with homework, to listening to a child read, to helping a teacher by preparing materials. Some specific ways in which parents are involved in Success for All schools are as follows.

Parent Involvement in School Governance

It is an old adage for most community organizers that for people to be very involved in an activity, they need to "own" it. Ownership is fostered by being involved in the development and implementation of any project. All too often, disadvantaged parents stay away from schools because they do not see the school as "theirs." More often, the school is viewed as yet another institution that is trying to do something to them. Instead, there needs to be a shift in thinking of the school as an institution that does things for and with parents. Ownership is greatly fostered if parents see themselves in the role of decision makers in the school.

One key way to have parents be decision makers is to ensure that they have a role in school governance. The creation of a Building Advisory Team is often particularly effective. This team is composed of teachers, administrators, and parents. They have the mandate to advise the principal on general school direction and planning. Some key tasks for the Building Advisory Team may be as follows:

- Review or develop a schoolwide discipline policy
- Set direction for parent involvement projects
- Evaluate the need for community services on site
- Review and implement homework guidelines
- Evaluate school climate

In general, the team evaluates the entire school climate and advises on general direction and goals. This team can meet between four and six times per year. When the team has made recommendations, they often work closely with the Family Support Team to ensure that programs are implemented.

In-School Volunteer Support

Parent involvement has traditionally been defined by participation as a volunteer in the school. This is an important, rewarding activity and can make a tremendous difference for financially strapped schools. Parents and other community members can engage in a wide range of activities that enhance school effectiveness.

One of the activities that Success for All schools implement is a Volunteer Listener program. The best way to learn to read is to read. Students in Success for All are encouraged to read at home every night. Family Support is actively engaged in promoting home reading and helping to ensure that students bring in their forms signed by parents that indicate that they are reading 20 minutes a night. Many schools encourage reading by having an incentive program in which students can earn a small prize or privilege by collecting enough signatures from parents or other adults. Some children may have parents who work at night or are unavailable for after-school reading time. Volunteers at these schools act as listeners for these students during lunch or free time. The volunteers may be parents, community members, local college or high school students, and so on. Many schools use volunteers from their local America Reads programs. Students can read to these volunteers and obtain extra certificates. The job of the volunteer listeners is to listen and to let the child know that he or she is doing a great job. Volunteer listeners are not tutors—they are present to encourage students to read and take pride in their reading. Both the volunteers and the students enjoy the additional one-to-one time during the school day. Students who just need extra practice can use the volunteer listeners in the building.

Some schools have used their volunteer listeners to celebrate improvement in reading. Volunteer listeners listen to several children read and give awards to their reading buddies. In one school, the parents bought and decorated special chairs that the children sit in when they read to the volunteer listeners.

Some schools have set up a homework room in which parents and teachers help children after school. This is especially beneficial when there are children who find it difficult to complete home assignments or do not have a quiet place to work. Parents can elect to have their child attend the after-school homework room 1 or more days per week. Generally, at least one parent and one teacher supervise and provide homework help when needed.

Many schools have implemented a Breakfast Reading Club. Some parents or volunteer listeners are available first thing in the morning to listen to students read and to sign off on Read and Respond forms for students who are unable to read at home.

Other In-School Parent Volunteer Activities

Parents in most schools are encouraged and trained to participate in a wide variety of school activities. Parents help in the classroom, media center, cafeteria, and playground. Often, schools provide training in these areas and certificates for participation. Parents can provide invaluable service in all areas of the school, but most find direct interaction with children more rewarding than clerical tasks or other work that does not involve children.

Teacher and School Communication to Parents

A vital means of fostering the link between parents and schools is to make consistent efforts to increase teacher and school communication to the parent. This communication models for everyone the perception that parents are an integral part of the school community. It helps to cement the mind-set for staff as well as parents that families need to be valued, and involved in the daily activities of the school. Parents who perceive the school as working to involve them say that the school is a good one (see Epstein, 1995). In addition, parents give teachers who frequently contact them high ratings. Fostering this sense of a positive school community is crucial to effective parent-school partnerships.

In many schools, most parents only hear from teachers and schools at the yearly parent-teacher conference or when their child is in trouble. Frequent communication between teacher and parent is a bad sign, something to be avoided. This sets a negative tone for all interaction. All too often, parents feel that no news is good news and cringe when the phone rings or school personnel stop by. There is a temptation to avoid the school, particularly for parents whose children are having difficulty. Of course, this only reinforces the school's belief that "the parents who most need to be here never come."

The more frequently parents are contacted, the more parents are involved in the daily functioning of the school, and the more parents are given good news about their child, the more likely they will be involved in the school. In Success for All, school personnel routinely make welcoming visits for new students and conduct fall information visits. Teachers send home Success Cards, newsletters, and good news notes. Informational meetings, often called "Second Cup of Coffee," occur on a regular basis in schools. In some schools, Second Cup of Coffee sessions provide coffee and pastries in the lobby to encourage parents to stop by and chat informally with Family Support personnel. In other schools, Second Cup of Coffee has evolved into regular meetings, with presentations on topics of concern to families. In all cases, the purpose is to create positive connections with families. Everyone shuns aversive experiences and there is nothing more aversive than hearing a barrage of negative things about your child. The goal of teacher and school communication is to alter the negative cycle and build a more positive connection.

Parent Involvement in Curriculum

Success for All schools place a strong emphasis on involving parents in supporting the curriculum at home. All students are urged to read to someone at home for 20 minutes each evening. Students are given Share Sheets and paperback books to bring home. Parents are asked to sign a form indicating that students have done their reading. In the fall, most schools have a Success for All Kick-Off Demonstration Night. This is designed to keep parents informed of the program of instruction that their child is receiving and give them tips on how to support the program at home. Students and teachers demonstrate the reading program.

Another standard part of family support is the Raising Readers program. The more aware parents are about the curriculum, the better they can support it at home. One way that parents become more aware is through the Raising Readers program. Raising Readers consists of a series of workshops in prekindergarten through second grade designed to familiarize families with the Success for All reading program and provide training so that parents can support reading skills at home. The program for prekindergarten and kindergarten is called Books and Breakfast; for first graders, Snacks and Stories; and for second graders, Chips and Chapters. A Spanish version of Raising Readers, *Creando Lectores,* is also widely used. In the upper grades, Raising Readers provides incentive programs for reading in a program called Navigating Novels. In addition to the workshop series, take-home libraries are provided with guides and extension questions to facilitate interactive reading at home.

The goal of the workshop series is not only to familiarize parents with the curriculum but also to provide parents with both the skills and materials needed to promote parent-child interaction around literacy. The content of each series of workshops is based on the curriculum for each grade level. At all grade levels, the key components of the structure are as follows:

- Parents attend with their children.
- Grade-level teachers explain and model a key component of the reading curriculum with the children.
- Teachers discuss how to help children at home with the identified skills.
- Parents and children practice with each other the skill modeled by the teacher.
- Parent and child create a "make and take" activity together to facilitate home practice of literacy skills.

A typical Raising Readers workshop would occur first thing in the morning. Family support personnel would have been involved in publicizing the workshop. Families receive several flyers, banners are posted outside the school, and sometimes personal calls are made to key classes or families to encourage participation. Generally, families arrive with their children, and the school provides coffee and pastries. The teacher models reading with the children and strategies to encourage listening comprehension. The parents use the same materials and practice the identified skills with their own child. Parents and children then are able to take home lending library books to use at home. Parents have been very enthusiastic about the program. Turnouts have consistently been high. Most schools report between 50% to 75% of parents participate in the workshops. In addition, parents report enjoying the take-home libraries. Typically, even the most-high-risk families want to help their children at home, and they report that this program has given them the information and support to do it.

Workshop nights for parents are often held throughout the school year to keep parents involved in curriculum support. Schools have experimented with teaching parents of prekindergarten students the STaR program and having parents make "big books" with their child. In addition, parents have been trained in cooperative learning and have formed teams in which to participate in designing school programs. The more parents can participate in the curriculum, the more enthusiastic they become.

Attendance

Family Support Teams also work to improve school attendance. Children need to attend school consistently in order to learn. Successful attendance strategies require a schoolwide approach. Success for All schools that have attendance problems (typically, less than 95% daily attendance) implement an attendance program that addresses three fundamental areas: (a) monitoring, (b) intervention, and (c) prevention.

A monitoring system is necessary to ensure that all children arrive safely at school and are accounted for early in the day. A comprehensive monitoring system does three things: (a) It increases the safety of students because all students are accounted for early, (b) it creates a school norm that all absences are important, and (c) it provides the necessary information for quick intervention on attendance problems. Effective monitoring systems allow school personnel to try to get the targeted child to school the same day. Attendance monitors use a record-keeping system that identifies students having attendance problems at a glance, enabling the school to follow up with at-risk absent children immediately.

Intervention also aims for quick response. We recommend hiring an attendance monitor who will be able to go into the community and meet with families. Through the use of this monitor, timely and effective outreach efforts are possible. This is particularly important for areas in which many families may not have phone service. If the monitor finds that an attendance problem does not improve or that a family has a variety of needs, the Family Support Team will provide case planning, further intervention, or referral. If the behavior causing attendance problems is to be changed, knowledge is not enough. Action is vital.

Prevention programs involve setting a schoolwide norm for attendance and putting in place programs that are proactive. Prevention programs include a wide range of incentive programs designed to reward individuals, classrooms, and families whose children consistently attend school. The best solution to any problem is to prevent it from occurring.

School-Based Intervention

The goal of Success for All's innovative curriculum, teaching strategies, and tutoring is to have every child achieve. However, some students cannot benefit as much as we hope from improved instruction because they have serious family, behavioral, or attendance problems. The school-based intervention component of the Family Support Team is designed to ensure that these children do not fall through the cracks. It is here that success for most must be translated into success for all.

Faculty, administration, or parents may refer a child to the Family Support Team. Referral forms are distributed early in the school year at parent and faculty meetings and are always available in the school office. Referrals are sent to the facilitator, who initially screens students to ensure that standard Success for All classroom strategies and tutoring are already in place; the Family Support Team is not a substitute for good classroom management and effective implementation of the basic instructional model.

Once a referral has been reviewed, the facilitator brings the case to the Family Support Team. Each case is assessed, a case manager assigned, and an action plan developed. The classroom teacher and the parent must be involved in the development of an action plan. If necessary, the case manager can schedule a meeting with a parent after the initial team assessment. To develop effective action plans, the team uses materials that are designed to promote solution-oriented thinking. Teams can become stymied by the endless problems possible in tough cases. Family Support Teams use Solution Sheets, which are designed to focus the team on the most important problems that are likely to be solvable by the school and to move the team forward with small-step solutions that involve school, family, and community. This approach necessitates that teams become adept at finding strengths and resources. Family Support is committed to the notion that people change from their strengths, not from their weaknesses. Solutions therefore are often found if teams are adept at identifying strengths and resources as well as problems.

After an action plan has been developed, the referral source is given a copy of the plan and encouraged to notify the team if any progress or deterioration is noticed. The team regularly reviews all cases to ensure that progress is being made or to adjust the action plan so it is more effective.

The process of school-based intervention is diagrammed in Figure 6.2.

Service Integration Between Community and School

Many students and families in Success for All schools have problems that require services from a range of community agencies. Often, families are unable or unwilling to access these services. Schools and community agencies have found that families are more likely to make use of needed services if the service is provided in a familiar location. Schools have often been particularly successful locations. On-site services are also helpful for the schools. Quicker intervention with better follow-through and feedback are possible when agencies are available on site.

Family Support Teams try to be aware of local services and make referrals, whether the services are on or off site. If a family is without heat or shelter, for example, it is the job of the Family Support Team to provide information and help families obtain needed services. This assistance may involve more than just providing a referral. Families often do not obtain community services because of problems with transportation or because of their inability to negotiate the labyrinth of large bureaucratic institutions. The team may help families with these problems and provide as much assistance as possible to make sure that the family is able to follow through on the referral. The Family Support Team members can also check to make sure that referrals led to services and that these services solved the problem. For example, if a

Figure 6.2. School-Based Intervention

SCHOOL-BASED INTERVENTION

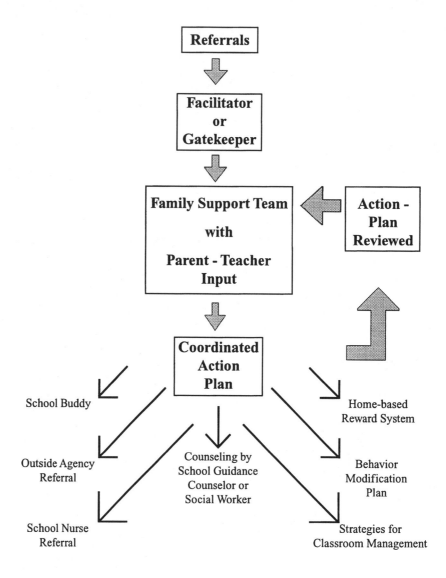

child needs eyeglasses, the Family Support Team might check to see that the family and social agencies have gone through all the steps that lead to the child being in school every day with glasses on.

Teams assess community services that are most often needed by the students and families in their community. Special attention is paid to services that may strongly affect student performance. Once a team has assessed these needs, it becomes aware of how to obtain those services in the community and investigates if it

Figure 6.3. Service Integration

SERVICE INTEGRATION

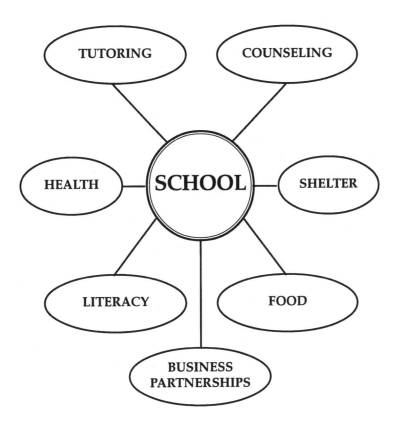

is possible to provide some of those services on site. A few common examples are shown in Figure 6.3 and descriptions follow.

Health: Some schools have obtained an on-site nurse practitioner from the local health department to help with sick or injured children and to do injections and physicals. All teams, however, know how to obtain needed medical care for students. In particular, it is important to know how to quickly obtain required shots, glasses, and eye and hearing exams. Family Support Teams try to ensure that these services are provided to students in a timely manner.

Counseling: Some Success for All schools have linked with community family counseling agencies to provide on-site family counseling. One school has linked with a drug and alcohol prevention program to provide groups for children of substance abusers. Community mental health programs are increasingly trying to provide some satellite services at schools and may have programs in the school area. Family Support Teams usually know about counseling programs in the community, particularly programs with no fee or sliding fee scales.

Food: If a child is hungry, he or she can't learn. Some schools link with a local agency to become a food distribution site for its community. Parents who have rarely been in the school building can come regularly to pick up food and thereby become acquainted with the school.

Shelter: Providing housing to needy families is problematic in most cities. Family Support Teams usually know the emergency shelters in town and try to work with the family to support the child while a family is homeless or in temporary living situations. It is better for a student to be supported at his old school while the family is trying to obtain permanent housing. The fewer upheavals for the student the better during this time. Family Support Teams have been instrumental in helping to plan transportation and additional supports for homeless students.

Tutoring: Success for All schools work with local universities, high schools, retirement groups, or churches to obtain additional tutoring for their students. In particular, the federal America Reads program is helping recruit reading tutors in every community. These volunteers may serve as listeners or, if they are able to devote enough time, they may tutor marginal students or older students who do not qualify for Success for All tutoring. Tutoring and volunteer listening are most effective if they are on site, and these groups are often happy to provide tutoring at the school. If a team is going to begin to make community linkages, this is often a good place to start.

Literacy: Parent literacy affects the academic success of students. Several Success for All schools have begun to work with local literacy groups to provide parent literacy programs on site. In general, parents involved in these school-based programs also participate in volunteer activities during the school day. Some schools also offer after-school computer programs for parents and children.

Business linkages: Local businesses have become more involved in supporting education over the past few years. Business leaders are increasingly aware that schools produce the workers of tomorrow and that the effectiveness of their own enterprises depends on the ability of schools to deliver quality employees. Consequently, both small and large businesses have made real commitments to local schools. Success for All schools have found that effective partnerships have occurred when schools energetically approach local businesses and structure some specific ways in which the business partners can help. Sometimes, effective linkages fail to develop because the partner is unclear about how much of a commitment they are making and what sort of help is needed. Just asking a business to be a partner and to help the school or just asking for money may be too vague. A clearly organized presentation of needs, some suggested ideas by the school of projects that the business partner could participate in, and ways to highlight the partnership to the community have generally been more successful approaches. Some examples of activities of local business involvement in Success for All schools are as follows:

- Providing incentives for attendance or reading (fast food restaurants, local movie rental stores, and convenience stores have often been large providers of small incentives for school programs)
- Providing additional tutoring for students
- Donating furniture for parent rooms or reading corners
- Providing mentorship programs or after-school club activities
- Providing public relations material for parents and community for special school projects (for example, local photographers have taken pictures of students involved in Success for All activities; partners have provided T-shirts or buttons to publicize special projects to families as part of outreach education about Success for All)

Getting Along Together: A Social-Problem-Solving Curriculum

The ability to think critically and solve interpersonal problems peacefully is an essential skill. Preparing children to become productive adults means not only providing excellent academic instruction but also reinforcing the social-problem-solving skills that are necessary for lifelong success. Teamwork, with its concomitant demands for sophisticated negotiation and decision making, is not only a cornerstone of Success for All but also a crucial skill in the modern workplace. In a world that is increasingly interconnected and a society that is multicultural, the ability to appreciate diversity, listen accurately to others, and solve differences peacefully is essential. The Getting Along Together curriculum (Haxby, Lasaga-Flister, & Magri, 1999) provides students with instruction and practice in all these social-problem-solving skills.

Children who have the ability to master academic material may end up failing because they lack the problem-solving skills necessary to successfully adjust to the school setting. For these students to achieve success, it is critical that they be taught these skills early in their school careers. Overtly teaching the behaviors to be successful problem solvers rather than punishing those students who fall short in this skill is crucial for both prevention and early intervention of problems that can lead to school failure.

The Getting Along Together program provides three components for students to develop problem-solving skills: (a) Learn About It is a set of classroom lessons fo-

Figure 6.4. Think It Through

Think It Through

<u>Conflict Stoppers</u>
1.   Share
2.   Taking Turns
3.   Apologize
4.   Ignore
5.   Make Amends
6.   Compromise
7.   Laugh it Off
8.   Flip a Coin
9.   Wait Until Later
10.   Get Help
11.   Talk it Out

What is the Problem?

What is My "I" Message?

How does the other person feel?

What could I do differently to solve the problem?

cusing on key social-problem-solving skills that are designed to be done during the first 2 weeks of the school year, while students are being assessed for placement in reading groups, (b) Think It Through is a set of guide sheets designed to help students begin to self-talk their way through interpersonal problems, and (c) Talk It Out uses a problem-solving model called the Peace Path, which enables students to talk out their difficulties in a positive way either at a weekly Class Council meeting, at a Roundtable at the back of the classroom, or at other points throughout the school day.

Learn About It

There are 2 weeks of social-problem-solving units available for all grades. The first week focuses on listening skills, and the second week is on conflict resolution. These lessons are designed to be taught within the reading time block. Each lesson is linked to a STaR or Listening Comprehension book. The teacher uses these books to highlight a particular social-problem-solving skill and conduct a team activity designed to provide students with an opportunity to practice the skill. For example, each lesson provides opportunities for students to reflect on the skills they are learning and homework to be able to practice those skills at home.

Think It Through

Students experiencing a problem in school need opportunities to calm down, think through their behavior, and make a well-reasoned decision about future behavior. Think It Through sheets are designed to give students time to reflect and to guide them through a self-talk process that encourages them to develop prosocial decision-making skills. Think It Through sheets are always kept at the back of the classroom at the Roundtable. Schools often keep them in the guidance office or in the main office for students experiencing difficulty throughout the day. In addition, bus drivers, cafeteria workers, and other school personnel may keep these sheets to dispense to students if necessary. The more opportunities a student has to practice talking themselves through problems in a positive way, the more automatic and accomplished the skill becomes.

Talk It Out

There are two structured opportunities for students to practice a conflict resolution process. Once a week, every teacher holds a brief Class Council meeting. This is an opportunity for both the teacher and the students to identify positive classroom behaviors and solve classroom problems. Second, at the back of every classroom, there is a designated Roundtable. Think It Through sheets (see Figure 6.4) are kept at the Roundtable, and there is a suggestion box for topics for the weekly Class Council meeting. A student who is experiencing a problem with another student or in the class can go to the Roundtable at any time, fill out a Think It Through sheet, and have an opportunity to talk through their difficulties.

Whether at a Class Council meeting or at the Roundtable, students are taught to use a conflict resolution process called the Peace Path (see Figure 6.5). The Peace Path is designed to be an engaging, concrete way for students to practice step-by-step conflict resolution skills. Initially, the Peace Path is placed on the floor, and students physically walk through the process. Older students may dispense with the Peace Path but incorporate just the step-by-step Peace Path discussion. In any case,

Figure 6.5. The Peace Path

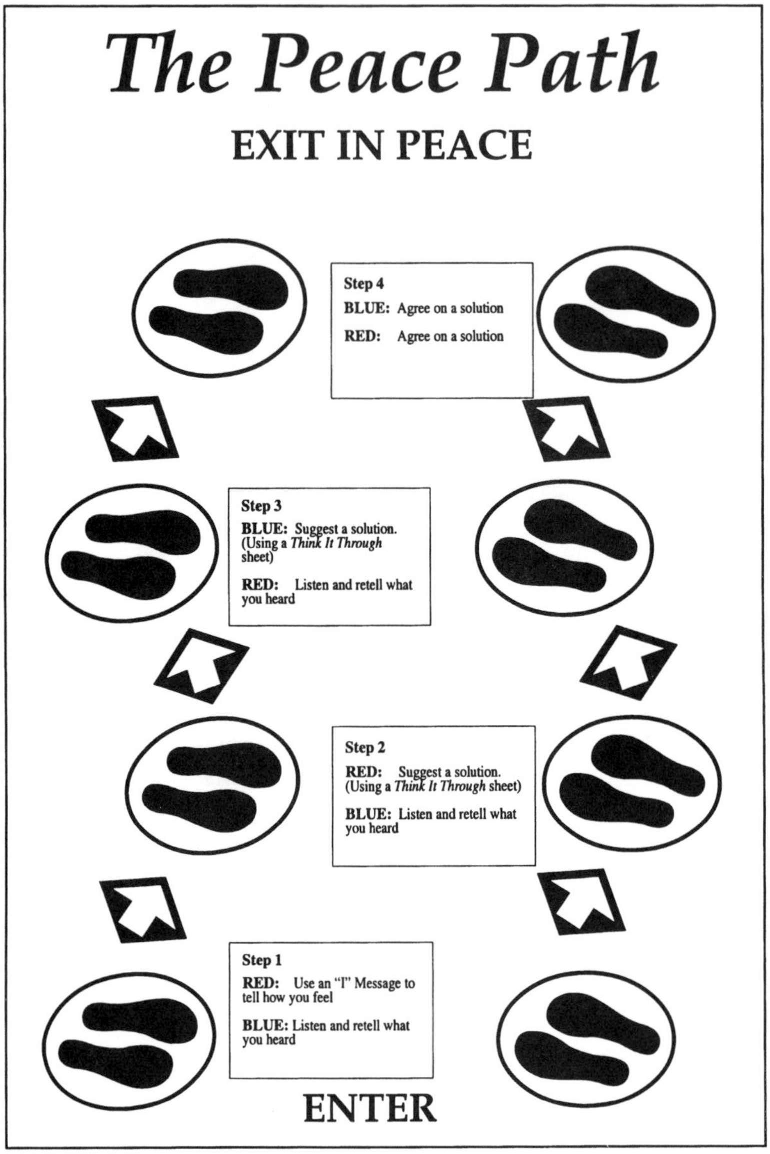

The Peace Path

EXIT IN PEACE

Step 4
BLUE: Agree on a solution
RED: Agree on a solution

Step 3
BLUE: Suggest a solution.
(Using a *Think It Through* sheet)
RED: Listen and retell what you heard

Step 2
RED: Suggest a solution.
(Using a *Think It Through* sheet)
BLUE: Listen and retell what you heard

Step 1
RED: Use an "I" Message to tell how you feel
BLUE: Listen and retell what you heard

ENTER

students are taught and provided ongoing practice in this win-win conflict resolution model.

Many schools have expanded this process and used the Peace Path throughout the building. Schools have painted Peace Paths on the playground or placed them in the gym or cafeteria. Schools that provide consistent and relentless modeling of this process have seen students who may have arrived at school with limited social-problem-solving skills make real gains and become positive and productive team members.

For more on family support and integrated services in Success for All and Roots & Wings, see Haxby, Lasaga-Flister, Madden, & Slavin, 1999.

Note

1. This vignette, a composite of experiences with many children and families involved in Success for All Schools, is adapted from Madden et al. (1993).

7

Facilitators and the Change Process

The implementation of Success for All or Roots & Wings requires substantial change in school organization and practices. It affects curriculum, instruction, assessment, early childhood programs, Title I, special education, promotion and retention policies, parent involvement, relations with health and social service agencies, and internal school governance. It requires the active participation of every member of an existing staff; Success for All schools are rarely able to select staff specifically for the program. It requires dramatic changes in daily teaching methods for teachers who may have decades of experience doing something else and for those who are new to teaching. It requires a change in beliefs about the school's ability and responsibility to ensure the success of every child, no matter what.

How does all this change come about? How do Success for All and Roots & Wings enter a school, solicit the enthusiastic participation of school staffs, train staff in program procedures, monitor and improve implementation over time, assess progress toward desired goals, and maintain coordination among the many pieces of the program? These are extremely important questions that we have had to address as we scaled up Success for All from a pilot program to become a replicable, reliably effective model for school change. This chapter discusses our practices and experiences with implementation of change in a wide variety of schools.

Establishing Success for All in New Sites

As noted in Chapter 1, there are (as of 1999-2000) 1,500 schools in 400 districts in 48 states implementing Success for All or Roots & Wings in collaboration with the Success for All Foundation. In addition, adaptations of Success for All are being implemented in Canada, Mexico, Britain, Australia, and Israel. The majority of U.S. schools are inner-city Title I schools serving very disadvantaged African American or Latino populations, but many are rural, many have white majorities, and some do not even qualify for Title I. Many students in Success for All have limited English proficiency. Schools and districts involved in Success for All and Roots & Wings have sought us out, usually after reading about or visiting schools already implementing the program.

Our procedures for negotiating with districts vary according to the district's characteristics and needs, but there are several procedures we insist on. One is the clear support of the district's administration. This involves a number of financial conditions (see Chapter 9) as well as a commitment to allow the Success for All or Roots & Wings schools to deviate from district policies (if necessary) on such matters as curriculum, Title I, special education, and promotion and retention.

We require that schools submit an application that commits them to provide the support necessary for successful implementation. Another requirement is a process by which principals are given a free choice to participate or not, and then in schools with strongly committed principals, teachers must have an opportunity to vote (by secret ballot) on whether or not to participate. We require that at least 80% of teachers buy in. In practice, most votes are more like 90% to 95% positive, but we insist on the exercise because we think it is essential that the teachers know that they had a free choice and that any individual disgruntled teachers know that their colleagues were overwhelmingly in favor of the program. Most often, project staff make a presentation to the interested schools (who have already done some investigation about Success for All) in the winter or spring before the program is to begin and then give the staffs a week or more to discuss, debate, read, and (if possible) send a delegation to visit existing schools. We do everything we can to see that teachers are fully informed, have all of their questions answered, and are not pressured into voting for the program.

When Success for All or Roots & Wings enters a district for the first time, we recommend starting with no more than five schools and then expanding in future years. For the pilot schools, we try to avoid any conditions (such as substantial additional funding) that could not be replicated elsewhere in the district. We have found that if pilot schools operate with extraordinary funding or other special circumstances, the conditions are difficult to maintain over time. Some schools receive as much as $50,000 per year to cover start-up costs, but more than this can be counterproductive in the long run. Overwhelmingly, the costs of Success for All and Roots & Wings are covered by Title I, plus state compensatory education, bilingual, and special education funds. Starting in 1998, many schools have received start-up funding to implement Success for All from the U.S. Department of Education's Comprehensive School Reform Demonstration (see Chapter 9).

At the end of the school selection process, we typically have schools with principals and staffs that have freely chosen to participate, in districts in which the central administration is unambiguously supportive. We have learned that this buy-in process is essential. When rough times come (and they always do), everyone involved in an innovation needs to remember that they chose the path they are on.

Professional Development

The philosophy of professional development behind Success for All and Roots & Wings is that although initial training is important, real change in teachers' practices takes place in the classroom, not the workshop. We consider professional development to be a process that never ends. Teachers in Success for All and Roots & Wings schools are constantly refining their instructional methods, learning new strategies, discussing their methods with other teachers, visiting each other's classes, and using assessments of student progress to guide changes in their teaching methods.

Initial training for a staff new to Success for All is ordinarily provided in July or August for a September start-up. This training is typically scheduled for 3 days. Beyond an orientation to the program and some team building among the school staff members, the main focus of initial training is on the changes in curriculum and instruction teachers will be making right away, as soon as school starts. Roots & Wings schools almost always start with the reading components and are therefore identical to Success for All schools in their first year. This means that almost all schools start with Early Learning for preschool and kindergarten, Reading Roots for first grade, and Reading Wings for teachers of students reading at the 2nd grade level or above. Tutors (who also teach a reading class if they are certified teachers) also participate in the Reading Roots training. They later receive their own 2 days of training on strategies for assessment and tutoring of at-risk students.

Around midyear, writing and language arts are usually introduced for teachers of Grades 1 to 6, and KinderRoots for kindergarten teachers. Roots & Wings schools would typically implement WorldLab or MathWings in the second implementation year (see Chapter 5), adding the remaining element in the third year. Along the way, training sessions are held on such topics as classroom management, cooperative learning, bilingual issues, family support, pacing, assessment, special education, and other topics, and to refine and extend topics presented earlier.

The training makes extensive use of simulations and demonstrations. For example, in learning how to use cooperative teams in Reading Wings, teachers work in teams themselves. In STaR and Reading Roots training, the teachers pretend to be teachers and students in the classroom. In addition, video tapes depicting each of the program elements are shown to the teachers. Teachers are always told the theories behind what they are learning, but the main emphasis is on giving them active, hands-on, pragmatic experience with strategies that will work.

After initial training, the main responsibility for staff development passes to the school-based facilitator, and the role of Success for All Foundation staff focuses more on enhancing the facilitator's and principal's skills than on direct teacher training. The facilitator's function in Success for All and Roots & Wings and the role of Success for All Foundation staff in maintaining quality implementations are described in the following sections.

The Facilitator

The first and most important decision a school makes after it has been designated as a Success for All or Roots & Wings school is to select a facilitator (see Madden, Cummings, & Livingston, 1995). The facilitator is the linchpin of the entire program; the effectiveness of the program depends to a substantial degree on his or her skills as a change agent. Facilitators are typically very experienced teachers, usually with backgrounds in reading, early childhood, or Title I. A good facilitator is one who has the respect of his or her colleagues, enormous energy and interpersonal skills, and a deeply felt certainty that every child can learn. Most Success for All and Roots & Wings schools have full-time facilitators, but a few (in very small schools) have half-time facilitators who do some tutoring in the afternoon.

A 5-day training session for new school facilitators and principals is held in a few locations each spring and summer. We strongly encourage new facilitators to spend as much time as possible visiting experienced schools and shadowing their facilitators so that they can learn firsthand what facilitators do.

Defining the precise place of the facilitator within the school's organizational structure is a delicate process. The facilitator must be seen as a friend and supporter to the teachers and therefore should not have a formal or informal role in teacher evaluation. Teachers should always be glad to see the facilitator in their classrooms and should feel free to share problems as well as successes. The facilitator must resist the principal's natural temptation to put them in a role like that of a vice principal. Facilitators need to be observing classes and organizing meetings of key staff, not collecting lunch money or monitoring the playground. They need to spend their time working as change agents, not facilitating the school's routine day-to-day operations.

The overarching responsibility of every facilitator is to ensure that the program achieves its goals—that it delivers *success,* not just services. This means that the facilitator is constantly checking on the operation of the program and its outcomes. Is every teacher proficient in implementing the curriculum? Is every teacher moving rapidly enough to bring all students to grade level? Is every teacher using effective classroom management techniques? Are the tutors supporting students' success in the regular classroom? Is the Family Support Team succeeding in reaching out to parents, and are they on top of any recurring attendance problems? Most important, is every child on a path to success, and if not, are all staff members involved working in a coordinated way to get the student on track? The facilitator operates to make sure that no child is being forgotten and that all staff are working together effectively.

The facilitator has three main responsibilities. One is to provide coaching and follow-up to help teachers and tutors implement changes in curriculum and instruction. Another is to help make sure that the teachers, tutors, family support staff, and principal are all coordinating their activities around the success of all children and that they are talking and planning together. Last, the facilitator manages the 8-week assessment program (see Chapter 2), using assessment information to help make grouping decisions, to decide who needs tutoring, and identify individual children who are not making adequate progress and to help staff explore options for serving these children.

Coaching

Perhaps the most important role the facilitator plays within a Success for All or Roots & Wings school is as a coach or change agent to help teachers and tutors effectively implement changes in curriculum and instruction. They carry out this role in a variety of ways.

The most common way facilitators coach teachers is through classroom visits and follow-up discussions. Some facilitators schedule their visits in advance, whereas others simply tell teachers they may be dropping by in a given week, which allows for more flexibility. Sometimes, facilitators may just stop in for a few minutes, give teachers a "thumbs up" sign or other indication of progress, and then move on; at other times, facilitators may observe teachers for a longer time and then schedule a time to sit down with the teacher to discuss the teacher's needs.

Classroom visits are extremely important in monitoring change. Regardless of the amount or quality of professional development, teachers need feedback on how they are doing in their own classes, and they need suggestions and help targeted to their own particular classroom problems.

Facilitators often teach demonstration lessons. They may arrange coverage so that they can assemble a few teachers at the same time for a lesson in one teacher's class, or they may do a short demonstration for one teacher. Alternatively, many facilitators identify a teacher who is doing an excellent job with a particular part of an instructional program and cover other teachers' classes while they watch the expert teacher's lesson. A facilitator may videotape outstanding lessons to show to the teachers later on. In doing this, a facilitator tries to find something outstanding in the work of every teacher. For example, Ms. Smith may demonstrate her STaR lesson, Ms. Jones her partner reading, and Mr. Williams his writing lesson. Seeing other teachers' solutions to the same problems they are confronting is enormously useful to teachers, and the process of using teachers within the same building as "experts" for each other helps build professionalism and cohesiveness among the staff.

In all of their coaching work, facilitators try to communicate respect and approval for teachers and try to avoid coming across as a supervisor or evaluator. This is why we insist that facilitators not be asked to provide principals with information that could be used in formal evaluations. That is also why we train facilitators to accentuate the positive, recognize good teaching rather than dwell on deficits or errors, and involve teachers in solving each other's problems rather than pretending to be the only expert in the building.

Whereas the facilitator's main role in professional development is to follow up on training by coaching teachers, facilitators also provide more formal training sessions. For example, following the main training sessions conducted by Success for All Foundation staff, school-based facilitators may conduct staff development sessions on classroom management, cooperative learning, or other topics, depending on their expertise and the school's needs. Facilitators have a particularly important training role with teachers who are new to the school or are new to teaching.

Maintaining Coordination

In programs as complex as Success for All or Roots & Wings, there is a need to be sure that all of the program components and services are working together toward the same objectives. One of the facilitator's major tasks is to see that classroom teachers, tutors, family support staff, and other school staff are communicating with each other and are supporting each other's efforts rather than simply providing services and hoping that others will fill in gaps. The facilitator monitors the flow of information between tutors and reading teachers and between family support staff and teachers and tries to find ways to overcome any barriers to open communication.

Component Team Meetings

The facilitator also helps teachers help each other by scheduling meetings twice a month at which teachers and tutors can discuss what they are doing and build their expertise. Schools schedule common planning times or regular after-school meeting times for teachers implementing a given component (e.g., Reading Roots, Reading Wings, Early Learning, Tutoring). In these meetings, specific issues may be addressed or the facilitator may draw out the teachers, asking them to share successes and problems and to make supportive and useful suggestions to each other. Facilitators may show videotapes of excellent lessons or describe from their notes an outstanding lesson to illustrate some point. These meetings are critical in maintaining continuous growth in implementation quality for teachers.

Managing 8-Week Assessments and Exploring Options for Children Having Difficulties

As noted in Chapter 2, 8-week assessments play a crucial role in the Success for All and Roots & Wings reading program. An important (and time-consuming) part of the facilitator's role is to manage the 8-week assessment program. This involves making sure that teachers have the tests they need, collecting tests after they are given, organizing test data, and using data to suggest alternative placements or services for individual children.

For example, the facilitator looks for children who could be accelerated to a higher reading group, children who appear to be in need of tutoring, and children who are currently receiving tutoring but may be able to exit from tutoring. Collaborative decisions about group placements and tutoring are made by the facilitator and the teacher or tutor (or both) involved. Facilitators may set aside time to observe a struggling student during reading class or tutoring time in order to suggest alternative teaching strategies or materials. The 8-week assessments provide a regular opportunity to examine and adjust the reading program for all students. It is the facilitator's job to see that the data are collected and then used to help ensure the success of every child.

A key goal of the Success for All and Roots & Wings program is to keep students with learning problems out of special education and to keep them from being retained. However, this does not simply mean throwing problems back on the teachers or "socially promoting" failing students. Instead, a Success for All or Roots & Wings school tries every strategy possible to meet students' needs so they can keep up with their age-mates.

The facilitator leads the effort to intervene before a student is assigned to special education. Teacher referrals go to the facilitator before they go to a child study team. The facilitator then meets with the teacher and others to try to understand what the child's problem is and how it can be solved without involving the special education system. For example, if a child is exhibiting serious behavior problems, the facilitator, teachers, and Family Support Team may design a home-based reinforcement program. A child having a problem with one teacher may be transferred to another. The same approach is taken with children in danger of being retained.

A Day in the Life of a Success for All Facilitator[1]

It is 7:45 a.m. on an October Monday at Baltimore's Brighton-Early Elementary School, a Success for All school in its second year of implementation. Most of the school is still dark and deserted, but in the library, there is a spirited discussion going on. The Reading Roots teachers and tutors are having a component team meeting to discuss problems they are having. Quietly managing the meeting is Alice Lyle, the Success for All facilitator.

Various teachers bring up problems of pacing and classroom management and discuss individual children who are having particular problems. Ms. Lyle tries to get the teachers and tutors themselves to suggest solutions to their own and each others' problems. She volunteers to cover one teacher's class later in the week so the teacher can observe a colleague who has worked out an effective way to get students organized for partner reading and sets up a time to coteach a demonstration lesson with a new teacher who is having trouble with modeling reading strategies during Listening Comprehension lessons. She encourages the tutors to discuss the strategies they are using successfully with children, and the classroom teachers think of ways they can support those strategies in reading class. At 8:15, the meeting ends, and teachers go to their classrooms to prepare for the students' arrival.

The building principal, Mr. Walker, is supervising the free breakfast program in the cafeteria. Ms. Lyle joins him there to catch up with him "on the fly" on several issues, including those she discussed with the first-grade team. During the brief homeroom and announcement period, Ms. Lyle brings boxes of soft-cover trade books to two of the third-grade teachers who have requested them for their home reading program.

At 8:45, reading period begins. To the sounds of "Reading Jogs Your Mind" played over the loudspeaker, children change classes for reading. Ms. Lyle is pleased to see that the changing of classes is going very smoothly, and she smiles and gives a "thumbs up" sign to several teachers who are monitoring the process in the hall.

When the children are settled, Ms. Lyle starts her "Monday Stroll" through the building. She visits all the classes briefly, just long enough to see what lesson each teacher is on and to get a flavor of what is happening. She keeps notes on a clipboard, identifying issues to bring up with teachers later on. After the stroll, Ms. Lyle spends time with two fourth-grade teachers who are using Reading Wings for the first time this year. During her class visits, Ms. Lyle listens to children read, models how to monitor partner reading, praises students who are working well in their cooperative groups, models preventative classroom management strategies by moving close to a pair of students who are giggling to each other, and signals to the teacher that she likes what she's seeing.

In her Monday stroll and other brief classroom visits, Ms. Lyle is identifying teachers who need more intensive help. Later in the week, she will meet with these teachers, discuss any problems, and collaboratively work out a plan. The plan could include having Ms. Lyle teach a demonstration lesson, having her cover a class so the teacher could observe another teacher, or a series of observation sessions followed by feedback and additional observations.

At 10:15, the reading lesson ends, and students return to their homerooms. Ms. Lyle checks in with a preschool teacher who had asked for help with her STaR program and then looks in briefly on two kindergarten classes that are doing thematic units on African American History. At 10:45, Ms. Lyle visits a tutor who is experiencing a great deal of trouble with one child. In the observation, she notices that the child is squinting at the page. After the child leaves, she suggests to the tutor that the child may need glasses, and she makes a note to mention this to the Family Support Team.

At 11:00, the Family Support Team meets. It is attended by the principal, the school's social worker, the parent liaison, and a second-grade teacher, as well as Ms. Lyle. The teacher is there to discuss a problem she is having with two children. One has inconsistent attendance, frequently coming to school late or not at all. Another is constantly getting into fights. The team first discusses the truant child. After trying out several ideas, they decide to have the social worker meet with the child's mother and to arrange to call her at 9:00 each day the child is absent. In addition, they propose to ask a neighbor who walks her child to school every day to stop by and pick up the child each morning. The teacher suggests a behavior contract system for the child who gets into fights, focusing on rewarding the child with a point for each activity completed during team activities. The parent liaison agrees to meet with the child's parents and to set up a system in which the teacher will send home a note each day the child gets five points. The parents will be given ideas for fun things to do with the child when he brings home a "good day" note.

After the teacher returns to her class, Ms. Lyle brings up the child who seems to need glasses, and the group discusses how to get vision screening for all children and how to get glasses from the local Lion's Club for those who cannot afford them. They also discuss upcoming "parent evenings," additional ways to involve parents in the school, and other topics.

It is now 11:45—lunch time. As usual, it's a working lunch for Ms. Lyle. Today, she meets with the school's special education resource teacher to plan a workshop on strategies teachers can use in the classroom to help students with learning disabilities. The special education teacher teaches a reading class composed of students with and without individual education plans, and she tutors identified special education students in the afternoon. However, much of her job is preventing students from being referred to special education by helping classroom teachers and tutors meet students' needs. Ms. Lyle and the special education teacher discuss several children who are having serious learning problems and brainstorm strategies to adapt to their needs without entering the formal special education referral system.

After lunch, Ms. Lyle videotapes two tutoring sessions. The videos will be sent to the school's lead Success for All Foundation trainer for feedback and suggestions and used in telephone conferences with Foundation staff to help Ms. Lyle build her own skills in noticing and responding to effective and ineffective tutoring strategies. Afterwards, she meets with a third-grade teacher to plan an observation the next day. She drops in on a "Read-In" going on for first graders, where parent volunteers and some students from the middle school across the street are listening to first graders read. At 1:45, she meets a student who is new to the school and gives him an informal reading inventory to place him in a reading group. She then briefly visits all of the fourth grades, which are beginning to use MathWings.

Immediately after school, Ms. Lyle has a brief meeting with the 5th-grade teachers to discuss their writing program. They are having their students prepare class "mystery books" to be read to the school at a winter assembly. They discuss some problems they are having with the peer editing process, and Ms. Lyle promises to visit their classes to see if she can make some suggestions.

At 3:30, Ms. Lyle has a cup of coffee with the principal, Mr. Walker, who has had an equally exhausting day. She tells him all the good things she's seen that day and discusses vision screening, an upcoming workshop on classroom management, and some issues around special education and Title I. At last, Ms. Lyle goes home, where she will spend part of the evening going over the results of the first 8-week reading assessments to identify children who need to be in different reading groups, need tutoring, or are not making adequate progress.

Is every facilitator's day as full as this one? Most facilitators would say that Ms. Lyle's day is, if anything, an easy one, because there were no crises in it. What our experience with facilitators tells us is how much it takes to bring about systemic change throughout high-poverty elementary schools. Nothing less than the extraordinary efforts of talented facilitators whose entire job is to bring about change will ensure the full implementation of a program as comprehensive as Success for All.

Maintaining Program Integrity: The Success for All Foundation Role

When Success for All began in Baltimore, the role of our staff at Johns Hopkins University was much like that of school-based facilitators. We conducted training, monitored implementation, attended Building Advisory Committee and Family Support Team meetings, and so on. When we expanded beyond Baltimore, our role had to change substantially (Slavin, 1994). We now have full-time trainers located in various parts of the country. In addition, our focus is now on enabling schools to manage Success for All on their own. We still conduct the initial training of teachers and facilitators, but our function after the initial training is directed toward empowering the school's staff to solve its own problems as much as possible.

Trainers from the Success for All Foundation and regional partners are responsible for the initial training provided to new Success for All and Roots & Wings schools. They then work with the new schools to help them implement the program over time. Two trainers visit new schools for about 6 days in the first implementation year and 2 to 4 days in later years to conduct additional training and to monitor implementation.

After the initial training, our efforts in new Success for All schools focus on enhancing the skills of the school-based facilitators to manage the programs on their own. For example, in visits to the schools, our trainers spend time in classes and tutoring sessions with the school-based facilitators. The main purpose of these visits is to help the school-based facilitators see what our trainers see. They share observations and insights to come to a common understanding of what portions of each teacher's lessons are good, what portions are in need of improvement, and what strategies the school-based facilitators might try to improve the teachers' skills.

These visits are supplemented by frequent telephone contacts between our staff and the school-based facilitators. In addition, we sometimes use speaker phones at the schools to enable our facilitators to have "meetings" with several school staff members, and we are beginning to have school-based facilitators videotape teachers' lessons and send them to us so that our staff can offer feedback and suggestions. In addition, school-based facilitators send us monthly reports to keep our staff informed of the program's progress and problems.

Maintaining the integrity of the program while allowing it to meet the different needs of different schools and communities is a constant, dynamic process. Part of this process takes place in the early negotiations, when our staff works with district and building administrators to adapt the model to district resources, needs, and interests. When the program is under way, there are frequent questions about adaptations and alterations to meet the needs of specific groups of children or local circumstances.

In addition to training and supporting implementation of Success for All and Roots & Wings, our staff has several other roles. We are continually working to develop and improve our curriculum materials, teachers' manuals, and training materials and procedures. Our research and development staff leads the development activities, but some of our trainers have one or more areas of curricular expertise in which they do some development.

We are very conscious of the problems of scaling up a program from pilot to national dissemination without watering down the program or losing the features that made it effective in its early sites. We are trying at every stage to maintain the quality and integrity of the model by building on our strengths and insisting on systems that ensure top-quality implementation at every participating school without being so rigid or prescriptive that the program cannot adapt to meet local needs.

Networking

Building a national network of Success for All and Roots & Wings schools is one of the most important things we're trying to do at the Success for All Foundation. An isolated school out on the frontier of innovation can sometimes hang on for a few years, but systemic and lasting change is far more likely when schools work together as part of a network in which school staff share a common vision and a common language, share ideas and technical assistance, and create an emotional connection and support system. This is the main reason we have annual conferences for experienced and new sites. At the annual conferences, we provide valuable information on new developments and new ideas (most of which we have gotten directly from the schools we work with). We are also trying to build connections between the experienced schools so that they can share ideas on issues of common interest and build significant relationships with other schools pursuing similar objectives, and we are also trying to create an esprit de corps, a pride in what we are all trying to do together, an understanding and acceptance of the struggle needed to achieve the goal of success for every child.

In addition to national conferences, there are many other things we do to build an effective support network. We publish a newsletter, Success Story, which focuses on new ideas and outstanding accomplishments of our schools. In our conversations with schools, we are constantly putting schools in touch with other schools to help them with specific issues, such as bilingual education, year-round schedules, use of Title I funds in nonschoolwide circumstances, use of special education funds to support tutoring, and so on.

One of the most common activities of local support networks for Success for All and Roots & Wings is regular meetings among key staff. Most often, it is facilitators or facilitators and principals together who meet about once a month to discuss common problems and explore ways to help each other. Sometimes, principals or family support teams meet separately from time to time to discuss issues of particular concern to them.

For more on the scaling up of Success for All and Roots & Wings, see Slavin and Madden (1999a).

Note

1. This vignette is a composite of the experiences of several facilitators in several Success for All schools. It is primarily the work of Alta Shaw and Lynne Mainzer, both of whom have been building facilitators and Success for All trainers. All names, including that of the school, are fictitious.

8

Research on Success for All and Roots & Wings

One of the guiding principles in the development of Success for All and Roots & Wings is an emphasis on rigorous evaluation. The elements of our programs are themselves derived from current research on reading, writing, math, science, and social studies; on early childhood, second language learning, and special education; and on parent involvement, professional development, and school change, among many others. However, it is not enough for a program to be based on good research: It must also be rigorously and repeatedly evaluated in many schools over meaningful periods of time in comparison to similar control schools.

Success for All is arguably the most extensively evaluated school reform model ever to exist. It was originally conceived, developed, and evaluated within a research center, currently called the Center for Research on the Education of Students Placed at Risk, at Johns Hopkins University, under federal funding that required extensive and rigorous evaluation. Furthermore, the majority of studies of Success for All have been carried out by researchers who are not at Johns Hopkins University. Experimental-control comparisons have been made by researchers at eight universities and research institutions other than Johns Hopkins, both within the United States and in five other countries. Taken together, dozens of studies have compared Success for All and control schools on individually administered standardized tests, such as the Woodcock and Durrell, and on state accountability measures, both norm-referenced tests and state performance assessments. Based on the amount, quality, and positive outcomes of this research, Success for All was cited as one of only two elementary comprehensive designs that met the highest standards for research base in a review of 24 programs done by the American Institutes of Research (Herman, 1999). The same conclusion was reached in a study commissioned by the Fordham Foundation (Traub, 1999).

Longitudinal evaluations of Success for All were begun in its earliest sites, six schools in Baltimore and Philadelphia. Later, third-party evaluators at the University of Memphis, Steve Ross, Lana Smith, and their colleagues, added evaluations in Memphis, Houston, Charleston (South Carolina), Montgomery (Alabama), Fort Wayne (Indiana), Caldwell (Idaho), Tucson (Arizona), Clover Park (Washington), Little Rock (Arkansas), and Clarke County (Georgia). Studies focusing on English-language learners in California have been conducted in Modesto and Riverside by researchers at WestEd, a federally funded regional educational laboratory. Each of these evaluations has compared Success for All schools to matched comparison schools using either traditional methods or alternative reform models on measures of reading performance, starting with cohorts in kindergarten or in first grade and following these students as long as possible (details of the evaluation design will be discussed later). Vagaries of funding and other local problems have ended some evaluations prematurely, but many have been able to follow Success for All schools for many years. As of this writing, we have data comparing matched Success for All and traditional control schools on individual measures from schools in 13 U.S. districts, and other studies have compared Success for All to a variety of alternative reform models, compared full and partial implementations of Success for All, and made other comparisons. In addition, there have been many studies involving group-administered standardized tests, including both national norm-referenced tests and state criterion-referenced tests used in state accountability programs. Experimental-control comparisons have also been carried out in Canada, England, Australia, and Israel.

Studies Comparing Success for All to Matched Control Groups

The largest number of studies has compared the achievement of students in Success for All schools to that of children in matched comparison schools using traditional methods, including locally developed Title I reforms. Schools implementing the Reading Recovery tutoring model were included as "traditional controls," because only a small proportion of students received tutoring; however, in each case, special analyses compared children tutored in Success for All and those tutored in Reading Recovery (those comparisons are discussed in a later section). The only studies excluded are a few in which there were pretest differences between Success

TABLE 8.1 Characteristics of Success for All Schools in Experimental-Control Group Comparisons

District, School	Enrollment	Percentage Receiving Free Lunch	Ethnicity (by percentage)	Date Began	Data Collected	Comments
Baltimore, Maryland						
B1	500	83	B-96, W-4	1987	88-94	First Success for All school; has additional funds first years
B2	500	96	B-100	1988	89-94	Had additional funds first 4 years
B3	400	96	B-100	1988	89-94	
B4	500	85	B-100	1988	89-94	
B5	650	96	B-100	1988	89-94	
Philadelphia, Pennsylvania						
P1	620	96	A-60, W-20, B-20	1988	89-94	Large ESL program for Cambodian children
P2	600	97	B-100	1991	92-93	
P3	570	96	B-100	1991	92-93	
P4	840	98	B-100	1991	93	
P5	700	98	L-100	1992	93-94	Study only involved students in Spanish bilingual programs
Charleston, South Carolina						
CS1	500	40	B-60, W-40	1990	91-92	
Memphis, Tennessee						
MT1	350	90	B-95, W-5	1990	91-94	Program implemented only in Grades K-2
MT2	530	90	B-100	1993	94	
MT3	290	86	B-100	1993	94	
MT4	370	90	B-100	1993	94	
Fort Wayne, Indiana						
F1	396	80	B-45, W-55	1991	92-94, 97-98	
F2	305	67	B-50, W-50	1991	92-94, 97-98	

TABLE 8.1 Characteristics of Success for All Schools in Experimental-Control Group Comparisons

District, School	Enrollment	Percentage Receiving Free Lunch	Ethnicity (by percentage)	Date Began	Data Collected	Comments
F3	588	82	B-66, W-34	1995	97-98	
Montgomery, Alabama						
MA1	450	95	B-100	1991	93-94	
MA2	460	97	B-100	1991	93-94	
Caldwell, Idaho						
CI1	400	20	W-80, L-20	1991	93-94	Study compared two Success for All schools to Reading Recovery school
Modesto, California						
MC1	640	70	W-54, L-25, A-17, B-4	1992	94	Large ESL program for students speaking 17 languages
MC2	560	98	L-66, W-24, A-10	1992	94	Large Spanish bilingual program
Riverside, California						
R1	930	73	L-54, W-33, B-10, A-3	1992	94	Large Spanish bilingual and ESL programs; year-round school
Tucson, Arizona						
T1	484	82	L-54, W-34, B-69, A-5	1995	95-96	Compared to locally developed schoolwide projects
T2	592	43	W-73, L-23, B-1, A-1	1995	95-96	Compared to locally developed schoolwide projects and Reading Recovery
Little Rock, Arkansas						
LR1	302	73	B-80, W-20	1997	98-99	
LR2	262	79	B-95, L-5	1997	98-99	
Clarke Co., Georgia						
CL1	420	70	B-80, W20	1995	97	
CL2	488	72	B-78, W-22	1995	97	

for All and control groups of more than 30% of a standard deviation (e.g., Ross & Casey, 1998a, 1998b; Wang & Ross, 1999a, 1999b).

Table 8.1 summarizes demographic and other data about the schools involved in the experimental-control evaluations of Success for All.

A common evaluation design, with variations due to local circumstances, has been used in most Success for All evaluations carried out by researchers at Johns Hopkins University, the University of Memphis, and WestEd. Each Success for All school involved in a formal evaluation was matched with a control school similar in poverty level (percentage of students qualifying for free lunch), historical achievement level, ethnicity, and other factors. Schools were also matched on district-administered standardized test scores given in kindergarten or on Peabody Picture Vocabulary Test (PPVT) scores given by the evaluators in the fall of kindergarten or first grade.

The measures used in the evaluations were as follows:

Woodcock Reading Mastery Test.   Three Woodcock scales, Word Identification, Word Attack, and Passage Comprehension, were individually administered to students by trained testers. Word Identification assesses recognition of common sight words, Word Attack assesses phonetic synthesis skills, and Passage Comprehension assesses comprehension in context. Students in Spanish bilingual programs were given the Spanish versions of these scales.

Durrell Analysis of Reading Difficulty.   The Durrell Oral Reading scale was also individually administered to students in Grades 1 through 3. It presents a series of graded reading passages that students read aloud, followed by comprehension questions.

Gray Oral Reading Test.   Comprehension and passage scores from the Gray Oral Reading Test were obtained from students in Grades 4 and 5.

Analyses of covariance with pretests as covariates were used to compare raw scores in all evaluations, and separate analyses were conducted for students in general and, in many studies, for students in the lowest 25% of their grades at pretest.

The figures presented here summarize student performance in grade equivalents (adjusted for covariates) and effect size (ES; proportion of a standard deviation separating the experimental and control groups), averaging across individual measures. Neither grade equivalents nor averaged scores were used in the analyses, but they are presented here as a useful summary.

Each of the summarized evaluations follows children who began in Success for All or Roots & Wings in first grade or earlier, in comparison to children who had attended the control school over the same period. Students who started in it after first grade are not considered to have received the full treatment (although they are of course served within the schools).

Results for all experimental-control comparisons in all evaluation years are averaged and summarized in Figure 8.1, using a method called multisite replicated experiment (Slavin et al., 1996a, 1996b; Slavin & Madden, 1993).

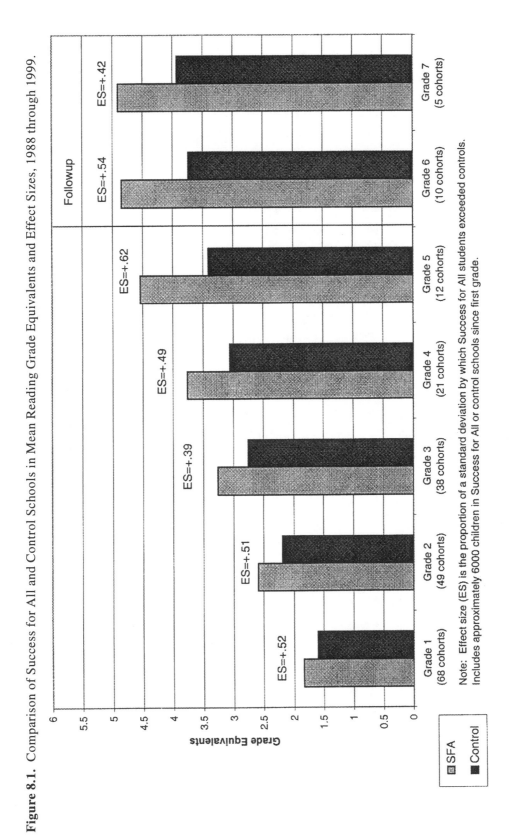

Figure 8.1. Comparison of Success for All and Control Schools in Mean Reading Grade Equivalents and Effect Sizes, 1988 through 1999.

Note: Effect size (ES) is the proportion of a standard deviation by which Success for All students exceeded controls. Includes approximately 6000 children in Success for All or control schools since first grade.

For more details on methods and findings, Slavin and Madden (1999), Slavin, Madden, Dolan, and Wasik (1996), and the full site reports.

Reading Outcomes

The results of the multisite replicated experiment evaluating Success for All are summarized in Figure 8.1 for each grade level, 1 through 5, and for follow-up measures into Grades 6 and 7. The analyses compare cohort means for experimental and control schools. A cohort is all students at a given grade level in a given year. For example, the Grade 1 graph compares 68 experimental to 68 control cohorts, with cohort (50-150 students) as the unit of analysis. In other words, each bar is a mean of scores from more than 6,000 students. Grade equivalents are based on the means and are only presented for their informational value. No analyses were done using grade equivalents.

Statistically significant ($p = .05$ or better) positive effects of Success for All (compared to controls) were found on every measure at every grade level, 1 through 5. For students in general, ESs averaged around a half standard deviation at all grade levels. Effects were somewhat higher than this for the Woodcock Word Attack scale in first and second grades, but in Grades 3 through 5, ESs were more or less equivalent on all aspects of reading. Consistently, ESs for students in the lowest 25% of their grades were particularly positive, ranging from ES = +1.03 in first grade to ES = +1.68 in fourth grade. Again, cohort-level analyses found statistically significant differences favoring low achievers in Success for All on every measure at every grade level. A follow-up study of Baltimore schools found that positive program effects continued into Grade 6 (ES = +0.54) and Grade 7 (ES = +0.42), when students were in middle schools.

Quality and Completeness of Implementation

It was no surprise that effects of Success for All are strongly related to the quality and completeness of implementation. In a large study in Houston, Nunnery et al. (in press) found that schools implementing all program components obtained better results (compared to controls) than did schools implementing the program to a moderate or minimal degree.

In this study, 46 school staffs were allowed to select the level of implementation they wanted to achieve. Some adopted the full model, as ordinarily required elsewhere; some adopted a partial model; and some adopted only the reading program, with few if any tutors, and half-time facilitators or no facilitators. Many of the schools used the Spanish bilingual form of Success for All and were assessed in Spanish.

Figures 8.2 and 8.3 summarize the results. The figures show ESs comparing Success for All to control schools on individually administered measures. On the English measure (Figure 8.2), ESs were very positive for the schools using the full program (ES = +0.47), less positive for those with a medium degree of implementation (ES = +0.31), but for those implementing the fewest program elements, ESs were slightly negative (ES = – 0.13), indicating that the control groups achieved somewhat better scores. Among schools teaching in Spanish, there were too few certified teacher-tutors for any school to qualify as a high implementer (due to a shortage of teachers). However, medium implementers scored very well (ES = +.31), whereas low implementers scored less well (ES = +.19; see Figure 8.3).

A Memphis study (Ross, Smith, Lewis, & Nunnery, 1996; Ross, Smith, & Nunnery, 1998) compared the achievement of eight Success for All schools to that of four schools using other restructuring designs, matched on socioeconomic status and PPVT scores. Each pair of Success for All schools had one school rated by observers as a high implementer and one rated as a low implementer. In the 1996 cohort, first-grade results depended entirely on implementation quality. Averaging across the four Woodcock and Durrell scales, every comparison showed high-implementation Success for All schools scored higher than their comparison schools, whereas low-implementation Success for All schools scored lower (Ross et al., 1996). However, by second grade, Success for All schools exceeded comparison schools, on average, and there was less of a clear relationship with the original implementation ratings, perhaps because implementation quality changed over the 2-year period. Similarly, the 1997 first-grade cohort did not show a clear pattern with respect to quality of implementation.

A Miami study (Urdegar, 1998) evaluated Success for All, two integrated learning systems computer programs (CCC and Jostens), and Reading Mastery on the Stanford Achievement Test's Reading Comprehension scale. None of the programs were associated with higher achievement gains than matched controls. However, program implementation was very poor in the Success for All schools, particularly in that there were few or no tutors in most schools. Also, a pretest, given 8 months before the posttest, was used as a covariate, even though the programs had been used for several years in most schools. The pretest is likely to reflect some or all of the program's impact over time, making the analysis of covariance difficult to interpret.

An early study by a separate team of Johns Hopkins researchers also found mixed outcomes in a study with serious implementation problems. This study, in Charleston, South Carolina, compared one school to a matched control school. However, the researchers failed to obtain the required 80% vote in favor of the program, implementation was very poor, and Hurricane Hugo had ripped the roof off of the school, closing it for many weeks and disrupting it for many more. Despite this, most kindergarten and 1st-grade measures favored Success for All, and retentions in grade were significantly diminished. However, 2nd-grade and 3rd-grade measures did not favor the Success for All school (Jones, Gottfredson, & Gottfredson, 1997).

Cooper, Slavin, and Madden (1998), in an interview study, found that high-quality implementations of Success for All depended on many factors, including district and principal support, participation in national and local networks, adequacy of resources, and genuine buy-in at the outset on the part of all teachers.

Figure 8.2 Houston Independent School District: 1996 First-Grade Effect Sizes by Implementation Level—English

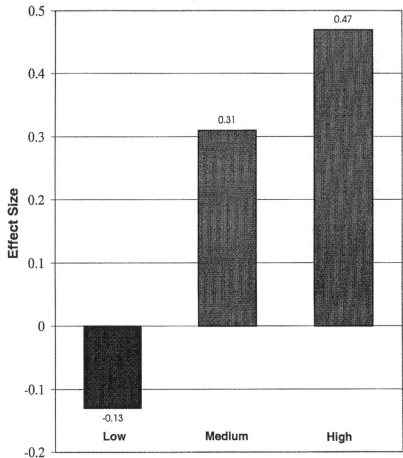

Effects on District-Administered Standardized Tests

The formal evaluations of Success for All have relied on individually administered assessments of reading. The Woodcock and Durrell scales used in these assessments are far more accurate than district-administered tests and are much more sensitive to real reading gains. They allow testers to hear children actually reading the material of increasing difficulty and to respond to questions about what they have read. The Woodcock and Durrell are themselves nationally standardized tests and produce norms (e.g., percentiles, normal curve equivalents, and grade equivalents), just like any other standardized measure.

However, educators often want to know the effects of innovative programs on the kinds of group-administered standardized tests they are usually held accountable for. To obtain this information, researchers have often analyzed standardized or state criterion-referenced test data comparing students in experimental and control

Figure 8.3 Houston Independent School District: 1996 First-Grade Effect
Sizes by Implementation Category—Spanish

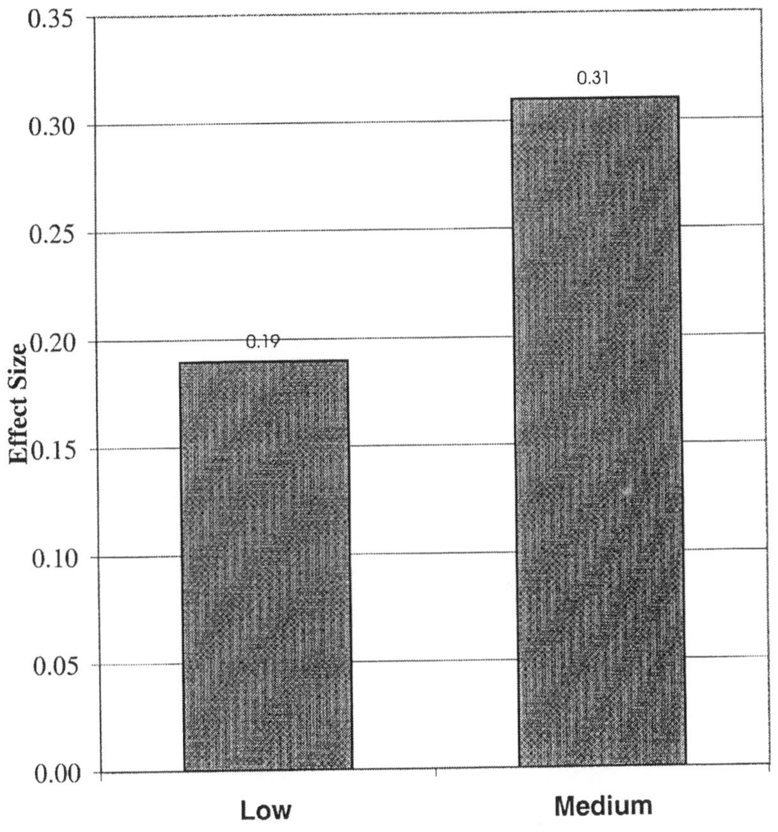

schools. The following sections briefly summarize findings from these types of
evaluations.

Memphis, Tennessee

One of the most important independent evaluations of Success for All and Roots
& Wings was a study carried out by researchers at the University of Tennessee-
Knoxville for the Tennessee State Department of Education (Ross, Sanders, Wright,
& Stringfield, 1998). William Sanders, the architect of the Tennessee Value-Added
Assessment System (TVAAS), carried out the analysis. The TVAAS gives each
school an expected gain, based primarily on school poverty levels, and compares it
to actual scores on the Tennessee Comprehensive Assessment Program (TCAP).
TVAAS scores above 100 indicate gains in excess of expectations; those below 100
indicate the opposite. Sanders compared TVAAS scores in eight Memphis Success
for All schools to those in (a) matched comparison schools and (b) all Memphis
schools.

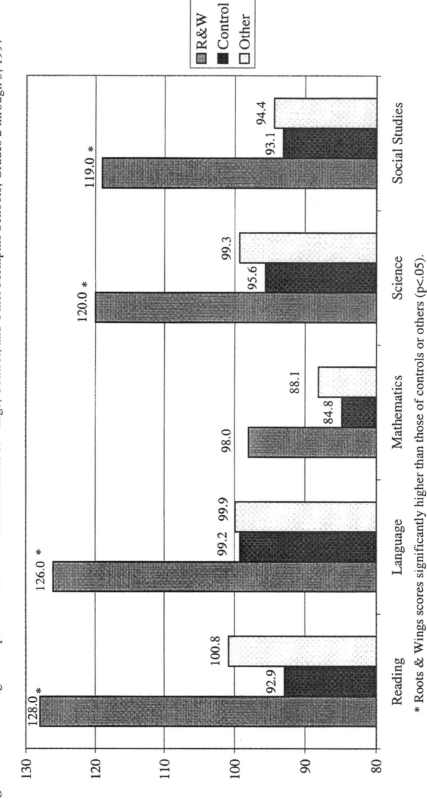

Figure 8.4. Percentage of Expected Gain on TVAAS for Roots & Wings, Control, and Other Memphis Schools, Grades 2 through 5, 1997

* Roots & Wings scores significantly higher than those of controls or others (p<.05). Tennessee Value-Added Assessment System (TVAAS) scores analyzed by William Sanders for the Tennessee State Department of Education. See Ross, Sanders, & Wright, 1998.

282

Figure 8.4 summarizes the results for all subjects assessed. At pretest, the Success for All schools were lower than both comparison groups on TVAAS. However, after 2 years, they performed significantly better than comparison schools in reading, language, science, and social studies. Whereas some schools had implemented aspects of WorldLab, none had implemented MathWings; despite this, even math scores nonsignificantly favored the Success for All schools.

A 3rd-year evaluation found that Success for All schools averaged the greatest gains and highest levels on the TVAAS of five restructuring designs (Co-NECT, Accelerated Schools, Audrey Cohen College, ATLAS, and Expeditionary Learning), as well as exceeding controls, averaging across all subjects (Ross, Wang, Sanders, Wright, & Stringfield, 1999).

The importance of the Memphis study lies in several directions. First, it is a completely independent evaluation that involved state assessment scores of the kind used in most state accountability systems. Second, it shows carryover effects of a program focused on reading, writing, and language arts into science and social studies outcomes.

An earlier study of Success for All schools in Memphis also showed positive effects on the TCAP. This was a longitudinal study of three Success for All and three control schools carried out by Ross, Smith, and Casey (1997a). On average, Success for All schools exceeded controls on TCAP reading by an ES of +0.38 in first grade and +0.45 in second grade.

State of Texas

Since 1994, the State of Texas has administered the Texas Assessment of Academic Success, or TAAS, in Grades 3, 4, and 5, and in writing in Grade 4. It also assessed fourth-grade reading in 1993. Recently, Texas put its TAAS scores for every school every year on the Internet, making it possible to compare Success for All schools throughout the state to gains in the state as a whole. The importance of this is that it makes possible an independent assessment of program outcomes; even if we compute the means, anyone with a list of Success for All schools and an Internet account can do the same analysis.

Reading data, analyzed by Eric Hurley and Anne Chamberlain, are summarized in Figure 8.5. The data, from 117 high-poverty Title I schools using Success for All throughout the state, are organized according to the year the program began, focusing on gains from the spring before program implementation to spring 1998, averaged across Grades 3 through 5. The gains for Success for All cohorts are compared to average gains in all other schools throughout the state over the same time periods. Because TAAS scores, expressed as the percentage of students meeting minimum expectations, have been gradually rising statewide, gains for Success for All and other schools are larger the longer the time period involved. However, Success for All schools have consistently gained more than other schools, with the relative advantage increasing with each year in the program. All differences between Success for All and state gains are statistically significant ($p < .05$), using school means as the unit of analysis.

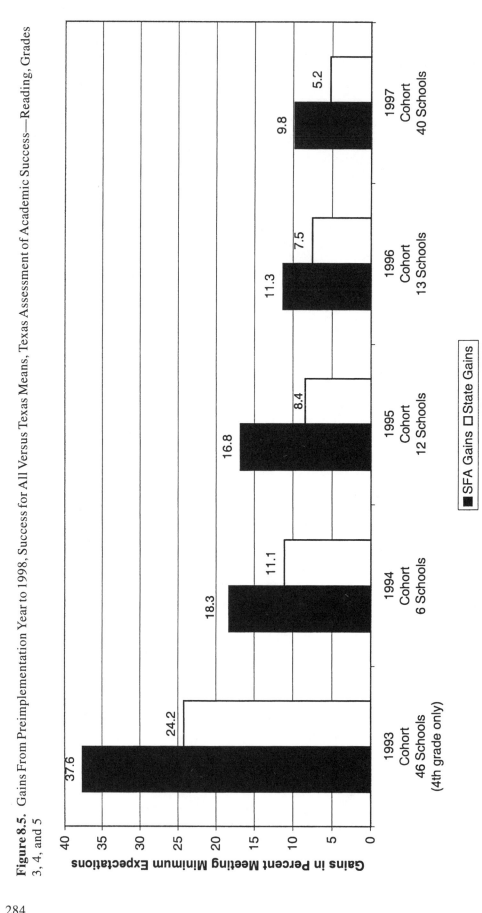

Figure 8.5. Gains From Preimplementation Year to 1998, Success for All Versus Texas Means, Texas Assessment of Academic Success—Reading, Grades 3, 4, and 5

In raw scores rather than gains, Success for All schools, far more impoverished than the state average, started far below state averages and then increased to near equality with state averages. For example, the 1993 cohort (Grade 4 only, as this was the only grade tested in 1993) began 32.5 percentile points behind the state in percentage meeting minimum standards on TAAS reading, but 5 years later was nearly indistinguishable from the state (88.1% passing for the state vs. 85.0% for 46 Success for All schools). Similar patterns were seen for the 1994, 1995, and 1996 cohorts, all of which started far below state means and, as of 1998, were within 1.4 to 3.8 percentile points of state means. The only cohort that did not close the gap to this extent was the most recent, the 1997 cohort (35 schools). This cohort started 17.3 percentile points behind the state and 1 year later was 12.8 points behind, a real improvement but not to virtual equality.

Houston, Texas

In Houston, Success for All was begun on a large scale in 1995, in two forms. One set of schools ($n = 46$) adopted Success for All as part of a study (Nunnery et al., in press) in which they were allowed to implement either the full program, the reading program only, or something in between. As noted earlier, the full-implementation schools obtained excellent outcomes on individually administered tests given to subsamples, in comparison to control schools, whereas moderate-implementation schools obtained less positive outcomes, and low-implementation schools did not differ from controls (recall Figures 8.2 and 8.3). After the first 2 years, the Houston district insisted that all Success for All schools take on the full model, but because of the incomplete start made by most schools, quality of implementation in these schools never reached the levels typical elsewhere.

In contrast, a set of schools in Houston is implementing Success for All as part of a larger program called Project GRAD (Ketelsen, 1994; McAdoo, 1998). Project GRAD, developed and led by a former CEO of Tenneco, works with entire feeder patterns of schools leading into a high school. At the elementary level, Project GRAD uses all Success for All elements but adds a math program called Move-It Math and a school climate program called Consistency Management/Cooperative Discipline (Freiberg, Stein, & Huang, 1995). Most important, Project GRAD schools receive the resources, assistance, and monitoring needed to fully implement Success for All, and in most cases, implementation quality in Project GRAD schools is at or above usual levels for urban Success for All schools.

Figure 8.6 shows TAAS gains for Project GRAD schools, other Houston Independent School District (HISD) Success for All schools, and the State of Texas. As the figure shows, Project GRAD schools ($n = 8$) gained significantly more than HISD Success for All schools ($n = 46$), which in turn gained significantly more than other Texas schools, in reading as well as writing at all grade levels. This result provides one more indication of the importance of high-quality implementation, as well as supporting the broader approach taken by Project GRAD.

Figure 8.6. Texas Assessment of Academic Skills, Gains in Percentage Meeting Minimum Expectations From Spring 1994 to Spring 1998, Houston Success for All Schools (N = 46) Versus Project GRAD Success for All Schools (N = 8), Grades 3 Through 5

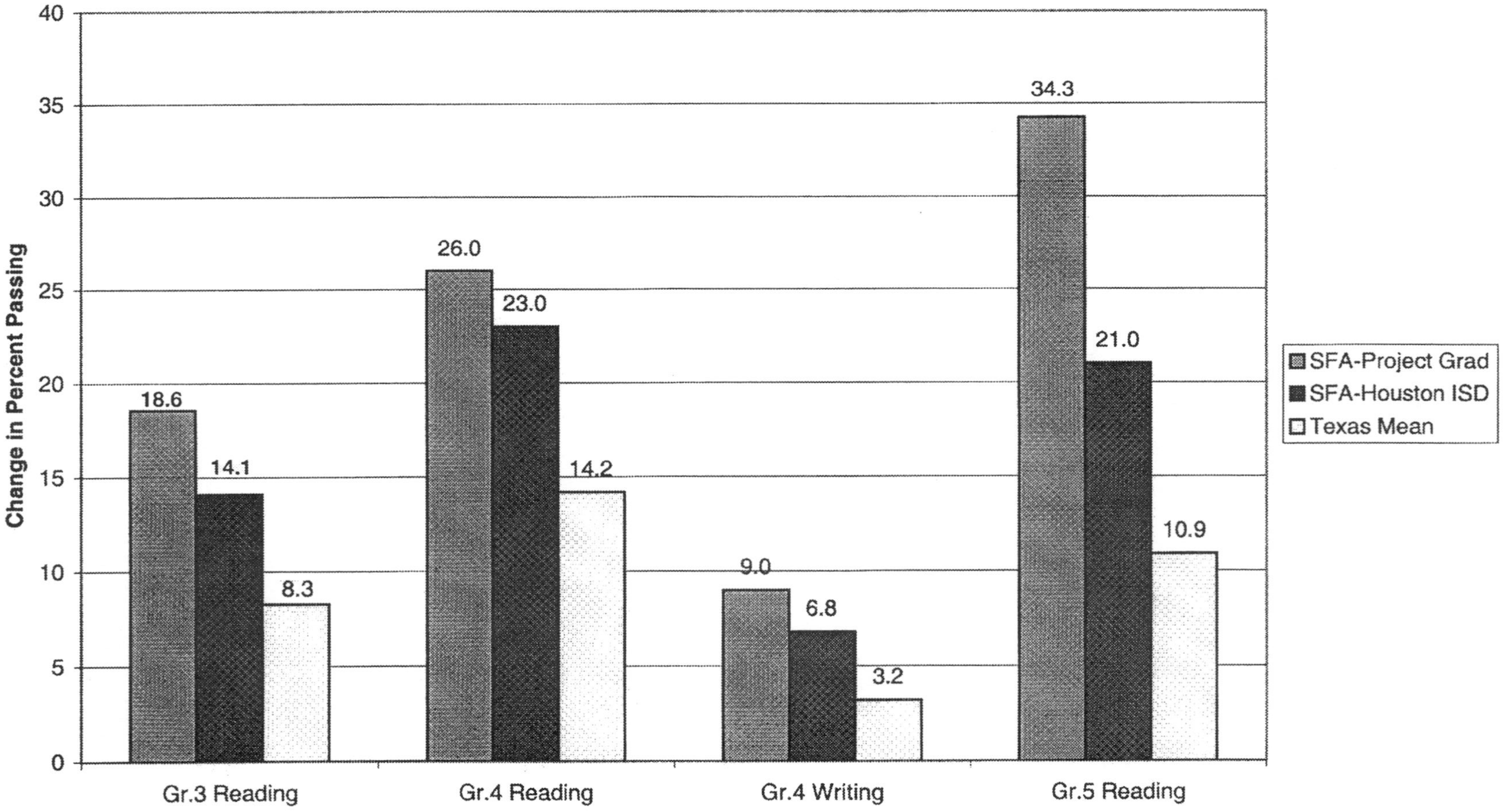

286

Baltimore, Maryland

A longitudinal study in Baltimore from 1987 through 1993 collected Comprehensive Test of Basic Skills (CTBS) scores on the original five Success for All and control schools. On average, Success for All schools exceeded control schools at every grade level. The differences were statistically and educationally significant. By fifth grade, Success for All students were performing 75% of a grade equivalent ahead of controls (ES = +0.45) on CTBS Total Reading scores (see Slavin, Madden, Dolan, Wasik, Ross, & Smith, 1994).

A critique of the Baltimore research was written by Venezky (in press), who observed that although both individually administered and standardized test scores did favor Success for All over the control group, neither Success for All nor controls were performing at grade level by fifth grade. Venezky also questioned whether the upper-elementary parts of the program contributed to overall effects. Still, Venezky recognized the effectiveness of the first-grade program and did not dispute the observation that experimental-control differences were important and were maintained throughout the elementary grades.

Flint, Michigan

Two schools in Flint, Michigan, began implementation of Success for All in 1992. The percentage of students passing the Michigan Educational Assessment Program (MEAP) in reading at fourth grade increased dramatically. Homedale Elementary had a pass rate of 2% in 1992, placing it last among the district's 32 elementary schools. In 1995, 48.6% of students passed, placing it first in the district. Merrill Elementary, 27th in the district in 1992 with only 9.5% of students passing, was 12th in 1995 with 22% passing. Over the same period, the average for all Flint elementary schools only increased from 18.3% passing to 19.3%.

Fort Wayne, Indiana

An evaluation in two schools in Fort Wayne, Indiana (Ross, Smith, & Casey, 1995), found positive effects of Success for All on the reading comprehension scale of the ISTEP, Indiana's norm-referenced achievement test. In first grade, the ES was +0.49 for students in general and +1.13 for the lowest-performing 25%. In second grade, ESs were +0.64, and in third grade, ES = +.13.

International Evaluations of Success for All Adaptations

Several studies have assessed the effects of adaptations of Success for All in countries outside of the United States. These adaptations have ranged from relatively minor adjustments to accommodate political and funding requirements in Canada and England to more significant adaptations in Mexico, Australia, and Israel.

The Canadian study (Chambers, Abrami, & Morrison, in press) involved one school in Montreal that was compared to a matched control school on individually administered reading measures. Results indicated significantly better reading performance in the Success for All school than in the control school both for special needs students (a large proportion of the Success for All students) and for other students. Similarly, a study of five Success for All schools in Nottingham, England, found that Success for All students gained more in reading than did students in a previous cohort, before the program was introduced, and gained more on Key Stage 1 (age 7) and Key Stage 2 (age 11) reading tests than did English schools overall (Harris, Hopkins, Youngman, Harris, & Wordsworth, in press; Hopkins, Youngman, Harris, & Wordsworth, 1999).

Because of language and cultural differences, the most significant adaptation of Success for All was made to use the program in Israel with both Hebrew-speaking children in Jewish schools and Arabic-speaking children in Israeli Arab schools, all in or near the northern city of Acre. The implementation involved community interventions focusing on parent involvement, integrated services, and other aspects in addition to the adapted Success for All model. In comparison to control groups, Success for All first graders performed at significantly higher levels on tests of reading and writing (Hertz-Lazarowitz, in press).

Australian researchers created a substantially simplified adaptation of Success for All, which they called SWELL. SWELL uses instructional procedures much like those used in Success for All but uses books adapted for the Australian context. Only the early grades are involved. Schools do not have full-time facilitators or family support programs, and they may or may not provide any tutoring. Two studies of SWELL found positive effects of the program on reading performance in comparison to control groups and to Reading Recovery schools (Center, Freeman, Mok, & Robertson, 1997; Center, Freeman, & Robertson, in press).

Last, a Mexican study in Juarez, near El Paso, Texas, found substantial gains on Spanish reading tests in three schools implementing an adaptation of Success for All (Calderón, in press).

The international studies of programs adapted from Success for All have importance in themselves, of course, but also demonstrate that the principles on which Success for All are based transfer to other languages, cultures, and political systems. In addition, they provide third-party evaluations of Success for All in diverse contexts, strengthening the research base for Success for All principles and practices.

Roots & Wings

A study of Roots & Wings (Slavin & Madden, 2000) was carried out in four pilot schools in rural southern Maryland and one school in San Antonio, Texas. In both, evaluations compared students' gains on state assessments to those for their respective states as a whole.

In the Maryland evaluation, the Roots & Wings schools served populations that were significantly more disadvantaged than state averages. They averaged 48% free and reduced-price lunch eligibility, compared to 30% for the state. The assessment tracked growth over time on the Maryland School Performance Assessment Program (MSPAP), compared to growth in the state as a whole. The MSPAP is a performance measure on which students are asked to solve complex problems, set up experiments, write in various genres, and read extended text. It uses matrix sampling, which means that different students take different forms of the test.

In both third-grade and fifth-grade assessments in all subjects tested (reading, language, writing, math, science, and social studies), Roots & Wings students showed substantial growth. As shown in Figures 8.7 and 8.8, by the third implementation year, when all program components were in operation, the State of Maryland gained in average performance on the MSPAP over the same time period, but the number of Roots & Wings students achieving at satisfactory or excellent levels increased by more than twice the state's rate on every measure at both grade levels.

After the 1995-96 school year, when funding for the pilot was significantly reduced, implementation dropped off substantially in the Maryland pilot schools, and MSPAP scores correspondingly failed to increase further and in some cases slightly declined. Still, 2 years after the end of full implementation, the total gains made by the Roots & Wings schools remained higher than those for the state as a whole in every subject at both grade levels except for fifth-grade language.

The first evaluation of Roots & Wings outside of Maryland took place at Lackland City Elementary School in San Antonio, Texas (see Slavin & Madden, 2000). This school served a very impoverished population, with 93% of its students qualifying for free lunch in 1998, up from 88% in 1994. Most of its students (79%) are Hispanic; 16% are white, and 5% African American.

Lackland City adopted Success for All in 1994-1995 and then added MathWings for Grades 3 through 5 in 1995-1996 and WorldLab and Primary MathWings in 1996-1997. In contrast to St. Mary's County, implementation of Roots & Wings at Lackland City continues to be strong.

Like Maryland, Texas uses a high-stakes performance measure: TAAS. Scores on the TAAS for Lackland City were compared to those for the state as a whole for Grades 3 through 5 reading and math and for Grade 4 writing. Scores are the percentages of students scoring above minimum standards.

Figure 8.9 summarizes TAAS gains from 1994 (pretest) to 1998. As in Maryland, the Roots & Wings schools gained substantially more than the state as a whole on each scale, with the largest absolute gains in math but the largest relative gains in reading and writing.

Changes in Effect Sizes Over Years of Implementation

One interesting trend in outcomes from comparisons of Success for All and control schools relates to changes in effect sizes according to the number of years a

(Continues on page 294)

Figure 8.7. Maryland School Performance Assessment Program: Gains in Percentage of Students Scoring Satisfactory or Better, St. Mary's County Roots & Wings Schools Versus State Means, Grade 3, 1993 through 1996 (full implementation)

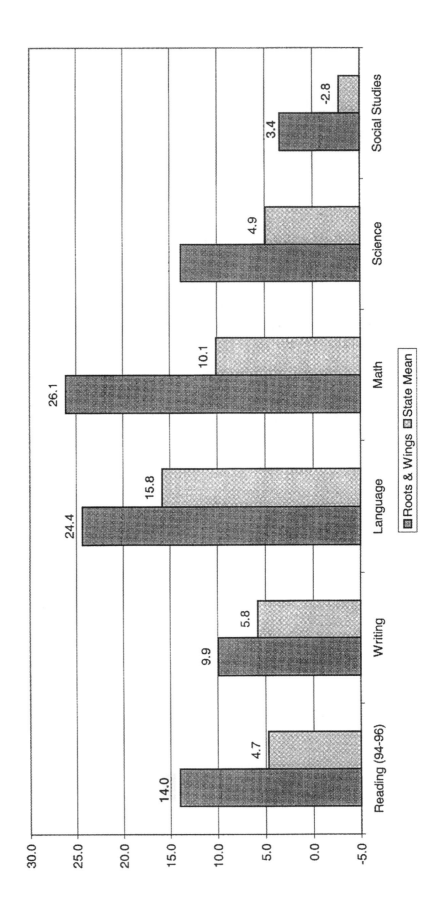

Figure 8.8. Maryland School Performance Assessment Program: Gains in Percentage of Students Scoring Satisfactory or Better, St. Mary's Ccounty Roots & Wings Schools Versus State Means, Grade 5, 1993 through 1996 (Full Implementation)

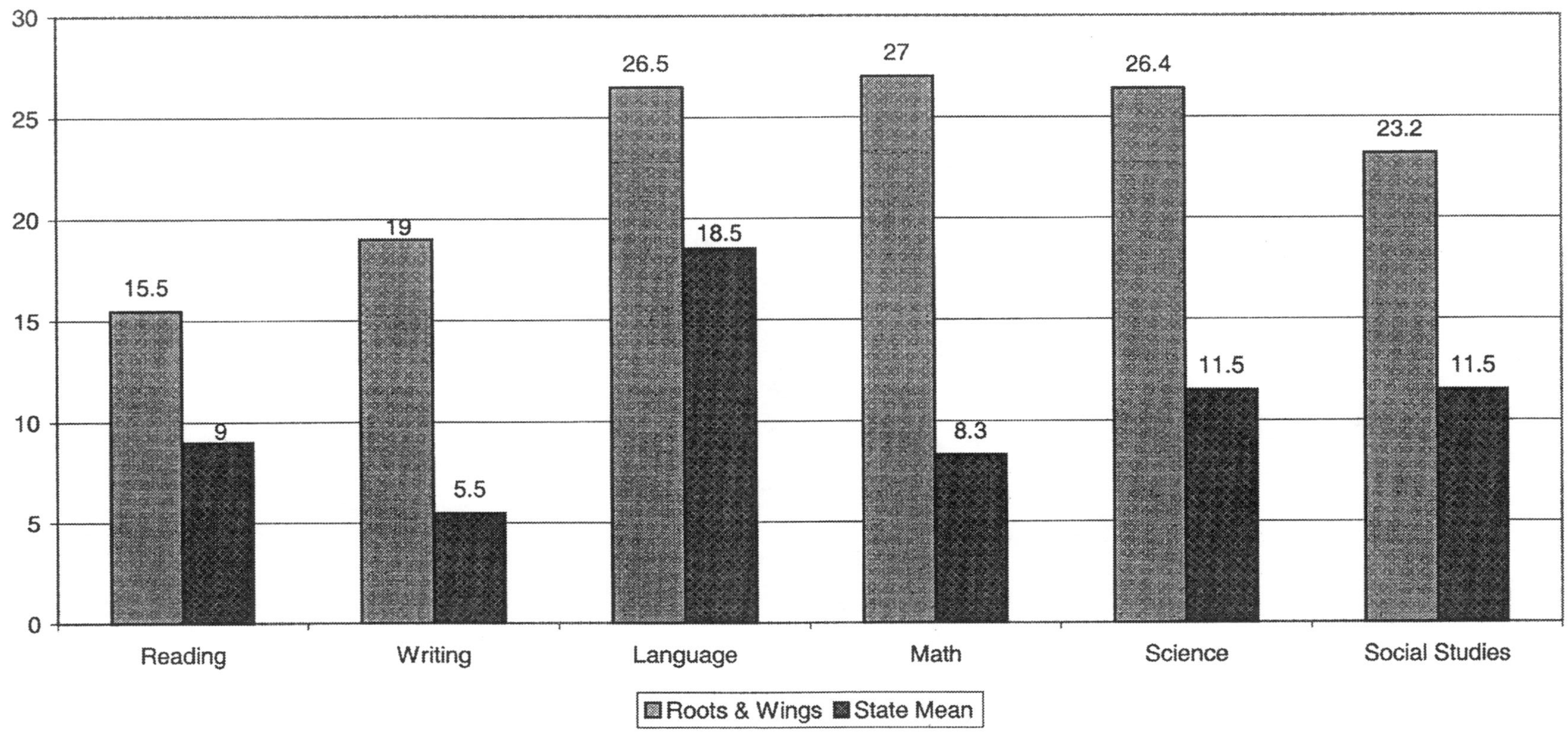

Figure 8.9. Texas Assessment of Academic Skills: Gains in Percentage of Students Meeting Minimum Expectations, Lackland City Elementary School Versus State of Texas, Grades 3 Through 5, 1995 to 1998

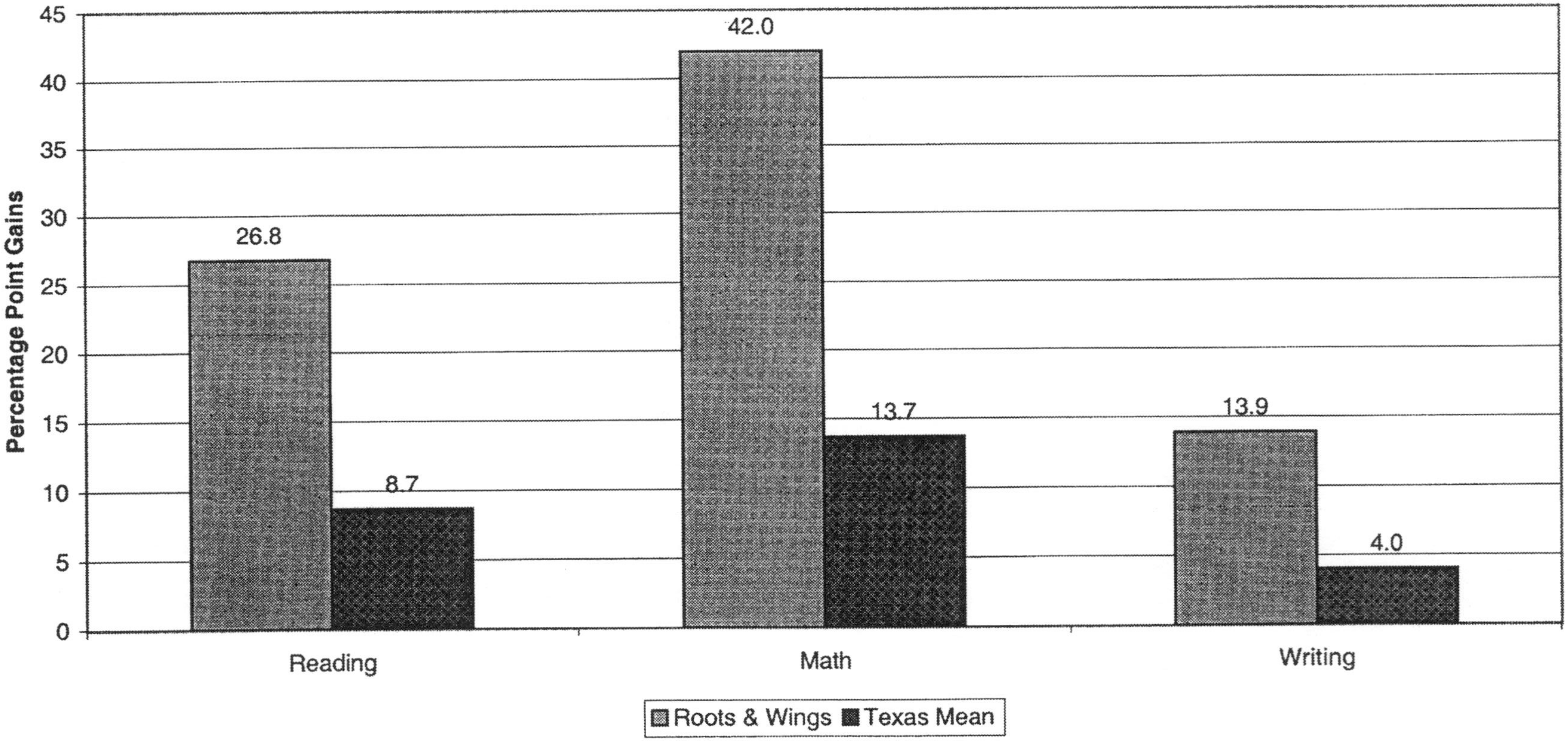

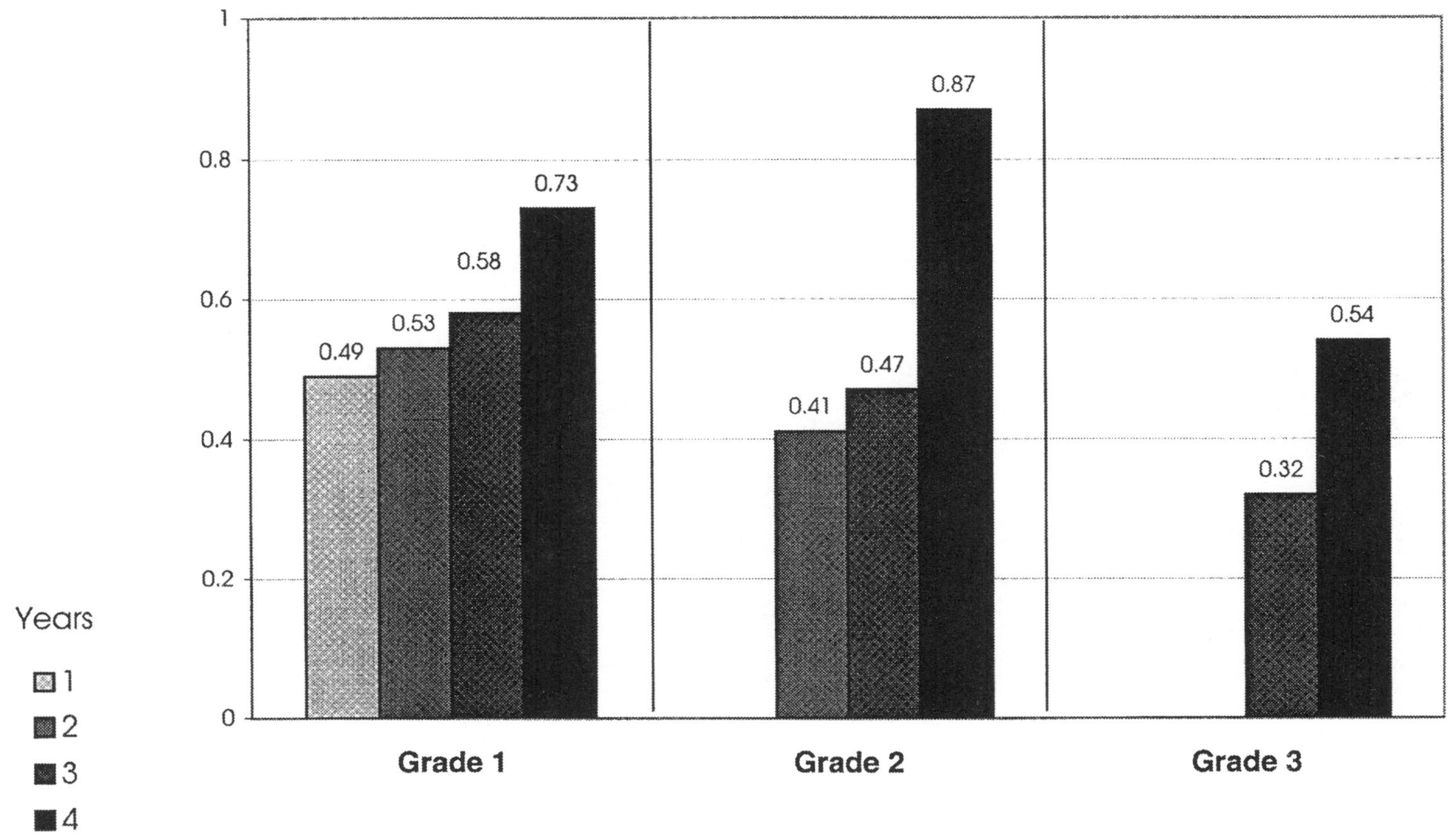

Figure 8.10. Effect Sizes Comparing Success for All and Control Schools According to Implementation Year

school has been implementing the program. Figure 8.10, which summarizes these data, was created by pooling ESs for all cohorts in their first year of implementation, all in their second year, and so on, regardless of calendar year.

Figure 8.10 shows that mean reading ESs progressively increase with each year of implementation. For example, Success for All first graders score substantially better than control first graders at the end of the first year of implementation (ES = +0.49). The experimental-control difference is even higher for first graders attending schools in the second year of program implementation (ES = +0.53), increasing to an ES of +0.73 for schools in their fourth implementation year. A similar pattern is apparent for second-grade and third-grade cohorts.

The data summarized in Figure 8.10 show that although Success for All has an immediate impact on student reading achievement, this impact grows over successive years of implementation. Over time, schools may become increasingly able to provide effective instruction to all of their students, to approach the goal of success for *all*.

Success for All and English Language Learners

The education of English language learners is at a crossroads. On one hand, research on bilingual education continues to show that children who are initially taught in their home language and then transitioned to English ultimately read as well or better in English than children taught only in English (August & Hakuta, 1997; National Academy of Sciences, 1998). Despite these findings, political pressure against bilingual education, most notably in California's Proposition 227, has mounted in recent years, based largely on the fact that Latino children perform less well than Anglo children on achievement tests, whether or not they have been initially taught in Spanish.

Although language of instruction is an essential concern for children who are acquiring English, the *quality* of instruction (and corresponding achievement outcomes) is at least as important, whatever the initial language of instruction may be. There is a need for better programs for teaching in the home language and then transitioning to English and for better programs for teaching English language learners in English with support from English as a second language strategies. Both development and research on Success for All have focused on both of these issues.

Six studies have evaluated adaptations of Success for All with language minority children (see Slavin & Madden, 1999b). Three of these evaluated *Éxito Para Todos* ("Success for All" in Spanish), the Spanish bilingual adaptation, and three evaluated a program adaptation incorporating English as a second language strategies.

Bilingual Studies

One study compared students in *Éxito Para Todos* to those in a matched comparison school in which most reading instruction was in English. Both schools served extremely impoverished, primarily Puerto Rican student bodies in inner-city Philadelphia. It is no surprise that *Éxito Para Todos* students scored far better than control students on Spanish measures. More important was the fact that after transitioning to all-English instruction by third grade, the *Éxito Para Todos* students scored significantly better than controls on measures of *English* reading. These differences were significant on Word Attack but not on Word Identification or Passage Comprehension.

An evaluation of *Éxito Para Todos* in California bilingual schools was reported by Livingston and Flaherty (1997), who studied three successive cohorts of students. On Spanish reading measures, *Éxito Para Todos* students scored substantially higher than controls in first grade (ES = +1.03), second grade (ES = +0.44), and third grade (ES = +.23). However, the second- and third-grade differences almost certainly understate the true effects; the highest-achieving students in the bilingual programs were transitioned early to English-only instruction, and the transition rate was twice as high in the *Éxito Para Todos* classes as in the controls.

A large study in Houston compared limited-English-proficient (LEP) first graders in 20 schools implementing *Éxito Para Todos* to those in 10 control schools (Nunnery et al., in press). As an experiment, schools were allowed to choose Success for All/*Éxito Para Todos* as it was originally designed or to implement key components. The analysis compared three levels of implementation: high, medium, and low. None of the *Éxito Para Todos* programs were categorized as "high" in implementation, as a bilingual teacher shortage made it impossible to hire certified teachers as Spanish tutors, a requirement for the "high implementation" designation. Medium-implementation schools significantly exceeded their controls on all measures (mean ES = +0.24). Low implementers exceeded controls on the Spanish Woodcock Word Identification and Word Attack scales but not on Passage Comprehension (mean ES = +0.17).

One additional study evaluated Bilingual Cooperative Integrated Reading and Composition, which is closely related to *Alas Para Leer,* the bilingual adaptation of Reading Wings. This study, in El Paso, Texas, found significantly greater reading achievement (compared to controls) for English language learners in Grades 3 through 5 transitioning from Spanish to English reading (Calderón, Hertz-Lazarowitz, & Slavin, 1998).

ESL Studies

Three studies have evaluated the effects of Success for All with English language learners being taught in English. In this adaptation, ESL strategies (such as total physical response) are integrated into instruction for all children, whether or not they are limited in English proficiency. The activities of ESL teachers are closely coordinated with those of other classroom teachers so that ESL instruction directly supports the Success for All curriculum, and ESL teachers often serve as tutors for LEP children.

The first study of Success for All with English language learners took place in Philadelphia. Students in an Asian (mostly Cambodian) Success for All school were compared to those in a matched school that also served many Cambodian-speaking children. Both schools were extremely impoverished, with nearly all children qualifying for free lunches.

At the end of a 6-year longitudinal study, Success for All Asian fourth and fifth graders were performing far ahead of matched controls. On average, they were 2.9 years ahead of controls in fourth grade (median ES = +1.49), and 2.8 years ahead in fifth grade (median ES = +1.33). Success for All Asian students were reading about a full year above grade level in both fourth and fifth grades, whereas controls were almost 2 years below grade level. Non-Asian students also significantly exceeded their controls at all grade levels (see Slavin & Madden, 1999b).

The California study described earlier (Livingston & Flaherty, 1997) also included many English language learners who were taught in English. Combining results across three cohorts, Spanish-dominant English language learners performed far better on English reading measures in Success for All than in matched control schools in first grade (ES = +1.36) and second grade (ES = +0.46) but not in third grade (ES = +0.09). As in the bilingual evaluation, the problem with the third-grade scores is that many high-achieving children were transitioned out of the ESL designation in the Success for All schools, reducing apparent experimental-control differences. Corresponding ESs for students who spoke languages other than English or Spanish were +0.40 for first graders, +0.37 for second graders, and +0.05 for third graders.

An Arizona study (Ross, Nunnery, & Smith, 1996) compared Mexican American English language learners in two urban Success for All schools to those in three schools using locally developed Title I reform models and one using Reading Recovery. Two socioeconomic school strata were compared, one set with 81% of students in poverty and 50% Hispanic students and one with 53% of students in poverty and 27% Hispanic students. Success for All first graders scored higher than controls in both strata. Hispanic students in the high-poverty stratum averaged 3 months ahead of the controls (1.75 vs. 1.45). Hispanic students in the less impoverished stratum scored slightly above grade level (1.93), about 1 month ahead of controls (1.83).

The effects of Success for All for language minority students are not statistically significant on every measure in every study, but the overall impact of the program is clearly positive, both for the Spanish bilingual adaptation, *Éxito Para Todos,* and for the ESL adaptation. What these findings suggest is that whatever the language of instruction may be, student achievement in that language can be substantially enhanced using improved materials, professional development, and other supports.

Comparing Success for All and Reading Recovery

Reading Recovery is one of the most extensively researched and widely used innovations in elementary education. Like Success for All, Reading Recovery provides one-to-one tutoring to first graders who are struggling in reading. Research on Reading Recovery has found substantial positive effects of the program as of the end of first grade, and longitudinal studies have found that some portion of these effects maintain at least through fourth grade (DeFord, Pinnell, Lyons & Young, 1987; Lyons, Pinnell, & DeFord, 1993; Pinnell, Lyons, DeFord, Bryk, & Seltzer, 1994).

Schools and districts attracted to Success for All are also often attracted to Reading Recovery, as the two programs share an emphasis on early intervention and a strong research base. Increasing numbers of districts have both programs in operation in different schools. One of the districts in the Success for All evaluation, Caldwell, Idaho, happened to be one of these. Ross, Smith, Casey, and Slavin (1995) used this opportunity to compare the two programs.

In the Caldwell study, two schools used Success for All and one used Reading Recovery. All three were very similar rural schools with similar ethnic makeups (10%-25% Hispanic, with the remainder Anglo), proportions of students qualifying for free lunch (45%-60%), and sizes (411-451). The Success for All schools were somewhat higher than the Reading Recovery school in poverty and percentage of Hispanic students. In 1992-1993, one of the Success for All schools was in its second year of implementation and the other was a new school that was in its first year (but had moved a principal and some experienced staff reassigned from the first school). Reading Recovery was in its second year of implementation.

The study compared first graders in the three schools. Students in the Success for All schools performed somewhat better than students in the Reading Recovery school overall (ES = +.17). Differences for special education students were substantial, averaging an ES of +.77. Special education students were not tutored in the Reading Recovery school and were primarily taught in a separate resource room. These students scored near the floor on all tests. In contrast, Success for All special education students were fully mainstreamed and did receive tutoring, and their reading scores, though still low, showed them to be on the way toward success in reading.

Excluding the special education students, there were no differences in reading performance between tutored students in the Success for All and Reading Recovery schools (ES = .00). In light of earlier research, these outcomes suggest that both tutoring programs are effective for at-risk first graders.

A second study, by Ross, Nunnery, and Smith (1996), also compared Success for All and Reading Recovery. This study, in an urban Arizona school district, compared first graders in three matched schools, in which 53% of students qualified for free lunch, 27% were Hispanic, and 73% were Anglo. One of the schools used Success for All, one used Reading Recovery, and one used a locally developed Title I schoolwide project.

Results for the overall sample of first graders strongly favored Success for All. Averaging across four individually administered measures, Success for All students scored well above grade level (GE = 2.2). Those in the Reading Recovery school averaged near grade level (GE = 1.7), slightly below the control school (GE = 1.8). ESs (adjusted for pretests) comparing the Success for All and Reading Recovery schools averaged +0.68, and ESs compared to the locally developed schoolwide project averaged +0.39.

Focusing on the children who actually received one-to-one tutoring, the differences were dramatic. On Peabody Picture Vocabulary Tests given at pretest, the students tutored in the Reading Recovery school scored 41% of a standard deviation higher than students tutored in the Success for All school. Yet at the end of the year, the Reading Recovery students were essentially nonreaders, with an average grade equivalent of 1.2. In contrast, the students tutored in Success for All scored at grade level (GE = 1.85). The mean ES for this comparison, ES = 2.79, is inflated by a huge difference in Word Attack, but even excluding this scale, the ES mean is +1.65.

The difference between the Idaho and the Arizona findings is probably due in part to the nature of the broader school programs, not just to differences in the tutoring models. The Arizona Reading Recovery school had a program strongly influenced by whole language, and the tutored children performed very poorly on Word Attack measures. In contrast, the Idaho Reading Recovery school used a more balanced approach so that these children were receiving some phonics instruction in their regular classes.

Reading Recovery can be a powerful means of increasing the reading success of students having reading difficulties, but it needs to be implemented well and supplemented with high-quality instruction that includes a strong phonetic component if it is to produce significant reading gains. Because Success for All attends to classroom instruction as well as tutoring, it is able to ensure that the effects of one-to-one tutoring build on high-quality, well-balanced reading instruction, rather than expecting the tutors to teach children to read with little support from classroom instruction.

Comparisons With Other Programs

A few studies have compared outcomes of Success for All to those of other comprehensive reform designs.

As noted earlier, a study of six restructuring designs in Memphis on the TVAAS found that Success for All schools had the highest absolute scores and gain scores on the TVAAS, averaging across all subjects (Ross, et al., 1999). TVAAS is a measure that relates performance on the Tennessee Comprehensive Achievement Test to "expected" performance. The designs, in addition to Success for All, were Co-NECT, Accelerated Schools, Audrey Cohen College, ATLAS, and Expeditionary Learning.

A study in Clover Park, Washington, compared Success for All to Accelerated Schools (Hopfenberg & Levin, 1993), an approach that, like Success for All, emphasizes prevention and acceleration over remediation but, unlike Success for All, does not provide specific materials or instructional strategies to achieve its goals. In the first year of the evaluation, the Success for All and Accelerated Schools programs had similar scores on individually administered reading tests and on a writing test (Ross, Alberg, & McNelis, 1997). By second grade, however, Success for All schools were scoring slightly ahead of Accelerated Schools in reading and significantly ahead in writing (Ross, Alberg, McNelis, & Smith, 1998).

Success for All
and Special Education

Perhaps the most important goal of Success for All is to place a floor under the reading achievement of all children, to ensure that every child performs adequately in this critical skill. This goal has major implications for special education. If the program makes a substantial difference in the reading achievement of the lowest achievers, then it should reduce special education referrals and placements. Furthermore, students who have IEPs indicating learning disabilities or related problems are typically treated the same as other students in Success for All. That is, they receive tutoring if they need it, participate in reading classes appropriate to their reading levels, and spend the rest of the day in age-appropriate, heterogeneous homerooms. Their tutors or reading teachers are likely to be special education teachers, but otherwise, they are not treated differently. One-to-one tutoring in reading, plus high-quality reading instruction in the mainstream at the student's appropriate level, should be more effective than the small-group instruction provided in special education classes. For this reason, we expect that students who have been identified as being in need of special education services will perform substantially better than similar students in traditional special education programs.

The philosophy behind the treatment of special education issues in Success for All is called *neverstreaming* (Slavin, 1996a). That is, rather than waiting until students fall far behind, are assigned to special education, and then may be mainstreamed into regular classes, Success for All schools intervene early and intensively with students who are at risk, to try to keep them out of the special education system. Once students are far behind, special education services are unlikely to catch them up to age-appropriate levels of performance. Students who have already failed in reading are likely to have an overlay of anxiety, poor motivation, poor behavior, low self-esteem, and ineffective learning strategies that are likely to interfere with learning, no matter how good special education services may be. Ensuring that all students succeed in the first place is a far better strategy, if it can be accomplished. In Success for All, the provision of research-based preschool, kindergarten, and first-grade reading; one-to-one tutoring; and family support services are likely to give the most at-risk students a good chance of developing enough reading skills to remain out of special education or to perform better in special education than would have otherwise been the case.

The data relating to special education outcomes clearly support these expectations. Several studies have focused on questions related to special education. One of the most important outcomes in this area is the consistent finding of particularly large effects of Success for All for students in the lowest 25% of their classes. Whereas ESs for students in general have averaged around + 0.50 on individually administered reading measures, ESs for the lowest achievers have averaged in the range of +1.00 to +1.50 across the grades. In the longitudinal Baltimore study, only 2.2% of third graders averaged 2 years behind grade level, a usual criterion for special education placement. In contrast, 8.8% of control third graders scored this poorly. Baltimore data also showed a reduction in special education placements for learning disabilities of about half (Slavin, Madden, Karweit, Dolan, & Wasik, 1992). A study of two Success for All schools in Fort Wayne, Indiana, found that for a 2-year period, 3.2% of Success for All students in Grades K through 1 and 1 through 2 were referred to special education for learning disabilities or mild mental handicaps. In contrast, 14.3% of control students were referred in these categories (Smith, Ross, & Casey, 1994).

Taken together, these findings support the conclusion that Success for All both reduces the need for special education services (by raising the reading achievement of very low achievers) and reduces special education referrals and placements. Both of these outcomes have significant consequences for long-term costs of educating students placed at risk; these are discussed in Chapter 9.

Another important question concerns the effects of the program on students who have already been assigned to special education. Here again, there is evidence from different sources. In the study comparing Reading Recovery and Success for All described earlier, it so happened that first graders in special education in the Reading Recovery group were not tutored but, instead, received traditional special education services in resource rooms. In the Success for All schools, first graders who had been assigned to special education were tutored one to one (by their special education teachers) and otherwise participated in the program in the same way as all other students. As noted earlier, special education students in Success for All were reading substantially better (ES = +.77) than special education students in the comparison school (Ross et al., 1995). In addition, Smith et al. (1994) combined first-grade reading data from special education students in Success for All and control schools in four districts: Memphis, Fort Wayne (Indiana), Montgomery (Alabama), and Caldwell (Idaho). Success for All special education students scored substantially better than controls (mean ES = +.59).

Teachers' Attitudes Toward Success for All

Three studies have examined teachers' attitudes toward Success for All using questionnaires. Ross, Smith, Nunnery, and Sterbin (1995) surveyed teachers involved in six restructuring designs, including Success for All, and found that Success for All schools had the most positive attitudes toward the success of the implementation. However, all designs were rated relatively positively, and there was more variation among schools implementing the same designs than between models.

Rakow and Ross (1997) studied teacher attitudes in five Success for All schools in Little Rock, Arkansas. Once again, responses varied widely from school to school, but overall effects were very positive. For example, 70% of teachers agreed that Success for All was having a positive effect in their schools, and 78% felt "positively about using the Success for All model."

Datnow and Castellano (in press) also examined teachers' attitudes in extensive observations and interviews in three California schools with substantial Latino majorities. They described 64% of the teachers as "supportive" or "strongly supportive," 28% "accepting," and 8% (three teachers) "opposed." Among the "accepting" teachers were some teachers who personally did not like the program but still felt it was working for their children.

Perhaps the best indicator of teacher support for Success for All is not from a study but from a vote. In spring 1999, the San Antonio Independent School District, responding to a severe budget shortfall and a change of superintendents, required teachers in all schools using restructuring designs to vote on whether to keep these designs or to return to the district's program. A vote of 80% in favor was required to keep the program. Across 24 Success for All schools, the average vote in favor was 81% positive. In contrast, votes for the five other designs (37 schools) averaged 36.5% positive.

Conclusion

The results of evaluations of dozens of Success for All schools in districts in all parts of the United States and five other countries clearly show that the program increases student reading performance. In almost every study, Success for All students learned significantly more than matched control students. Significant effects were not seen on every measure at every grade level, but the consistent direction and magnitude of the effects show unequivocal benefits for Success for All students. Effects on district-administered standardized tests and criterion-referenced tests used in state accountability programs reinforced the findings of the studies using individually administered tests. Large impacts have been seen on the achievement of limited-English-proficient students in both bilingual and ESL programs and on both reducing special education referrals and improving the achievement of students who have been assigned to special education. Research on Roots & Wings, particularly on MathWings, has also begun to show positive effects on a variety of state accountability measures.

The Success for All evaluations have used reliable and valid measures, in particular, individually administered tests that are sensitive to all aspects of reading: comprehension, fluency, word attack, and word identification. Positive effects on state accountability assessments and on other standardized measures have also been documented many times. Performance of Success for All students has been compared to that of students in matched control schools, who provide the best indication of what students without the program would have achieved. Replication of high-quality experiments in such a wide variety of schools and districts is extremely unusual. As noted earlier, reviews of research by the American Institutes of Research (Herman, 1999) and by the Fordham Foundation (Traub, 1999) found Success for All to be one of only two comprehensive elementary reform models to have rigorous, frequently replicated evidence of effectiveness.

An important indicator of the robustness of Success for All is the fact that of the more than 1,100 schools that have used the program for periods of 1 to 9 years, only about three dozen have dropped out. This usually takes place as a result of a change of principals, major funding cutbacks, or other substantial changes. Hundreds of other Success for All schools have survived changes of superintendents, principals, facilitators, and other key staff; major cuts in funding; and other serious threats to program maintenance.

The research summarized here demonstrates that comprehensive, systemic school-by-school change can take place on a broad scale in a way that maintains the integrity and effectiveness of the model. The schools we have studied are typical of the larger set of schools currently using Success for All and Roots & Wings in terms of quality of implementation, resources, demographic characteristics, and other factors. Program outcomes are not limited to the original home of the program. The widely held idea based on the RAND study of innovation (Berman & McLaughlin, 1978; McLaughlin, 1990) that comprehensive school reform must be invented by school staffs themselves is certainly not supported in research on Success for All or Roots & Wings. Although the program is adapted to meet the needs of each school, and whereas school staffs must agree to implement the program by a vote of 80% or more, Success for All and Roots & Wings are externally developed programs with specific materials, manuals, and structures. The observation that these programs can be implemented and maintained over considerable time periods and can be effective in each of their replication sites certainly supports the idea that every school staff need not reinvent the wheel.

9

Success for All,
Roots & Wings,
and School Reform

Success for All and Roots & Wings are clearly having a substantial impact on the schools that are implementing them. This is, of course, important in itself. However, the experience of developing and disseminating these programs, and in particular, the research on their outcomes, have important implications for school reform that go beyond these schools. Success for All and Roots & Wings provide what may be the best evidence available that well-structured, comprehensive programs can be replicated on a substantial scale and can ensure success for a large proportion of children who would otherwise need long-term remedial and special education services. This chapter discusses the implications of research on Success for All and Roots & Wings for compensatory education, special education, and school reform in general.

Can Success for All and Roots & Wings Work at Scale?

The practical and policy consequences of research on Success for All and Roots & Wings would be minimal if the program depended on conditions unlikely to be replicated in schools beyond our pilot sites. Yet this is obviously not true; the program currently exists in over 1,500 schools in 48 states and is continuing to expand (see Slavin & Madden, 1999c). Clearly, successful implementation of the program does not depend on the existence of handpicked staff, charismatic principals, or unobtainable resources. The 1,500 schools are highly diverse and are located in all parts of the United States, from California to Alaska to Texas to Florida to Indiana. This is not to say that every school serving disadvantaged students can successfully implement the program. It does require a clear commitment from the district, principal, and staff to a very different way of organizing their schools. However, it is our belief and experience that with adequate support from their central administrations, the majority of Title I elementary schools want to implement a program such as Success for All and are capable of doing so.

The most important impediments to the widespread use of Success for All and Roots & Wings are not any lack of willingness or skill on the part of school staffs but rather revolve around the cost of the program and around our ability to provide training and support to large numbers of schools. Chapter 7 described how we have expanded our training and support capacity by establishing regional training sites and by helping develop school districts' own capacities to support the program.

The following sections discuss several questions relating to the cost of Success for All and Roots & Wings. First is a discussion of what the costs are. This is followed by discussion of mid-term to long-term savings brought about by the program.

Costs

Most of the costs of Success for All are in reallocations of staff from other functions to provide a facilitator and some number of tutors. Beyond this, current costs (for the 2000-2001 school year) for materials and training average $75,000 for the first year, $30,000 for the second year, and $25,000 for the third year, for a school of 500 students just implementing Success for All. In Roots & Wings schools, costs remain around $75,000 for three years and then diminish.

Success for All and Roots & Wings have been implemented with widely varying constellations of resources. Most schools fund the program by reconfiguring existing Title I support, sometimes supplemented by funds or personnel from special education, state compensatory education, or bilingual education or ESL programs. Some schools have received grants of at least $50,000 per year from the Comprehensive School Reform Demonstration (CSRD) program to help implement Success for All (see discussion to follow). However, the great majority of funding, even in CSRD schools, comes from Title I. Schools may obtain grants or other short-term funding to help them with the initial costs of training and materials, but most do not. Few of

TABLE 9.1 Typical Staffing Needs (FTEs) for Success for All or Roots & Wings Schools at Different Title I Eligibility Levels

	Percentage of Students Eligible for Title I		
	75%	*50%*	*25%*
Facilitator	1.0	1.0	1.0
Tutors[a]	5.0	3.0	2.0
Family Support Specialist[b]	1.0	1.0	1.0

a. Certified teachers serve as tutors. High-quality paraprofessionals or retired teachers can be added to this number or substituted for some tutors if at least one certified teacher-tutor is available to supervise others and work with children with the most serious problems.
b. Social worker, counselor, or parent liaison

the current Success for All schools have much more funding than what they would have had without the program.

Staffing Needs

The number of staff needed in Success for All and Roots & Wings (other than classroom teachers) is typically the same as the staff already available in the school, but staff roles change significantly. In general, Title I (and often special education) staff become tutors, and one position is set aside for the facilitator. Table 9.1 shows typical staff configurations for Success for All and Roots & Wings schools of 500 students with various levels of Title I eligibility (and corresponding levels of Title I funds).

The Success for All and Roots & Wings curricula and instructional programs could theoretically be used without tutors, family support staff, and other staff. However, based on our research that indicates that the full model, well implemented, is far more effective than partial models (e.g., Nunnery et al., in press), we insist that schools interested in Success for All implement something close to our vision of a school in which very few students fail or require special or remedial education, and this requires tutors and other staff. In our experience, most high-poverty schools, especially Title I schoolwide projects, can implement Success for All or Roots & Wings using Title I, state compensatory education, bilingual, and special education resources. Schools with fewer disadvantaged students and, therefore, fewer Title I dollars, often require funds from elsewhere: desegregation funds, state funds, foundation or government grants, and so on. Costs generally diminish over time as the need to provide remedial services for older children diminishes. We have found that it is not a good idea for schools to try to obtain grants to fund the *continuing* costs of the program, as they then have to continually fight to maintain their funding. However, short-term grants (such as CSRD) to help with start-up costs can be very helpful.

Alternatives for Reducing the Costs
of Success for All and Roots & Wings

The variations in staff and other resources among different Success for All schools has enabled us to examine the contribution made by many key program elements to program outcomes. Our conclusion at present is that to guarantee the success of *every* child requires greater funding. In a study comparing schools with additional funding beyond Title I to schools just using their Title I resources, the fully funded schools had overall achievement effects only slightly better than those obtained in less well-funded locations, but they had more positive effects on the performance of the most at-risk students (those in the lowest 25% at pretest) and on such outcomes as retentions and special education placements (see Slavin et al., 1992). For the students with the greatest difficulties, the provision of adequate tutoring and family support services was crucial for success, but a small number of such students in each school absorbed enormous person-hours.

Having adequate resources also enabled the schools to avoid the use of expensive alternative services, such as special education and retention. For example, a student who was struggling at the end of first grade might be promoted to second grade and given continued one-to-one tutoring and family support. In a school without adequate support services, the same child would likely be retained or referred to special education. Retention rates and special education placements for children with learning disabilities have been substantially reduced by the program, leading to savings that are not immediately apparent but that reduce real education costs in the long run.

Without question, the most important resources for students with the most serious difficulties are the tutors. The effects of Success for All for the lowest 25% of students are closely associated with the number and quality of tutors. In high-risk schools, we recommend having enough tutors to serve 30% of first graders, 20% of second graders, and 10% of third graders. Originally, we insisted on the use of certified teachers as tutors. However, in schools that cannot afford enough certified tutors, we have recommended a mix of certified, paraprofessional, and volunteer tutors. These schools have at least one certified teacher tutor who works with the students with the most severe and unusual reading problems and also supervises the paraprofessional and volunteer tutors. Reducing the number of qualified tutors does reduce the capacity of the program to ensure success for *all,* but schools can still make a substantial difference in student achievement by implementing the curricular and instructional components of the program and using a mix of certified and noncertified tutors.

The impact of additional family support staff has been clearly seen on student attendance. Family support interventions have also been crucial for individual children who have had serious behavior problems, health problems, or other family related problems, and family support plays an important role in finding alternatives to special education placements. The impact of family support on overall reading scores is probably small, but if Success for All is to truly mean *all,* family support is a critical component. Most schools create family support teams within their existing staff rather than adding staff for this purpose, but the team is most effective if there is a full-time staff person dedicated to family support. Our analyses of family support programs indicate that they vary widely from school to school depending on level of support, staffing patterns, and community involvement and needs.

Because all Success for All and Roots & Wings schools have facilitators, we cannot assess the contribution they make to program outcomes. However, our experience tells us that they are essential. The changes in instruction, curriculum, support services, and other features of the elementary program are so extensive that there must be someone whose sole job is to ensure that all elements of the program are well implemented, well coordinated with each other, and focused on the success of every child. We have experimented with half-time facilitators (who tutor in the afternoon), but we recommend against this, based on experience as well as research (see Nunnery et al., in press), especially in the early stages of program implementation.

To summarize, we believe based on our research to date that much of the overall impact of Success for All or Roots & Wings can be achieved through improvements in curriculum and instruction, with the provision of a full-time facilitator critical to success in implementation. For the lowest-achieving students, tutors are clearly essential, as is family support. When hard choices have to be made, we emphasize the importance of tutors and the facilitator in addition to curriculum change, professional development, and a basic family support program (at least guaranteeing acceptable levels of attendance) as minimum requirements for an adequate implementation.

Savings Brought About by Success for All and Roots & Wings

Whereas the costs of Success for All or Roots & Wings must be primarily justified as an investment in children, it is important to note that the program typically brings about many savings:

Retentions

Many Success for All schools have substantially reduced their rate of retentions (Slavin et al., 1992). Reducing retentions has an important effect on educational costs. A retained child is receiving a very expensive intervention; one more year of school. Every time an elementary school retains 25 to 30 students, it must eventually hire an additional teacher, supply an additional classroom, and so on. When Success for All started in 1987, retention rates in many urban districts often approached 20%. Research on the negative effects of retention (Shepard & Smith, 1989) caused most districts to lower their retention rates, but now there is a new trend toward grade-to-grade promotion standards, promoted by the Clinton Administration and many governors and mayors, and retention rates are once again rising. This makes the cost savings brought about by Success for All's reductions in retention rates particularly important.

Special Education

Success for All schools have been able to reduce special education placements for learning disabilities by about half (see Slavin, 1996b). The additional cost of serving such students averages around $3,500 per year. If over a period of years, the number of children in special education for learning disabilities could be cut from 8% to 4%, the annual savings in a school of 500 students would be $70,000. In addition, reducing the number of assessments for special education (a national average of $1,800) from 8% to 4% would add a savings of $36,000 per year. Most schools report fewer referrals, and the referrals they do receive tend to be more accurate, thereby reducing unnecessary assessments (see Slavin, 1996b).

Supplanted Training and Materials

Success for All and Roots & Wings materials and training often take the place of other staff development and materials. For example, Success for All reading replaces basal texts for Grades K and 1 and workbooks for all grades. MathWings and WorldLab completely replace math, science, and social studies texts, respectively. Therefore, the costs of Success for All and Roots & Wings are rarely additional costs to the school but instead replace other expenditures for the same purposes.

Long-Term Savings

The preceding discussion only deals with short-term to midterm savings realized by the school or school system. To these savings must be added the likely savings to society over the long term in costs of welfare, police, prisons, and so on. The link between school success and life success, and between these and the need for expensive social services, is well established. To the degree that Success for All ultimately reduces delinquency, dropout, teen pregnancy, or other problems strongly associated with school failure in low-income communities, its savings to society could far outweigh any costs of implementation (see Barnett & Escobar, 1977). Research on prevention suggests that the links between early school achievement and mental health are strong.

Success for All is a practical, replicable, and effective program for improving the performance of disadvantaged elementary students. It is expensive, but with reallocations of Title I, special education, and other funds, most school districts serving many disadvantaged students can afford a credible form of the model. Immediate and long-term savings introduced by Success for All may ultimately offset most of the program's cost. For these reasons, Success for All is a cost-effective means of bringing all children in disadvantaged schools to acceptable levels of reading performance.

Implications of Success for All
for Compensatory Education

Once upon a time (or so the story goes), there was a train company experiencing a high rate of accidents. The company appointed a commission to look into the matter, and the commission issued a report noting its major finding, which was that when accidents occurred, damage was primarily sustained to the last car in the train. As a result of this finding, the company established a policy requiring that before each train left the station, the last car was to be uncoupled!

All too often in its 35-year history, compensatory education has primarily pursued a "last car" strategy in providing for the needs of low-achieving students. The attention and resources of Title I and its predecessor, Chapter 1, have mostly gone into identifying and remediating the damage sustained by individual children. Yet, the fault lies not in the children but in the system that failed to prevent the damage in the first place, just as the damage to the last car was due to the train system and had nothing to do with the last car in itself.

The 1994 reauthorization of Chapter 1 as Title I created unprecedented opportunities for high-poverty schools to fundamentally reform themselves. In particular, it reduced the free-lunch criteria for schools to qualify as schoolwide programs from 75% to 50%. The 1999 reauthorization reduced this requirement further, to 40% free lunch. Schoolwide programs can use their Title I resources flexibly to meet the needs of all children and to provide extended professional development for all staff. More than ever before, Title I schools can select programs that match their visions of excellence and implement that program with adequate professional development, materials, and flexibility. Yet, all too many Title I schools are still not taking advantage of the flexibility they have. They are continuing to invest in pullout remedial teachers and instructional aides, neither of which has much evidence of effectiveness for student achievement (Puma, Jones, Rock, & Fernandez, 1993).

Title I can be much more than it has been in the past. It can be an engine of change in the education of disadvantaged children (see Slavin, 1999). It can ensure the basic skills of virtually all children; it can help our nation's schools put a floor under the achievement expectations for all children so that all children will have the basic skills necessary to profit from regular classroom instruction. It can help schools move toward teaching a full and appropriate curriculum for all students but particularly for those who by virtue of being "at risk" too often receive a narrow curriculum emphasizing isolated skills. It can make the education of disadvantaged and at-risk students a top priority for all schools.

Preventing Early Reading Failure

Perhaps the most important objective of compensatory education should be to ensure that children are successful in reading the first time they are taught and never become remedial readers. The importance of reading success in the early grades is apparent to anyone who works with at-risk students. The consequences of failing to learn to read in the early grades are severe. For example, disadvantaged students who have failed a grade and are reading below grade level are extremely unlikely to graduate from high school (Lloyd, 1978). Retentions and special education referrals are usually based on early reading deficits.

Trying to remediate reading failure after it has occurred is very difficult, because by then, students who have failed are likely to be unmotivated, have poor self-concepts as learners, and be anxious about reading. Reform is needed at all levels of education, but no goal of reform is as important as seeing that all children start off their school careers with success, confidence, and a firm foundation in reading. Success in the early grades does not guarantee success throughout the school years and beyond, but failure in the early grades does virtually guarantee failure in later schooling.

A growing body of evidence from several sources indicates that reading failure in the early grades is preventable. The outcomes summarized in Chapter 8 show that Success for All has been able to dramatically reduce the number of students who fail to learn to read. Reading Recovery (Pinnell, DeFord, & Lyons, 1988), which provides at-risk first graders with one-to-one tutoring from specially trained certified teachers, has been found to substantially increase these students' achievement and to sustain these improvements into the later elementary grades. This and other evidence suggest that reading failure is preventable for nearly all children, even a substantial portion of those who are typically categorized as learning disabled (see Slavin, 1996b).

If reading failure can be prevented, it must be prevented. Title I is the logical program to take the lead in giving schools serving disadvantaged students the resources and programs necessary to see that all children learn to read.

Enhancing Regular Classroom Instruction

One of the most fundamental principles of Title I has been that compensatory funds must be focused on the lowest-achieving students in qualifying schools. In principle, this makes sense, in that it avoids spreading Title I resources too thinly. But in practice, this requirement has led to many problems, including a lack of consistency or coordination between regular and Title I instruction, disruption of children's regular classroom instruction, labeling of students who receive services, and unclear responsibility for children's progress (Allington & Johnston, 1989; Allington & McGill-Franzen 1989; Stein, Leinhardt, & Bickel, 1989).

The best way to prevent students from falling behind is to provide them with top-quality instruction in their regular classrooms. A substantial portion of Title I funds should be set aside for staff development and adoption of programs known to be effective by teachers in Title I schools. For example, by hiring one less aide, schools could instead devote about $20,000 per year to staff development, a huge investment in terms of what schools typically spend but a small one in terms of what many Title I schools receive. The educational impact of one aide could never approach that of thorough and intelligent implementation of effective curricula and instructional practices in regular classrooms throughout the school. For the cost of three aides, a school could pay all of the nonpersonnel costs of Success for All. For this amount of money, a school could pay for extensive inservice, in-class follow-up, and release time for teachers to observe each other's classes and to meet to compare notes, as well as purchase needed materials and supplies. The achievement benefits of effective classroom instruction all day would far outweigh the potential benefits of remedial services.

There are many examples of programs that have been much more successful for low-achieving students than remedial services. In reviews of the literature on effective programs for students at risk (Slavin & Fashola, 1999; Slavin, et al., 1989; Slavin, Karweit, & Wasik, 1994), we identified several such programs, including a variety of continuous-progress models, cooperative learning, and peer tutoring. Programs directed at improving classroom management skills also often increase achievement. In addition to particular classroom methods, comprehensive, whole-school reform programs, such as James Comer's (1988) School Development Program and the New American Schools Development Corporation programs (as well as Success for All and Roots & Wings), can be funded by Title I.

Success for All provides one demonstration of how a schoolwide emphasis on staff development and adoption of effective practices can be implemented under Title I funding and can greatly affect the learning of all students. Title I must help create a situation in which eligible schools are able to select from among a set of programs known to be effective and are then able to use their funds to obtain inservice, follow-up, and materials—whatever is needed to ensure top-quality implementation of whatever methods the schools has chosen.

Of course, Title I should not only be a staff development program. There is still a need for service targeted to individual children (for example, to provide tutoring to first graders having difficulty reading). However, without major investment in staff development, those who provide Title I services will always be trying to patch up individual children's deficits without being able to affect the setting in which students spend the great majority of their day, the regular classroom. Under current regulations, schools can use Title I dollars for staff development, but this rarely goes into the kind of training, follow-up, and assessment needed to effectively implement validated programs. Far more typical are 1-day workshops with no follow-up.

Obey-Porter Comprehensive School Reform Demonstration

Perhaps the best model of what Title I should become, and the most important development in whole-school reform in recent years, has been the creation in 1997 of CSRD, introduced by Congressmen David Obey (D-Wisconsin) and John Porter (R-Illinois). In its first round of funding, CSRD provided $150 million, most of which was awarded to schools to help them with the start-up costs of adopting a proven, comprehensive design. Schools were able to apply to their states for grants of at least $50,000 per year for up to 3 years. Recently, CSRD funding has been increased, and CSRD-type language has been inserted into the main Title I law.

In the CSRD legislation, 17 programs were named as examples of comprehensive designs. These included all eight NASDC programs, Success for All and Roots & Wings, Accelerated Schools, the School Development Program, the Coalition of Essential Schools, Direct Instruction, and several less widely disseminated programs. Schools were not limited to these, and in the first round of funding, a wide variety of programs was funded; fewer than half of the grants were to implement programs on the list of 17. Of grants made by the states, about 322 (17%) have gone to Success for All and Roots & Wings, 7% to Accelerated Schools, and 11% (collectively) to the seven NASDC designs other than Success for All and Roots & Wings.

CSRD is providing an enormous boost to the comprehensive school reform movement, which was already expanding rapidly before CSRD. The most obvious impact is on schools that have received CSRD grants. However, the impact is much broader than this. First, the entire awareness process being carried out by states in collaboration with regional laboratories is making a far larger set of schools aware of comprehensive programs. Even those schools that never apply for CSRD, and those that apply but are not funded, are now aware that comprehensive programs exist and that they are valid, approved expenditures of Title I funds. State departments of education, and especially their Title I offices (which are mostly running the CSRD competitions), now have staff who are deeply aware of comprehensive school reform models and may suggest them to Title I schoolwide projects entirely separate from the CSRD process. Similarly, the regional laboratories are playing a key role in the awareness and buy-in process for CSRD and are learning about comprehensive reform models and how to disseminate them in the process.

CSRD: Early Evidence of Effectiveness

Although the CSRD process is just now getting under way, there are early indicators that this strategy could make a substantial and widespread difference in student achievement. Of course, the first indicator is the evidence of effectiveness for the comprehensive models themselves (see American Institutes for Research, 1999; Northwest Regional Educational Laboratory, 1998; Slavin & Fashola, 1998). Furthermore, an independent evaluation of schools implementing a variety of reform models (mostly NASDC programs) in Memphis found that students in these schools were performing substantially better than were students in matched control schools (Ross et al., 1998).

Implications for Special Education Policy

For more than 30 years, the most important debates in special education research and policy have revolved around the practice of mainstreaming, particularly mainstreaming of students with mild academic handicaps, such as those identified as learning disabled. From early on, most researchers and policymakers have favored mainstreaming academically handicapped students to the maximum extent possible (Leinhardt & Pallay, 1982; Madden & Slavin, 1983), and the passage of PL 94-142 in 1975 put the federal government squarely behind this effort. Since that time, students with academic disabilities have certainly spent more time in general education classes than they did before, but the number of students identified for special education services has risen dramatically. Since 1975, the proportion of students categorized as learning disabled has risen more than 250%, whereas the category of educable mental retardation has diminished only slightly (U.S. Department of Education, 1998).

Despite the increase in mainstreaming, significant proportions of both special and general education teachers have never been comfortable with the practice. The movement toward full inclusion, which includes an even broader range of students in general education classes, has increased this discomfort. At the school level, holding mainstreaming or inclusion in place is often like holding together two positively charged magnets; it can be done but only if external pressure is consistently applied. General education teachers are quite naturally concerned about the difficulty of teaching extremely heterogeneous classes, and special education teachers, seeing themselves as better trained to work with academically handicapped students and more concerned about them, are often reluctant to send their students into what they may perceive as an inappropriate environment.

Solutions to the problems of mainstreaming academically handicapped children have generally been built around attempts to improve the capacity of the general classroom teacher to accommodate the needs of a heterogeneous classroom (Zigmond et al., 1995). For example, forms of individualized instruction (Slavin, 1984b; Wang & Birch, 1984), cooperative and peer-mediated instruction (Jenkins, Jewell, Leceister, Jenkins, & Troutner, 1990; Slavin, Stevens, & Madden, 1988), and teacher consultation models (Idol-Maestas, 1981) are based on the idea that to fully integrate academically handicapped students, teachers need new programs and skills.

Improving the capacity of the general education classroom to meet diverse needs is an essential part of a comprehensive strategy to serve academically handicapped students, but it is not enough. The problem is that once a child is academically handicapped (or significantly behind his or her peers for any reason), neither mainstreaming nor special or remedial education are likely to bring the child up to age-appropriate achievement norms. For most academically handicapped children, mainstreaming may only be the least unappealing of many unappealing options.

The Success for All and Roots & Wings models propose a markedly different approach to the education of students who are likely to become academically handicapped. The key focus of these models is an emphasis on prevention and on early, intensive, and untiring intervention to bring student performance within normal limits. We call this approach "neverstreaming" (Slavin, 1996a) because its intention is to see that nearly all children remain in the mainstream by intervening to prevent the academic difficulties that would lead them to be identified for separate special education services.

Success One Year at a Time

One key concept underlying neverstreaming is that instructional programs must help students start with success and then maintain that success at each critical stage of development.

First, all students should arrive in kindergarten with adequate mental and physical development. This requires investments in prenatal and infant and toddler health care, parent training, early stimulation programs for at-risk toddlers, effective preschool programs, and so on.

The next critical juncture is assurance that all students leave first grade well on their way to success in reading and other critical skills. This requires effective kindergarten and first-grade instruction and curriculum, family support programs, and one-to-one tutoring or other intensive interventions for students who are having difficulties in reading.

Actually, success in passing from each grade level to the next might be considered a critical requirement for neverstreaming at all levels; programs and practices must be directed toward doing whatever it takes to see that all children make it each year. As students move into second and third grade and beyond, this would mean continuing to improve regular classroom instruction, monitor student progress, and intervene intensively as often as necessary to maintain at-risk students at a performance level at which they can fully profit from the same instruction given to students who were never at risk.

The idea here is to organize school and nonschool resources and programs to relentlessly and systematically prevent students from becoming academically handicapped from their first day of school (or earlier) to their last (or later). Rather than just trying to adapt instruction to student heterogeneity, neverstreaming attacks the original problem at its source, attempting to remove the low end of the performance distribution by preventing whatever deficits can be prevented, intensively intervening to identify and remediate any remaining deficits, and maintaining interventions to keep at-risk students from sliding back as they proceed through the grades.

Is Neverstreaming Feasible?

For neverstreaming to be a viable concept, we must have confidence that prevention and early intervention can, in fact, bring the great majority of at-risk students to an acceptable level of academic performance and prevent unnecessary special education referrals. Several recent developments in research on programs for students at risk of academic difficulties have shown the potential of prevention and early intervention to keep students in the early grades from starting the process of falling behind that often ultimately results in assignment to special education. As noted earlier, there is a growing body of evidence to suggest that reading failure is fundamentally preventable for a very large proportion of at-risk students. Reading failure is a key element of the profile of most students identified as learning disabled (Norman & Zigmond, 1980).

The findings to date of the Success for All evaluations illustrate the potential of prevention and early intervention to keep students from falling far behind their age-mates, to keep them from failing, and to keep them from being assigned to special education for learning disabilities. Most Success for All and Roots & Wings schools serve very disadvantaged student populations; many experience problems with truancy, inadequate health care, parental poverty, drug involvement, and other problems that are unusual even among urban schools. Yet in these schools, even the lowest achievers are well on their way to reading, are being promoted, and are staying out of special education. More typical schools without many of these challenges should be able to ensure that virtually all nonretarded students are successful in reading and other basic skills and can therefore stay out of separate special education programs.

How Many Students Can Be Neverstreamed?

It is too early to say precisely what proportion of the students now identified as having academic handicaps can be neverstreamed, which is to say prevented from ever having learning deficits serious enough to warrant special education. It may be that as our knowledge and experience grow, it will become possible to avoid special education for the great majority of students currently categorized as learning disabled, about 5% of all students aged 6 to 17 (U.S. Department of Education, 1998), plus some proportion of those identified as mildly mentally retarded and behaviorally handicapped.

Looking at data from Success for All, it is clear that even the very lowest-achieving third graders are reading at a level that would allow them to participate successfully in regular classroom instruction. In extremely disadvantaged Baltimore schools, only 4% of Success for All third graders scored 2 years below grade level, one third the proportion in the control schools (Slavin et al., 1992). With continuing improvements in curriculum and instruction through the fifth grade, these third graders should all complete their elementary years with an adequate basis in reading, and this should greatly increase their chances of success in the secondary grades. There is no reason to believe that similar strategies in mathematics, spelling, writing, and other subjects would not have similar impacts, particularly to the degree that success in these areas depends on reading skills.

The number of students who can be neverstreamed is dependent not only on the effectiveness of prevention and early intervention but also on the degree to which general education can become better able to accommodate student differences. For example, use of cooperative learning, individualized instruction, and other strategies can also increase the ability of classroom teachers to meet individual needs. In one sense, the idea of neverstreaming is to work from two sides at the same time: making the classroom better able to accommodate individual differences and reducing the severity of deficits in the first place to make accommodation of differences much easier.

The Role of Special Education in a Neverstreamed World

At the policy level, one practical means of beginning to emphasize neverstreaming would be to require that no child be assigned to special education for a reading disability unless he or she had been given a year of one-to-one tutoring from a qualified tutor. This, plus other reforms in instruction and curriculum, would greatly reduce the number of children who end up with IEPs indicating learning disability. However, there will always be students who will continue to need top-quality special education services, such as those who are retarded or severely emotionally disturbed, as well as those with physical, speech, or language deficits and those with severe learning disabilities. The goal of Success for All is to keep special education "special." In a neverstreamed school, traditionally configured special education services would still be provided to these students, with an emphasis on prevention and early intervention and on providing services in the least restrictive environment. This approach allows special education to return to its focus on more severely impaired students, those truly in need of *special* services.

Special education also has a key role to play in providing consultation to classroom teachers on such issues as adapting instruction to accommodate diverse needs and learning styles, improving classroom management, and assessing students. For example, even students who are reading well may have learning and behavior problems that classroom teachers may need help to accommodate. Special education consultants might include among their responsibilities working with individual children for brief periods to learn how to succeed with them and then returning them to their teachers and tutors. Many of our Success for All and Roots & Wings schools involve special education teachers as reading teachers during the 90-minute reading period, often serving primarily identified students. This greatly improves the reading-group options for students.

If neverstreaming were to become institutionalized on a broad scale, it would create a need for a new category of teachers—professional tutors. Effective tutoring is not simply a matter of putting one teacher with one student; there are several studies of tutoring that have found unsystematic forms of tutoring to have few effects on learning (see Wasik, 1997; Wasik & Slavin, 1993). The education and supervision of tutors might take place under the auspices of special education.

At the moment, neverstreaming should be seen as a goal rather than a well-developed policy. However, if this goal is to be realized, we need to focus our energies on research, development, evaluation, and demonstration to move toward a day when students with learning disabilities and other students at risk of academic handicaps can confidently expect what neither mainstreaming nor special education can guarantee them today: not only services but success.

Success for All Within the School Reform Movement

We are in a time in U.S. society where there is tremendous pressure to reform our schools. This pressure comes from constituencies at the national, state, and local community level. Reform efforts range from modest supplements to traditional classroom instruction to radical "break the mold" approaches to school change.

Success for All and Roots & Wings have many components that have been implemented in isolation in many educational environments. They benefit from past research that documents effective instructional programs for children at risk. One does not have to dig too deeply to recognize how the model has benefited from the development and research of others. For example, our tutoring model has benefited from the research on Reading Recovery, our family support team from Comer's School Development Program, our cross-grade regrouping from research on the Joplin Plan, and of course our instructional approaches draw extensively on our earlier research on the benefits of cooperative learning (Slavin, 1995). We have not tried to reinvent the educational wheel. However, we have put together many existing wheels to create a vehicle to optimize success for every child.

Success for All and Roots & Wings are among a growing number of school restructuring efforts. However, in many ways, they are quite distinct from other reform efforts. What is different about our model is not so much the individual strategies but the way these strategies are woven together as a comprehensive system of complementary parts. We start with effective instruction within the regular classroom. Next, a set of multistaged interventions are available whenever danger signs are noted. The model involves many changes in both the organization and curriculum of schools. It is based on the concept of relentlessness, which implies always having a back-up strategy to ensure success. In the case of Success for All and Roots & Wings, we believe the whole is indeed greater than the sum of its parts.

For many years, there has been much doubt among policymakers that research-based school change can take place on a broad scale. Many believe that only systemic changes in standards, assessments, frameworks, and legislation can make a difference, or that reform can only come from changes in school governance, as with vouchers or charter schools. Success for All, Roots & Wings, and other replicable school designs show that today's public schools can reform themselves within the current system. Systemic change is necessary and desirable, but it must be accompanied by professional development, materials, and school organization methods capable of enabling schools to confidently achieve new, higher standards. Charter schools and private schools need proven programs just as much as public schools do, and there are examples of both in the Success for All network. Success for All and Roots & Wings provide one model of how standards and school-by-school reform can work together.

Conclusion

Twenty years ago, Ronald Edmonds (1981, p. 56) put forth three assertions:

1. We can, whenever and wherever we choose, successfully teach all children whose schooling is of interest to us;
2. We already know more than we need to do that; and
3. Whether or not we do it must finally depend on how we feel about the fact the we haven't so far.

Edmonds's conclusions were based on his studies of effective and ineffective schools serving poor and minority children. His key assumption was that if the characteristics of effective schools could be implanted in less-effective schools, all children could learn. Yet, this transfer turned out not to be an easy one. Making a run-of-the-mill school into an outstanding one takes much more than telling staffs the characteristics of outstanding schools.

The greatest importance of the research on Success for All is that it brings us closer to making Edmond's vision a reality. Only when we have confidence that we can take a *typical* school serving disadvantaged children and ensure the success of virtually every child can we really force the essential political and policy question: If we know that we can greatly improve the educational performance of at-risk children, *are we willing to do what it takes to do so?*

The findings of research on Success for All and related prevention and early-intervention programs make it impossible to continue to say that the problems of education in high-poverty schools cannot be solved. The Success for All schools, which include some of the most disadvantaged schools in the United States, do not have hand-picked staffs or principals. If they can achieve success with the great majority of at-risk children, so can most schools serving similar children.

It takes money and time, but increasingly, the money is already in place as schools are given increasing flexibility in using Title I and special education funds. We have demonstrated that with sustained efforts over time, significant change can occur for the vast majority of students. What is most needed is leadership, a commitment at every level of the political process to see that we stop discarding so many students at the start of their school careers.

If we had an outbreak of a curable disease, we would have a massive outpouring of publicity and funding to do what is necessary to cure it. *Reading failure is a curable disease.* If we are a caring nation, or even if we are only a self-interested but far-sighted nation, the knowledge that reading failure is fundamentally preventable must have a substantial impact on our policies toward education for at-risk children.

There is much more we need to learn how to do and much more we need to learn about the effects of what we are already doing, but we already know enough to make widespread reading failure a thing of the past. Next September, another 6 million children will enter U.S. kindergartens. If we know how to ensure that all of them will succeed in their early schooling years, we have a moral responsibility to use this knowledge. We cannot afford to let another generation slip through our fingers.

References

Adams, M. J. (1990). *Beginning to read: Thinking and learning about print.* Cambridge: MIT Press.

Adams, M. J., Foorman, B. R., Lundberg, I., & Beeler, T. (1998). *Phonemic awareness in young children: A classroom curriculum.* Baltimore: Paul H. Brookes.

Allington, R. L., & Johnston, P. (1989). Coordination, collaboration, and consistency: The redesign of compensatory and special education interventions. In R . E. Slavin, N. L. Karweit, & N. A. Madden (Eds.), *Effective programs for students at risk.* Boston: Allyn & Bacon.

Allington, R. L., & McGill-Franzen, A. (1989). School response to reading failure: Instruction for Chapter I and special education students in grades two, four, and eight. *Elementary School Journal, 89*(5), 529-542.

American Institutes for Research. (1999). *An educator's guide to schoolwide reform programs.* Washington, DC: Author.

August, D., & Hakuta, K. (1997). *Improving schooling for language-minority children: A research agenda.* Washington, DC: National Research Council.

Barnett, W. S., & Escobar, C. M. (1977). The economics of early education intervention: A review. *Review of Educational Research, 57,* 387-414.

Barnett, S., Tarr, J., & Frede, E. (1999). *Early childhood education in the Abbott districts: The need for high quality programs.* New Brunswick, NJ: Rutgers University, Center for Early Education.

Berman, P., & McLaughlin, M. (1978). *Federal programs supporting educational change: A model of education change, Vol. 8: Implementing and sustaining innovations.* Santa Monica, CA: RAND.

Bredekamp, S., & Copple, C. (1997). *Developmentally appropriate practice in early childhood programs* (Rev. ed.). Washington, DC: National Association for the Education of Young Children.

Calderón, M. (in press). Success for All in Mexico. In R. E. Slavin & N. A. Madden (Eds.), *Success for All: Research and reform in elementary education.* Mahwah, NJ: Lawrence Erlbaum.

Calderón, M., Hertz-Lazarowitz, R., & Slavin, R. E. (1998). Effects of Bilingual Cooperative Integrated Reading and Composition on students making the transition from Spanish to English reading. *Elementary School Journal, 99*(2), 153-165.

Calkins, L. M. (1983). *Lessons from a child: On the teaching and learning of writing.* Exeter, NH: Heinemann.

Campbell, J. R., Donahue, P. L., Reese, C. M., & Phillips, G. W. (1996). *NAEP 1994 reading report card for the nation and the states.* Washington, DC: U.S. Department of Education, National Center for Education Statistics.

Center, Y., Freeman, L., Mok, M., & Robertson, G. (1997, March). *An evaluation of Schoolwide Early Language and Literacy (SWELL) in six disadvantaged New South Wales schools.* Paper presented at the annual meeting of the American Educational Research Association, Chicago.

Center, Y., Freeman, L., & Robertson, G. (in press). A longitudinal evaluation of the Schoolwide Early Language and Literacy Program (SWELL). In R. E. Slavin & N. A. Madden (Eds.), *Success for All: Research and reform in elementary education.* Mahwah, NJ: Lawrence Erlbaum.

Chambers, B., Abrami, P. C., & Morrison, S. (in press). Can Success for All succeed in Canada? In R. E. Slavin & N. A. Madden (Eds.), *Success for All: Research and reform in elementary education.* Mahwah, NJ: Erlbaum.

Comer, J. (1988). Educating poor minority children. *Scientific American, 259,* 42-48.

Cooper, R., Slavin, R. E., & Madden N. A. (1998). Success for All: Improving the quality of implementation of whole-school change through the use of a national reform network. *Education and Urban Society, 30*(3), 385-408.

Datnow, A., & Castellano, M. (in press). An "inside" look at Success for All. *Journal of Education for Students Placed at Risk.*

DeFord, D. E., Pinnell, G. S., Lyons, C. A., & Young, P. (1987). *Ohio's Reading Recovery program: Vol. 7, Report of the follow-up studies.* Columbus: Ohio State University.

Durrell, D., & Catterson, J. (1980). *Durrell Analysis of Reading Difficulty.* New York: The Psychological Corporation.

Edmonds, R. R. (1981). Making public schools effective. *Social Policy, 12,* 56-60.

Epstein, J. L. (1995). School/family/community partnerships: Caring for the children we share. *Phi Delta Kappan, 76,* 701-712.

Freiberg, H. J., Stein, T. A., & Huang, S. (1995). Effects of a classroom management intervention on student achievement in inner-city elementary schools. *Educational Research and Evaluation, 1*(1), 36-66.

Galda, L., Cullinan, B. E., & Strickland, D. S. (1993). *Language, literacy and the child.* Fort Worth, TX: Harcourt Brace.

Graves, D. (1983). *Writing: Teachers and children at work.* Exeter, NH: Heinemann.

Harris, A., Hopkins D., Youngman, M., & Wordsworth, J. (in press). The implementation and impact of Success for All in English schools. In R. E. Slavin & N. A. Madden (Eds.), *Success for All: Research and reform in elementary education.* Mahwah, NJ: Lawrence Erlbaum.

Harris, A., Hopkins, D., Youngman, M., & Wordsworth, J. (1999). Evaluation of the initial effects and implementation of Success for All in England. *Journal of Research in Reading, 22*(3), 257-270.

Haxby, B., Lasaga-Flister, M., Madden, N. A., & Slavin, R. E. (1999). *Success for All family support manual.* Baltimore: Success for All Foundation.

Haxby, B., Lasaga-Flister, M., Madden, N. A., Slavin, R. E., & Dolan, L. J. (1995). *Family Support Manual for Success for All/Roots & Wings.* Baltimore: Johns Hopkins University, Center for Research on the Education of Students Placed at Risk.

Haxby, B., Lasaga-Flister, M., & Magri, J. (1999). *Getting Along Together: Integrated units in social problem solving.* Baltimore: Success for All Foundation.

Herman, R. (1999). *An educator's guide to schoolwide reform.* Arlington, VA: Educational Research Service.

Hertz-Lazarowitz, R. (in press). Success for All: A model for advancing Arabs and Jews in Israel. In R. E. Slavin & N. A. Madden (Eds.), *Success for All: Research and reform in elementary education.* Mahwah, NJ: Lawrence Erlbaum.

Hohmann, M., & Weikart, D. P. (1995). *Educating young children.* Ypsilanti, MI: High/Scope Press.

Hopfenberg, W. S., & Levin, H. M. (1993). *The Accelerated Schools resource guide.* San Francisco: Jossey-Boss.

Idol-Maestas, L. (1981). A teacher training model: The resource/consulting teacher. *Behavior Disorders, 6,* 108-121.

Jenkins, J. R., Jewell, M., Leceister, N., Jenkins, L., & Troutner, N. (1990, April). *Development of a school building model for educating handicapped and at risk students in general education classes.* Paper presented at the annual convention of the American Educational Research Association, Boston.

Jones, E. M., Gottfredson, G. D., & Gottfredson, D. C. (1997). Success for some: An evaluation of the Success for All program. *Evaluation Review, 21*(6), 643-670.

Karweit, N. L. (1994). Can preschool alone prevent early reading failure? In R. E. Slavin, N. L. Karweit, & B. A. Wasik. (Eds.), *Preventing early school failure: Research on effective strategies* (pp. 78-101). Boston: Allyn & Bacon.

Karweit, N. L., & Coleman, M. A. (1991, April). *Early childhood programs in Success for All.* Paper presented at the annual convention of the American Educational Research Association, Chicago.

Karweit, N. L., Coleman, M. A., Waclawiw, I., & Petza, R. (1990). *Story telling and retelling (STaR): Teacher's manual.* Baltimore: Johns Hopkins University, Center for Research on the Education of Students Placed at Risk.

Ketelsen, J. L. (1994). *Jefferson Davis Feeder School Project.* Houston, TX: Tenneco Corporation, Project GRAD.

Kostelnik, M. J. (Ed.). (1991). *Teaching young children using themes.* Glenview, IL: Scott, Foresman.

Leinhardt, G., & Pallay, A. (1982). Restrictive educational settings: Exile or haven? *Review of Educational Research, 52,* 557-578.

Livingston, M., & Flaherty, J. (1997). *Effects of Success for All on reading achievement in California schools.* Los Alamitos, CA: WestEd.

Lloyd, D. N. (1978). Prediction of school failure from third-grade data. *Educational and Psychological Measurement, 38,* 1193-1200.

Lyons, C. A., Pinnell, G. S., & DeFord, D. E. (1993). *Partners in learning: Teachers and children in Reading Recovery.* New York: Teachers College Press.

Madden, N. A. (1995). *Reading Roots: Teacher's manual.* Baltimore: Success for All Foundation.

Madden, N. A. (1999). *Reading Roots: Teacher's manual.* Baltimore: Success for All Foundation.

Madden, N. A., Calderón, M., and Rice, L. B. (1999). *Lee Conmigo: Teachers' manual.* Baltimore: Success for All Foundation.

Madden, N. A., & Cummings, N., & Livingston, M. (1995). *Facilitator's manual for Success for All/Roots & Wings.* Baltimore: Johns Hopkins University, Center for Research on Effective Schooling for Disadvantaged Students.

Madden, N. A., Farnish, A. M., Slavin, R. E., Stevens, R. J., & Sauer, D. C. (1999). *CIRC Writing: Manual for teachers.* Baltimore: Success for All Foundation.

Madden, N. A., Rice, L. B., Livermon, B. J., Wasik, B. A., & Slavin, R. E. (1999). *KinderRoots teacher's manual.* Baltimore: Success for All Foundation.

Madden, N. A., & Slavin, R. E. (1983). Mainstreaming students with mild academic handicaps: Academic and social outcomes. *Review of Educational Research, 53,* 519-569.

Madden, N. A., Slavin, R. E., Farnish, A. M., Livingston, M. A., & Calderón, M. (1996). *Reading Wings: Teacher's manual.* Baltimore: Johns Hopkins University, Center for Research on the Education of Students Placed at Risk.

Madden, N. A., Slavin, R. E., Farnish, A. M., Livingston, M. A., & Calderón, M. (1999). *Reading Wings: Teacher's manual.* Baltimore: Success for All Foundation.

Madden, N. A., Slavin, R. E., Karweit, N. L., Dolan, L. J., & Wasik, B. A. (1993). Success for All: Longitudinal effects of a restructuring program for inner-city elementary schools. *American Educational Research Journal, 30,* 123-148.

Madden, N. A., Slavin, R. E., & Simons, K. (1999). *Effects of MathWings on student mathematics performance.* Baltimore: Johns Hopkins University, Center for Research on the Education of Students Placed at Risk.

Madden, N. A., Wasik, B. A., & French, M. M. (1999). *Success for All/Roots & Wings tutoring manual.* Baltimore: Success for All Foundation.

Madden, N. A., Wasik, B. A., & Petza, R. J. (1989). *Writing From the Heart: A writing process approach for first and second graders.* Baltimore: Success for All Foundation.

McAdoo, M. (1998). Project GRAD's strength is in the sum of its parts. *Ford Foundation Report, 29*(2), 8-11.

McLaughlin, M. W. (1990). The RAND change agent study revisited: Macro perspectives and micro realities. *Educational Researcher, 19*(9), 11-16.

National Academy of Sciences. (1998). *The prevention of reading difficulties in young children.* Washington, DC: Author.

National Council of Teachers of Mathematics. (1989). *Curriculum and evaluation standards for school mathematics.* Reston, VA: Author.

National Council of Teachers of Mathematics. (2000). *Printables and standards for school mathematics.* Reston, VA: Author.

Norman, C., & Zigmond, N. (1980). Characteristics of children labeled and served as learning disabled in school systems affiliated with Child Service and Demonstrated Centers. *Journal of Learning Disabilities, 13,* 542-547.

Northwest Regional Educational Laboratory. (1998). *Catalog of school reform models.* Portland, OR: Author.

Nunnery, J., Slavin, R. E., Ross, S. M., Smith, L. J., Hunter, P., & Stubbs, J. (in press). An assessment of Success for All program component configuration effects on the reading achievement of at-risk first grade students. *American Educational Research Journal.*

Pinnell, G. S., DeFord, D. E., & Lyons, C. A. (1988). *Reading Recovery: Early intervention for at-risk first graders.* Arlington, VA: Educational Research Service.

Pinnell, G. S., Lyons, C. A., DeFord, D. E., Bryk, A. S., & Seltzer, M. (1994). Comparing instructional models for the literacy education of high risk first graders. *Reading Research Quarterly, 29,* 8-38.

Puma, M. J., Jones, C. C., Rock, D., & Fernandez, R. (1993). *Prospects: The congressionally mandated study of educational growth and opportunity* (Interim report). Bethesda, MD: Abt.

Rakow, J., & Ross, S. M. (1997). *Teacher survey: Success for All, Little Rock City Schools, 1996-97.* Memphis, TN: University of Memphis, Center for Research in Educational Policy.

Ross, S. M., Alberg, M., & McNelis, M. (1997). *Evaluation of elementary school schoolwide programs: Clover Park School District year 1: 1996-97.* Memphis, TN: University of Memphis, Center for Research in Educational Policy.

Ross, S. M., Alberg, M., McNelis, M., & Smith, L. (1998). *Evaluation of elementary schoolwide programs: Clover Park School District, year 2: 1997-98.* Memphis, TN: University of Memphis, Center for Research in Educational Policy.

Ross, S. M., & Casey, J. (1998). *Longitudinal study of student literacy achievement in different Title I school-wide programs in Ft. Wayne community schools, year 2: First grade results.* Memphis, TN: University of Memphis, Center for Research in Educational Policy.

Ross, S. M., Nunnery, J., & Smith, L. J. (1996). *Evaluation of Title I Reading Programs: Amphitheater Public Schools. Year 1: 1995-96.* Memphis, TN: University of Memphis, Center for Research in Educational Policy.

Ross, S. M., Sanders, W. L., & Wright, S. P. (1998). *An analysis of Tennessee Value Added Assessment (TVAAS) performance outcomes of Roots and Wings schools from 1995-1997.* Memphis: University of Memphis.

Ross, S. M., Sanders, W. L., Wright, S. P., & Stringfield, S. (1998). *The Memphis Restructuring Initiative: Achievement results for years 1 and 2 on the Tennessee Value-Added Assessment System (TVAAS).* Memphis, TN: University of Memphis.

Ross, S. M., Smith, L. J. & Casey, J. P. (1995). *1994-1995 Success for All Program in Ft. Wayne, IN: Final Report.* Memphis: University of Memphis, Center for Research in Educational Policy.

Ross, S. M., Smith, L. J., & Casey, J. P. (1997). *Final report: 1996-97 Success for All program in Clarke County, Georgia.* Memphis, TN: University of Memphis, Center for Research in Educational Policy.

Ross, S. M., Smith, L. J., Casey, J., & Slavin, R. E. (1995). Increasing the academic success of disadvantaged children: An examination of alternative early intervention programs. *American Educational Research Journal, 32,* 773-800.

Ross, S. M., Smith, L. J., Lewis, T., & Nunnery, J. (1996). *1995-96 evaluation of Roots & Wings in Memphis city schools.* Memphis, TN: University of Memphis, Center for Research in Educational Policy.

Ross, S. M., Smith, L. J., & Nunnery, J. A. (1998, April). *The relationship of program implementation quality and student achievement.* Paper presented at the annual meeting of the American Educational Research Association, San Diego.

Ross, S. M., Smith, L. J., Nunnery, J. A., & Sterbin, A. (1995). *Fall, 1995 teacher survey results for the Memphis city schools restructuring designs.* Memphis, TN: University of Memphis, Center for Research in Educational Policy.

Ross, S. M., Wang, L. W., Sanders, W. L., Wright, S. P., & Stringfield, S. (1999). *Two- and three-year achievement results on the Tennessee Value-Added Assessment System for restructuring schools in Memphis.* Memphis, TN: University of Memphis, Center for Research in Educational Policy.

Schweinhart, L. J., Barnes, H. V., Weikart, D. P., Barnett, W. S., & Epstein, A. S. (1993). *Significant benefits: The High/Scope Perry preschool study through age 27.* Ypsilanti, MI: High/Scope Press.

Shepard, L. A., & Smith, M. L. (Eds.). (1989). *Flunking grades: Research and policies on retention.* Philadelphia: Falmer.

Slavin, R. E. (1984). Team assisted individualization: Cooperative learning and individualized instruction in the mainstreamed classroom. *Remedial and Special Education, 5*(6), 33-42.

Slavin, R. E. (1987). Ability grouping and student achievement in elementary schools: A best-evidence synthesis. *Review of Educational Research, 57,* 347-350.

Slavin, R. E. (1994). School and classroom organization in beginning reading: Class size, aides, and instructional grouping. In R. E. Slavin, N. L. Karweit, B. A. Wasik, & N. A. Madden (Eds.), *Preventing early school failure: Research on effective strategies.* Boston: Allyn & Bacon.

Slavin, R. E. (1995). *Cooperative learning: Theory, research, and practice* (2nd ed.). Boston: Allyn & Bacon.

Slavin, R. E. (1996a). Neverstreaming: Preventing learning disabilities. *Educational Leadership, 53*(5), 4-7.

Slavin, R. E. (1996b). Reforming state and federal policies to support adoption of proven practices. *Educational Researcher, 25,*(9), 4-5.

Slavin, R. E. (1999). *How Title I can become the engine of reform in America's schools.* Baltimore: Johns Hopkins University, Center for Research on the Education of Students Placed at Risk.

Slavin, R. E., & Fashola, O. S. (1998). *Show me the evidence: Proven and promising programs for America's schools.* Thousand, Oaks, CA: Corwin.

Slavin, R. E., & Fashola, O. S. (1999). Effective dropout prevention and college attendance programs for Latino students. In R. E. Slavin & M. Calderón (Eds.), *Effective programs for Latino students.* Hillsdale, NJ: Lawrence Erlbaum.

Slavin, R. E., Karweit, N. L., & Madden, N. A. (Eds.) (1989). *Effective programs for students at risk.* Boston: Allyn & Bacon.

Slavin, R. E., Karweit, N. L., & Wasik, B. A. (1994). *Preventing early school failure: Research on effective strategies.* Boston: Allyn & Bacon.

Slavin, R. E., Leavey, M., & Madden, N. A. (1984). Combining cooperative learning and individualized instruction: Effects on student mathematics achievement, attitudes, and behaviors. *Elementary School Journal, 84,* 409-422.

Slavin, R. E., & Madden, N. A. (1993, April). *Multi-site replicated experiments: An application to Success for All.* Paper presented at the annual meeting of the American Educational Research Association, Atlanta.

Slavin, R. E., & Madden, N. A. (1999a). *Disseminating Success for All: Lessons for policy and practice.* Baltimore: Johns Hopkins University, Center for the Research on the Education of Students Placed at Risk.

Slavin, R. E., & Madden, N. A. (1999b). Effects of bilingual and English as a second language adaptations of Success for All on the reading achievement of students acquiring English. *Journal of Education for Students Placed at Risk, 4*(4), 393-416.

Slavin, R. E., & Madden, N. A. (1999c). *Success for All/Roots & Wings: Summary of research on achievement outcomes.* Baltimore: Johns Hopkins University, Center for Research on the Education of Students Placed at Risk.

Slavin, R. E., & Madden, N. A. (2000). Roots & Wings: Effects of whole-school reform on student achievement. *Journal of Education for Students Placed at Risk, 5*(1 & 2), 109-136.

Slavin, R. E., Madden, N. A., Dolan, L. J., & Wasik, B. A. (1994). Roots and Wings: Inspiring academic excellence. *Educational Leadership, 52*(3), 10-13.

Slavin, R. E., Madden, N. A., Dolan, L., & Wasik, B. A. (1996). *Every child, every school: Success for All.* Thousand Oaks, CA: Corwin.

Slavin, R. E., Madden, N. A., Dolan, L., Wasik, B. A., Ross, S. M., Smith, L. J., & Dianda, M. (1996). Success for All: A summary of research. *Journal of Education for Students Placed at Risk, 1,* 41-76.

Slavin, R. E., Madden, N. A., Dolan, L., Wasik, B. A., Ross, S. M., & Smith, L. J. (1994). "Whenever and wherever we choose . . . :" The replication of Success for All. *Phi Delta Kappan, 75*(8), 639-647.

Slavin, R. E., Madden, N. A., Karweit, N. L., Dolan, L., & Wasik, B. A. (1992). *Success for All: A relentless approach to prevention and early intervention in elementary schools.* Arlington, VA: Educational Research Service.

Slavin, R. E., Madden, N. A., Karweit, N. L., Livermore, B. J., & Dolan, L. (1990). Success for All. First-year outcomes of a comprehensive plan for reforming urban education. *American Educational Research Journal, 27,* 255-278.

Slavin, R. E., Madden, N. A., & Stevens, R. J. (1989/1990). Cooperative learning models for the 3 R's. *Educational Leadership, 47*(4), 22-28.

Slavin, R. E., Stevens, R. J., & Madden, N. A. (1988). Accommodating student diversity in reading and writing instruction: A cooperative learning approach. *Remedial and Special Education, 9,* 60-66.

Smith, L. J., & Ross, S. M., & Casey, J. P. (1994). *Special education analyses for Success for All in four cities.* Memphis, TN: University of Memphis, Center for Research in Educational Policy.

Stein, M. K., Leinhardt, G., & Bickel, W. (1989). Instructional issues for teaching students at risk. In R. E. Slavin, N. L. Karweit, & N. A. Madden (Eds.), *Effective programs for students at risk.* Boston: Allyn & Bacon.

Stevens, R. J., Madden, N. A., Slavin, R. E., & Farnish, A. M. (1987). Cooperative Integrated Reading and Composition: Two field experiments. *Reading Research Quarterly, 22,* 433-454.

Traub, J. (1999). *Better by design? A consumer's guide to schoolwide reform.* Washington, DC: Thomas Fordham Foundation.

Urdegar, S. M. (1998). *Evaluation of the Success for All program, 1997-98.* Miami, FL: Miami-Dade Public Schools.

U.S. Department of Education. (1998). *Fiscal year 1999 budget summary.* Washington, DC: Author.

Venezky, R. L. (in press). An alternative perspective on Success for All. In K. Wong (Ed.), *Advances in Educational Policy* (Vol. 4). Greenwich, CN: JAI.

Wang, M. C., & Birch, J. W. (1984). Comparison of a full-time mainstreaming program and a resource room approach. *Exceptional Children, 51,* 33-40.

Wang, W., & Ross, S. M. (1996a). *Comparisons between elementary school programs on reading performance: Albuquerque Public Schools.* Memphis, TN: University of Memphis, Center for Research in Educational Policy.

Wang, W., & Ross, S. M. (1996b). *Results for Success for All Program, Alhambra (AZ) School District.* Memphis, TN: University of Memphis, Center for Research in Educational Policy.

Wang, W., & Ross, S. M. (1999a). *Comparisons between elementary school programs on reading performance: Albuquerque Public Schools.* Memphis, TN: University of Memphis, Center for Research in Educational Policy.

Wang, W., & Ross, S. M. (1999b). *Results for Success for All Program, Alhambra (AZ) School District.* Memphis, TN: University of Memphis, Center for Research in Educational Policy.

Warach, B. G., & Lazorchak, S. A. (1999). The role of etiquette in social skill development of preschoolers. *Delta Kappa Gamma Bulletin,* 41-46.

Wasik, B. A. (1997). Volunteer tutoring programs: Do we know what works? *Phi Delta Kappan, 79*(4), 282-287.

Wasik, B. A. (in press). Teaching the alphabet to young children. *Young Children.*

Wasik, B. A., & Bond, M. A. (1999). *Early learning: Teachers' manual for pre-kindergarten and kindergarten.* Baltimore: Success for All Foundation.

Wasik, B. A., & Slavin, R. E. (1993). Preventing early reading failure with one-to-one tutoring: A review of five programs. *Reading Research Quarterly, 28,* 178-200.

Zigmond, N., Jenkins, J., Fuchs, L. S., Deno, S., Fuchs, D., Baker, J. N., Jenkins, L., & Couthino, M. (1995). Special education in restructured schools: Findings from three multi-year studies. *Phi Delta Kappan, 76*(7), 531-540.

Index